Seeking Provence

Seeking Provence

Old Myths, New Paths

by
Nicholas Woodsworth

 ArmchairTraveller

HAUS PUBLISHING
London

Copyright © 2008 Nicholas Woodsworth

First published in Great Britain in 2008 by Haus Publishing Ltd, 26 Cadogan
Court, Draycott Avenue, London SW3 3BX
www.hauspublishing.co.uk

The moral rights of the author have been asserted.

A CIP catalogue record for this book is available from the British Library

ISBN 978-1-905791-55-2

Typeset in Garamond 3 by MacGuru Ltd
Printed by Graphicom in Vicenza, Italy
Jacket illustration: Getty Images

To Jany and Simon, true Mediterraneans

One

You can't trust northern light. When I woke early on the morning of my Career Discussion and looked out of the porthole, Limehouse Basin was bathed in sunshine. The sky, as was only proper for the fine English spring day it heralded, was a tincture of robin's-egg blue. I couldn't actually see much through the circle of glass set a foot or so above the waterline, but from there, at least, the signs looked good.

Limehouse's fleet of little craft – narrowboats, yachts and motor cruisers – floated tranquilly at their moorings, with nobody up yet to disturb the peace. The buildings that surrounded the basin, glass walls glistening in the sun, were quiet, too – this part of Docklands was so newly fashionable that some flats were still unoccupied. Even the water of the boat basin itself was motionless and reflective. It is a mixture of River Thames and Regent's Canal, for the basin sits on the bank of the river, joining the two, and is mucky even by London standards. But now, untroubled by the thrash of passing propellers, its smooth expanse mirrored the clean wash of the sky. With a little calm and clear light almost anything can look serene.

I thought I might as well try and look the same way, too. I had brought my Italian linen suit especially for this meeting, and now dragged it off its hanger. Generally I don't like suits, but I had a weak spot for this one. I had bought it years before in Naples. It was hand-stitched, tan-coloured, and went well with a blue shirt. In the honourable tradition of linen suits it looked comfortably and confidently wrinkled. It was not something a man would wear to offices in the City, where I was headed. It was the suit of someone who has just flown in from Somewhere Else. It was the suit of a global traveller. It belonged to an old hand who was relaxed, self-assured, and knew what was what. I didn't feel like any of those people. I felt like somebody about to lose his job. But if I stood the slightest chance of keeping it I thought I had better look the part. It took several tries to get my tie right.

By the time I was pouring coffee a corner of the sky had veiled over. By the time I had finished my second cup, not fifteen minutes later, a breeze had come up, the light had dwindled, and the London air grown dull and grey. What had looked stylish in cheerful sunlight a moment before now just looked old and wrinkled. With the departure of the bright weather my pumped-up pretence of optimism began to drain away. I'd had a growing feeling ever since being summoned to London the week before that my days were

2

numbered. No meeting with a name like 'Career Discussion' could do me any good.

I glanced at my watch yet one more time and decided I might as well get going. Lenny, my friend and owner of the boat I was a guest on, had left for work long before. Not everyone who owns a vessel at Limehouse Basin keeps the hours of the leisured classes. Lenny was a British Waterways canalman, as Cockney as they come, and he worked where he lived. Lenny operated the Limehouse boat locks. Even now I could see him busy on the far side of the basin, piloting a bizarre craft whose flailing paddle-wheels were picking up beer cans, plastic bags, take-away pizza boxes and the other assorted odds and ends that float about in English canals. Sometimes the murky waters gave up larger, unexpected surprises – bobbing televisions, supermarket shopping trolleys, Canada geese with plastic six-pack rings around their necks, entire living-room sofa sets. Once a leg belonging to a black woman – no other trace was ever found – turned up near Lenny's boat in a plastic bin bag. I scribbled a quick note to my friend, scrambled off his boat onto a floating pontoon, then headed for shore and the Docklands Light Railway.

The train swayed, the converted red-brick detritus of an industrial age passed by and I stared out of the window, rehearsing. Via colleagues, over the phone, and through the grapevine I'd heard all about my new boss. She had only been in the job a few weeks and already her section of the office was in turmoil. There were people emerging from staff meetings scratching their heads over new directives, people considering transfers, people who were given no choice but to clear out their desks and go. This was a woman who was ambitious, calculating and ruthless. This was a woman who believed that a New Broom Sweeps Clean.

When I emerged from Bank Station the sky was heavy and threatening. Halfway down Threadneedle Street the first drops of rain began to fall. I ran. By the time I was indoors the suave traveller, the experienced man of the world, had vanished. I looked dreadful. Not even the receptionist who sat in the polished-granite entrance foyer could suppress a smile. I swiped a security card, passed through an electronic turnstile, and proceeded on to my Career Discussion. So much for the portents of fine English spring mornings.

꙳

'How long did you say you have been in the same job?' the New Broom asked me again, blinking through her glasses in disbelief.

'Twelve years,' I repeated lightly. I tried to make twelve years sound like a bagatelle. I might reasonably expect yet another twelve years, my tone of voice implied, before the time came to even start thinking about changing jobs.

'And how many Career Discussions have you had in that period?'

'Ah. Mmmm ... Well, none, actually.'

'Unbelievable,' the Broom whispered to herself as she

continued jotting in the notepad on her lap. There was no desk. As duplicitous as London weather, she had pulled two chairs together as if for cosy conversation.

'You were aware that in this company a Career Discussion is required with every employee every six months, weren't you?' The tone was anything but cosy.

'No, I wasn't,' I lied.

'You did know it is standard practice to shift staff members to different posts every two to three years, didn't you?'

'No, I didn't,' I lied again.

'This is all highly irregular, and I'm afraid we're going to have to take some fairly rapid action,' said my new boss, shaking her head sorrowfully at the inefficiencies of her predecessors. 'You obviously have no idea how this company works. Don't you understand? You're blocking the system. How in God's name you've managed to remain this newspaper's travel writer for so long is beyond me.'

I knew how I had managed it, but I wasn't about to volunteer information to a hostile interrogator. I had simply slipped through the cracks of office life.

It was easy. For when you are never there your presence, and therefore your absence, is never noted. For the past twelve years I had lived out of suitcases and moved between one hotel, one restaurant, one destination and the next. I had filed travel stories from around the globe over a telephone modem. Flying visits to London were rare because they served no purpose at all – they simply cut down on work-time. At first I had kept a narrowboat as a sort of temporary floating base in the city, a place to hole up in between flights – that was how I had met Lenny. For years I had also had a desk and telephone in the paper's offices. I never used them.

Eventually, returning to the paper at all had come to seem a waste of time. London was not home. If anywhere was home – and I found myself questioning the concept more and more often – it was far to the south, in Aix-en-Provence. My wife Jany, slim and dark-haired, was a dyed-in-the-wool, *cent-pour-cent* Provençal, an *Aixoise* born and raised in the narrow streets of the town's oldest quarter. Her roots went deep and had never turned – she had never wanted to live anywhere else. And even if she, too, had grown increasingly doubtful about the viability of our life together, she still regarded us as a couple. So did I. She was certainly more fun to come home to than Lenny and a flotsam-filled canal.

So the visits to London diminished and eventually dried up almost entirely. I sold my narrowboat. My desk and telephone were forgotten, then assigned to somebody else. I carried on working hard and travelling hard, year after year. As a by-line I continued appearing in the paper's pages every week. As a flesh-and-blood person I had virtually ceased to exist.

That was one reason I managed to keep going so long. The other was that I loved what I was doing. It was adrenaline-producing and addictive. I could not think of anything more exciting than stepping off a plane in a new place and taking those first, tentative sniffs of unfamiliar air. No matter how many times you did it each exploration was the first exploration, each place a new place. I gave my work everything I had and no questions were asked. But now out of the blue questions were being asked, and the answers failing to satisfy.

'Have you ever applied for any job-training courses in the last decade?' the boss continued.

I shook my head.

'You were the paper's Africa correspondent before you disappeared into this job. Have you ever even thought about moving into other specialised areas of journalism again?'

I had prepared a speech days before, a classic if-the-pump-ain't-broke-why-try-to-fix-it line of defence. But I could see it was hopeless. My interviewer was looking at her watch and losing patience. She moved in for the kill.

'Just a moment. Tell me one thing. Have you got *any* career ambitions at all?'

By this point I had nothing to lose.

'Yes,' I said after a moment. 'The world is big and complicated. No two people, no two places in it, are alike. Trying to understand what makes people and places different has kept me busy until now. I haven't made a lot of headway but I enjoy trying anyway. Because unexpected things come out of those differences. Not all of them are bad. Some even make the world a happier place. I don't see why discovering those things can't keep me busy for a few years more.'

Blank-faced, my inquisitor looked at me long and hard and then delivered her considered opinion.

'I don't think,' she said, 'that I have ever met a journalist with a vaguer career plan in my entire life.'

She was probably right. I didn't have a career plan at all. With that verdict my Career Discussion – and my career, as far as I could make out – drew to a close.

～

At Limehouse, Lenny made me a cup of tea and we sat in his wheelhouse looking out at the basin and squally rain falling in sheets. Sodden and forlorn, boats floated on water the colour of dirty dishwater.

'What in God's name am I to do, Lenny?'

Now I don't want to give the impression that my friend Lenny was some sort of sage to whom in times of trouble one would naturally turn. Because he wasn't. Lenny was somewhere in his mid-thirties, but there were times when he hadn't the sense of an eight-year-old.

You could not trust him with food, for example. Fry-ups, especially. Leave eggs, chips, sausage, tomatoes or baked beans around his boat – together, or in any combination, in any quantity – and he would down the lot. But then he could consume anything. I had seen Lenny, as a sort of casual afterthought at the end of a Chinese restaurant dinner, fish about and with gusto devour piles of damp green tea leaves from the bottom of empty teapots.

Nor was his behaviour judicious when it came to women. Lenny, to put it mildly, was rugged-looking – he grew a two-day beard less than four hours after shaving. But if he failed to look caring and sensitive on the outside, inside Lenny was a softie. He had fallen in love with so many wildly inappropriate women – it is surprising how many young female CEOs go jogging along London canals – that he was now perpetually prepared for rejection. It had gotten so bad that recently he'd sworn off love altogether.

Lenny, in fact, was not even to be entirely trusted about his principal business in life, boats and canals. He was a complete professional when it came to other people's marine affairs. He could keep order amongst a dozen anxious boaters locking through Limehouse in bad weather on a falling tide. He knew a thousand things about pumps and batteries and cooling systems. He would repair a friend's motor, as he had mine countless times, in exchange for a pint down the road at the Barley Mow. But when it came to his own life afloat his imagination had entirely run away with him.

He had lived for years aboard a shabby and comfortable old wooden cruiser named the *Marino*. One night a rotten hull-plank had sprung and Lenny had felt his vessel settling rapidly into the canal muck beneath him. This was at a time when Lenny had still been conducting the occasional failed romance. A hoped-for conquest had been aboard that evening; she was never seen again, and the skipper's humiliation was great. The *Marino II* was nothing like its predecessor. Steel-hulled and designed by Lenny himself, she was conceived as an unsinkable, luxury floating palace, safe and suitable for the seduction of all and any women. Unfortunately, once Lenny had paid for the steel hull part of it, there was not much left over for the floating palace bit. The *Marino II* was an empty shell, lined with little more than injected-foam insulation. The interior, her owner hoped, would eventually be completed in the fullness of time. I had seen little change in the past five years.

But if food, sex and shelter were not Lenny's strong points, I still valued his opinion. For he was a man of great enthusiasms, someone who gave himself entirely to his passions and ideas. Perhaps I also liked him because, for all his East-End gab and street savvy, he was an outsider like me. Lenny's surname, like his boat's, was Marino. His full Christian name was Leonardo. Leonardo Marino had been born in London, but sometime prior to that wondrous event the Marino clan had emigrated to the British capital from the town of Ravello high on the Italian Amalfi coast. Muffled by the sound of Bow Bells but nonetheless perceptible, the bell tower of Ravello's Santissima Annunziata was still reverberating somewhere deep inside my friend's head. Who could say? Perhaps in the furthest recesses of his mind entire groves of fragrant lemon trees were blossoming above dazzling blue seas. Lenny was a Wopney, a Mediterranean Cockney, and sometimes he came out with the most perceptive and astonishing of pronouncements.

'Admit it, there's no easy choice, is there?' I said to him now. 'The travelling is finished and done with. The question is, do I stay on with the paper, move up to London and take a desk job I'd soon be bored to death with? Or do I chuck newspapering altogether for the pleasure of going off to live in penury in the sunny south of France?'

Slowly nodding his head, Lenny considered my dilemma.

'Tough call, innit?' he said. 'You'd be buggered if you did the one and flaming out of your mind if you did the other.'

This was not the sort of comfort I was looking for. But Lenny was right. It was tougher even than he knew. It wasn't just a job that had come to an end. As far as I was concerned it was existence itself. For travel hadn't simply let me slip through the crevices of office routine. Travel had dropped me through the cracks of ordinary life altogether.

I had never known anything else. I am Canadian, born in the coldest capital on the globe after Ulan Bator. But I hadn't stayed in Ottawa long. My father, like many other residents of that city of snowbanks and bureaucrats, had worked for the government. A member of the Canadian foreign service, he'd been posted from one country to another and the rest of the family had followed. By the age of six, in imitation of the servants, I was squatting on my heels in the kitchen-compound behind a villa in Saigon learning to hawk phlegm along with the best of them. At twelve, at the height of the apartheid era, I was being caned in proper public-school manner at an all-white Cape Town boarding school that preferred to imagine itself still in the Dickensian age. By

11

seventeen, high on Harar home-grown, I was cruising the troubled streets of Addis Ababa in a green Ford Mustang even as Haile Selassie's doomed imperial regime teetered and fell.

Who could return to a frozen and fusty northern city after growing up like that? After that who could return to any steady or conventional life at all? The answer, I'd discovered, was that I didn't have to. There are lives and professions that can accommodate even the most vagrant habits. I have always felt happiest in out-of-the-way places. Eventually I'd settled to foreign correspondence, a job that seemed to suit me. I moved on to travel writing, a job that seemed to suit me even better. Fifteen years later I was still travelling hard and writing hard for the same London paper.

There was no denying it was a privileged life. But full-time nomadism is an odd existence, and withdraws other privileges so taken for granted we barely think of them. Life on the move had given me the whole world, but it had also given me the feeling that I wasn't especially attached to anything in it. All places were different, but no one city, landscape, group of people or way of doing things appealed to me more than any of the others.

That was why I'd been immediately attracted to Jany. She was everything I wasn't. She had just about every Mediterranean trait understood in that catch-all term, *joie de vivre* – she was effervescent, gregarious, emotional, affirmative, pleasure-loving, loquacious, extravagant, jealous, impulsive, affectionate and demonstrative. But beneath the more ephemeral attributes there was something else, a rock-solid quality that to me was infinitely appealing: she had an absolute and unquestioning assurance of her place in the world. She had permanence.

But impermanence, too, can become a way of life and like any other, once established, hard to change. Every destination attracted me, especially the next one. I lived a fractured, disassociated life. The more time went by the more I felt the centrifugal force of my own movement pushing me further out into an orbit that left me less and less attached to the ordinary things of life. At the time it hardly seemed to matter. In my gypsy habits everything was an isolated and ever changing one-off, and I knew no other way of going about it.

'Maybe there's a third way,' Lenny now said, breaking into my thoughts. Apparently he had not quite finished his assessment of the situation.

'What's that, Len?'

'Nuffink.'

I waited for the rest. There wasn't any.

'What do you mean?'

'Wot I said,' Lenny replied. 'If I was you, I wouldn't do nuffink at all.'

Well, here, at least, was a novel concept.

'Now, who was it?' Lenny went on. 'I've got a quote. It's the real thing, the genuine dog's bollocks. I just can't remember who said it.'

I waited, knowing this might be important. Lenny had obviously given the matter some thought. Who had said what? Was it Livy, Lenin, David Livingstone, Ken Livingstone, Bruce Lee? You could never tell with Lenny.

'Ah, yeah, that's right,' he said, pleased that it had come back to him. 'It was the late, great Mae West, a late-night television favourite of mine. And a very wise woman she was, too. Always in sticky situations, always in complete control. Anyway, her piece of advice went like this.'

Dramatically, he cleared his throat. '"When in doubt," she said, "take a bath".'

We sat there in the silence, the rain pinging down onto Lenny's slowly rusting metal roof. Thirty seconds, perhaps a minute went by.

'Is that it?' I asked.

'That's it,' said Lenny. 'Great, innit?'

'What's it supposed to mean, for heaven's sake?'

But like all true helpers in life, Lenny knew when to stop helping. 'Think about it, me old son,' was all he said. 'Just think about it.'

I did think about it, a great deal. I thought about it all that night, staring up at foam insulation, and thought about it all next day, looking out at rain. On the following morning I took the train back into the City, and had a long chat with the paper's managing editor. That afternoon I was on a flight back to southern France.

Carefully stowed in the jacket pocket of my wrinkled linen

travelling suit was a written agreement – a leave of absence. With it came the choice of negotiating a return to the paper at its conclusion, or of not returning to the paper at all. At last it was time to stop travelling and to take off the suit. It was time, in fact, to take off everything. Lenny and Mae West had been right. A long bath was just the thing I needed.

But I was not aiming for immersion in any old tub. I was planning to sink slowly into the deep bath of all things Provençal, and there to wallow long and contemplatively.

It wasn't an idea that came spontaneously. In the first place I hadn't spent more than two weeks anywhere for years, and the prospect made me nervous. But beyond that I had a real problem with the whole idea of Provence itself.

In the early 1980s a former advertising executive left his own London life behind him, bought and renovated an old village house in the Luberon hills in Provence, and then wrote a book about it. Two years on the best-seller lists, translated into umpteen languages, Peter Mayle's *A Year in Provence* became a publishing phenomenon. It fixed, seemingly forever, a certain image of Provence in the minds of people around the world. It also spawned a Mediterranean travel-book genre – it had literary wanderers pulling up stakes and departing to write about unspoiled Latin settings from Tuscany to Andalusia. And they, in their turn, drew other admirers. Northern escapees poured into Provence seeking their own dream-villages, and soon there were not enough old farmhouses to go around.

It wasn't long before Provence became a countryside of worn-out clichés. These days you don't have to travel very far in any direction to realise that places once glamorized as idyllic are sometimes no longer idyllic at all. In the last quarter-century Provence has grown as fast as anywhere else. There are urban landscapes there disfigured by ugly housing estates and gigantic shopping centres. There are rural landscapes devoted to turning out tons of tasteless vegetables beneath endless acres of hothouse plastic. There are days on the *autoroute* when pollution levels are so high you are required to drive at reduced speed. There are other days on the *autoroute* when the pollution levels are low but the driving so nasty you swear you'll leave the country anyway. Nobody who reads Peter Mayle should for an instant believe that all Provence is one great happy, sun-soaked celebration of life. Why should it be? It's part of the real world, too.

Yet the French Midi, for all that, remains an extraordinary place. From 30,000 feet in the air I could cast my mind's eye over the horizon to the Provençal countryside. Just as the stories described, it was still replete with hilltop stone hamlets, lively markets, tiny cafés, country meals, splashing fountains, aromatic lavender, yellow sunflowers, fresh goats-cheese and geraniums sitting red on window sills. But it was these very things, as beautiful and earthy and vital as ever, that now made me hesitate. What bothered me was that in the post-Mayle era all these things were portrayed as the essentials of an indolent and pleasure-seeking way of life.

I have nothing against indolent pleasure-seeking. It is one of life's central pursuits and takes up much of the world's energy and ambition. But in the end the Provençal life sought by its expatriate celebrants wasn't so different from the life they purported to be escaping in the first place. I had seen too many SUVs parked outside too many quaint, multi-million-dollar Luberon farmhouses to believe most foreigners settled here for an older, simpler, Mediterranean existence. As a foundation for an entire way of being, lounging round the pool with a glass of chilled Bandol hardly seemed adequate.

Was Provence really just a stockbroker belt gone south, simply one more invitation to the Good Life? Or was it, as I hoped I would discover, something more? The overwhelming evidence notwithstanding, Peter Mayle had hardly invented the place – surely it had to exist in another, more authentic version. What was a year in Provence compared with 3,000 years in Provence? No place remains a centre of Mediterranean life for that long without leaving something of itself behind.

And in fact I had to look no farther than Jany and the large Provençal family I had married into to see hints of its ongoing survival in everything they did and said. Buried, sometimes obscure, often mystifying, an older existence still lay deeply anchored in them and the places they inhabited.

What does it mean to be Mediterranean? Are Mediterraneans really any different from anyone else? Is an older,

17

more fundamental way of life even worth learning today? The search for another Provence was a starting point that might lead to some obscure and out-of-the-way places, but beyond that I had little idea where I was headed. In one way it hardly mattered. Somewhere early on the glue that holds things together, the adhesive bonds that make them sensible and meaningful, had in my case failed to stick. I needed some of that glue.

There was a change in engine pitch, a slight downward-tilting of the aeroplane aisle, and through the window beside me the unmistakable profile of Mont Ventoux drifted into view. I was almost home.

Not far from a sunny and bright blue coast Jany was waiting for me. If I was headed for deep immersion I had no doubt the Mediterranean was the best place for it. Beneath its limpid surface were hidden things that even Lenny – wise man, canal man and discoverer of all manner of sub-surface wonders – could never dream of coming across in the opaque grey pool of Limehouse Basin. I fastened my seat belt and prepared to set down in deep waters.

Two

The news on my return to Provence was not encouraging. For some days preceding the annual Chauvin family reunion at Les Jean-Jean in mid-May Odette, Jany's mother, had complained of not feeling well. She said thought it was probably the cough medicine she was taking, or perhaps her new rheumatism treatment. On the night before the event itself she slept little and was up vomiting two or three times. Pale and shaky the next morning, she told Jany's father, René, that she was not up to attending the reunion – we were to go without her.

René immediately replied that if she were not going, well then, *ça alors*, he would not be going either. Whereupon Jany said she was not moving an inch without both of them. Which left us all decisionless and immobile, standing and looking at each other defiantly in René and Odette's driveway. I might have expected it. This was not a family short on Latin emotion.

But that was not all. In theory that left me, the sole foreigner, alone to face a formidable horde – an entire farmyard of in-laws fired up on pastis and yet more demonstrative Latin emotion. It was unthinkable. In the end Jany and I bundled both her parents into the back of the car, and Odette did not protest too much. For we suspected what I think she herself suspected – her indisposition, too, was due to emotion. After many years of family reunions this was the first at which her brother Robert would not be present.

There are few families I have met who are as closely tied as the Chauvins. They live scattered across Provence, but their nucleus, a dozen or more households, is centred in the narrow Dôa Valley running up into the hills behind the Vaucluse market town of Apt. Most of the stone houses, fields, orchards, vineyards and woods that climb the steep valleysides halfway between Apt and the little village of Rustrel belong to Chauvins. There they have lived, their feet solidly planted in the valley's bright, ochre-red soil, for at least 500 years. They still farm the same small, sloping plots, observe the same rural rhythms and rituals, share the same concerns over harvests and hailstorms. I cannot think of the Chauvins of Apt as separate families. They are a single clan, a Provençal hill-tribe.

Odette and Robert were especially close. They grew up together on Le Marronnier, their parents' farm, in what is now another age. Odette washed clothes in the spring-fed stone *lavoir* in the courtyard, Robert trudged the uneven fields behind a horse and iron plough. In 1940, the year the Germans occupied France, Odette left Le Marronnier to marry, and after the war settled down to help René run his brand new sports-fishing shop in Aix-en-Provence. In 1941, Robert, then aged 18 and two years Odette's junior, also left the farm. Called upon by the Vichy regime to contribute to the Nazi war effort, Robert was supposed to be heading for factory-work in Germany. Instead he took to the hills behind Apt with his gun and joined the Resistance.

He survived, but the war did not leave the Chauvins untouched. An entire branch of the family was annihilated, executed by the Nazis in a farmyard reprisal for the activities of the local *Maquis*. The price Robert paid was exacted more slowly. The cigarettes parachuted into the hills along with other supplies were just the start of it – his lungs never fully recovered from the years spent sleeping outdoors on cold and humid ground.

It was his lungs that now, six decades later, had finally given out on him. The most recent occasion on which the Chauvin tribe had congregated had been on a winter's day a few months before, to see Robert laid to the cold and humid ground one last time. Funerals, in fact, are the other great convocations at which Chauvins gather *en masse*. At 90, René, now the doyen of the family, had seen too many of them. They left him sad for days. The point of family reunions, he encouraged Odette by remarking as we drove north from Aix along winding roads into the countryside, is that they are happy. As gatherings go, they even up the score.

And strangely enough, once we were on the way Odette

no longer felt ill. She brightened up, became almost cheerful. Perhaps the weather had something to do with it – after the rains of spring and before the summer's fierce heat had browned the country off, Provence was looking its best.

Still young, the leaves on the grapevines were a tender green. Fields of winter wheat, already high and rippling, were beginning to turn tawny yellow. Scattered as if by a careless hand, swathes of crimson poppies grew randomly by the roadside, in ditches, in long slashes of colour across grassy pastures. In Rognes, Cadenet and other villages along the way, there were bright roses blooming on trellises, massed irises growing in thick garden banks. The whole country was vibrant with rich colour and drifting smells and the promises of the coming season.

Odette and René were as seduced by the passing scene as I was, but they might have made the trip blind – over the last half-century they had made this visit countless times. Odette needed Le Marronnier every now and then in an almost physical way – in her mind, at least, she had never ceased being a *paysanne*, a peasant woman from the open Vaucluse hill-country.

We crossed into the *département* of the Vaucluse over the wide, gravelly bed of the Durance River. René appraised it, fuller than usual with grey spring-melt from the Alps, with his practised fisherman's eye. But also with the eye of memory.

'In the Fifties, before we had the money to buy our first

22

car, we used to visit Apt on the weekends by bus,' he told me from the back seat as we streaked across the bridge toward the Luberon hills. 'The bus was old and creaky and the bridge at that time even creakier. Nobody was sure how strong it was, or how long it would last – the driver used to stop at one end, and we would all get down and walk across the wooden planking on foot. Then the bus would crawl across the bridge and pick us up on the other side.'

'At least there was a bus,' I heard Odette reply. Just being back in the Vaucluse seemed to pump her up. 'When my grandfather carried *fruit confit* from Apt to Marseilles by cart he didn't get to ride at all. He led the horse, and walked all the way. He walked back again, too, with the cart full of sugar for more *fruit confit*.'

'At least he got there,' René chuckled. 'Look at your grandmother. She spent her entire life just a hundred kilometres from Marseilles, and never once saw the sea.'

'I don't know that it was that much different for your own father,' Odette shot back. 'When the rest of us were out in the fresh air growing cherries and melons, he sat inside all day soldering tins to hold it.'

The exchange continued on the back seat as the fashionable village of Lourmarin, its chateau sand-blasted and its olive groves carefully groomed, sailed by on the left. Peter Mayle, its best known resident ex-pat, might even now, I thought, be sitting there on the terrace of the crowded Café l'Ormeau and reading the English papers. Further on, in the deep and narrow limestone defile that winds through the Luberon chain, we passed the medieval stone fortress of Buoux high above us. On this bright Saturday spring morning it, too, would be busy with visitors from around the world.

I breathed a small sigh of relief and drove on. All was right with Odette again, and we were on the way to our own busy, if less urbane, little gathering.

⌒

A kilometre or two past Le Marronnier, on the far side of Guy Chauvin's metal-working shop and Daniel Chauvin's vineyards, we veered off the road and into the shady little hamlet of Les Jean-Jean. There was often a car or two parked not far from the half-dozen houses that made up Les Jean-Jean, for the clear, ferruginous water that tumbled into a fountain from a spring there was medically reputed – people from up and down the Dôa Valley came to stock up on it by the bucketful. But today the entire hamlet was littered throughout with dozens of cars parked in insouciant and anarchical fashion. Nobody minded, of course – it was all in the family. Nobody would have minded, anyway – it is the way the people of the Midi always park.

We picked our way through the cars and made for a red marquee tent, the sort of big top you would find at a circus-ground, pitched beside Gérard Chauvin's farmhouse. The tent was bright, but in his specially chosen, festive Hawaiian shirt – hula-dancers and waving palm trees on a background of red hibiscus flowers – Gérard was even brighter.

He would have been hard to miss, anyway. He was only in his mid-forties, but for the last twenty years his hair had been snow-white. And although Jany's cousin was not much taller than she was, he somehow gave the impression of being a vast mountain of a man. From his silvery, shovel-shaped beard to the dusty farmyard boots he usually wore – today's sandals were a holiday exception – Gérard was solid and well anchored. The broad back, the great barrel-chest, the impressive girth of stomach, the powerful forearms – everything about him was bear-like.

And, indeed, as I stepped forward to kiss him – after anything more than twenty-four hours an embrace is standard in the Chauvin clan – I felt I was going into a clinch with a bear. Smack went a kiss on one cheek; thud went a kiss on the other; biff went a kiss on the first cheek again. At the same time I was having the life squeezed out of me. It was like being simultaneously head-butted and suffocated by a large animal. If there was one thing I was reassured by it was Gérard's eyes. They were friendly, generous and, rare in this southern countryside, clear blue. They actually twinkled. No matter what he was doing, no matter how tough times sometimes got, Gérard had a vast energy and appetite for life.

I liked him. In a country that stakes all on image and social convention, Gérard pleased himself doing exactly as he wished. He had little time for the hypocrisy of poseurs, for the machinations of government or the greed of big corporations. He detested power-seeking, corruption, favouritism, political string-pulling and privilege purchased by wealth. He had little time for rules, officials or authority of any kind. Gerard was a back-woods libertarian, a left-leaning sort of Provençal hillbilly.

So much for what he did not have time for. What he did have time for, and a great deal of it, was the land and what it produced. Of all the country people I had met in Provence no one else was quite as passionately involved, in a sleeves-rolled-up, toes-in-the-muck kind of way, in the production of good food. All up and down the valley Gérard's cousins grew superior fruits and vegetables – grapes and melons and cherries, aubergines and squashes and courgettes. But because he was Gérard and a bit ornery he did something different – he raised the finest free-range poultry instead.

His farmyard milled with tail-wagging ducks, flocks of chickens and gaggles of geese as white as his own beard. Inside the sagging doors of his outbuildings lived elegant spotted guinea fowl, fat, grain-fed pigeons, silky-eared rabbits. There were cotes, coops, hutches, byres and pens wherever you looked. There were bleating sheep; baying, long-eared hounds used just for hunting; goats and donkeys kept as pets. There was one enclosure that held a toothy, stiff-bristled wild boar that Gérard had rescued half-drowned from a swimming pool. The whole noisy, feather-fluttering operation appeared entirely chaotic – the farmyard was liberally strewn with straw, bird-droppings, and an astounding collection of clapped-out agricultural odds and ends. If Gérard could not resist bringing up every kind of animal he came across, he was equally incapable of refusing a home, whether they worked or not, to all things mechanical.

But the end product was incomparable. The poultry he sold at local farmer's markets were free of antibiotics, hormones, vitamin additives and any other aids to growth. They grew instead on Gérard's care and hard work and were, by universal consent, the best-tasting birds around.

But that was just the beginning. When Gérard was not looking after animals he was either out in the hills hunting them, in his kitchen transforming them into patés and hams, or in his dining room eating them. He was in love with food in all its various stages of preparation, a man wholly consumed by what he consumed. For Gérard any excuse to celebrate with food and drink and friends was good enough. Such a successful *bon vivant* was he that in his yard sat an ancient and weather-beaten transport truck – one could still faintly see the logo of a popular brand of Normandy butter floating ghost-like on its sides – converted to a fully equipped field-kitchen. Was there a marriage taking place somewhere in the community? A new baby to fête? A successful fishing trip to boast about? Then look no further – Gérard was your man. If a feast needed organising he could be counted on to turn up with anything from a brace of pheasants to a whole lamb ready to spit-roast over a bed of coals. Naturally, when it came to hosting a family reunion, Gérard was invariably called upon.

∽

'How many Chauvins this year?' I asked Gérard once he had let go of me. Each spring the reunion got a little bigger as three older family generations gave way to a steadily expanding fourth.

'Somewhere over a hundred so far,' he told me. 'But I can't get a good count of the children – the little buggers keep running around too fast.'

As I wandered over to a long table covered with refreshments I made a hasty calculation. Kissing one's in-laws, no matter how distantly related, was an indispensable part of these reunions. My own WASPish family shied away from public demonstrations of affection. But this was stronger than mere affection; this was tribal communion. If each Chauvin kissed one hundred other Chauvins three times on meeting and three times on parting, I thought, that was 600 kisses per person. Just why three kisses was the rule in this small valley I had no idea. Only thirty miles down the road in Aix two kisses was the norm. In some parts of Brittany four was par for the course. But no matter – multiply 600 kisses per person by the total number of Chauvins gathered, and that made 60,000 kisses in all. By any standard that was a lot of French kissing. I puckered up for an exchange with the bartender, Odette's second cousin, Janine. Then with a

28

glass of cloudy yellow pastis in hand I began to make the rounds.

Some of these Chauvins I had scarcely met before, and I kept finding myself in deep confusion. Was Aimé's cousin Louis's brother's son? Or was that a different Aimé? It didn't matter – we embraced each other anyway. But the ones I knew best were Robert's family, for I had been seeing them on and off since we had first met years before, on a Christmas day at Le Marronnier.

I had arrived in the country just seventy-two hours before and knew nothing at all of Provence. Lunch was a splendid affair, a celebration at which twenty-five family members had sat down to a long table and for four hours feasted on food the likes of which I had never seen before. There were small, bright red crayfish, salads garnished with truffles sniffed out of the earth by a family spaniel, wild boar hunted in the nearby hills, small thrush neatly trussed in butcher's string, wines from the vineyard behind the house.

Throughout there had been talk – village gossip, the price of artichokes, hunting stories, advice on goats' cheese, reminiscences of other Christmases, hard times, the war. And throughout I was speechless, largely because I had few words of French at easy command, but also because I was overwhelmed. Here was a whole universe of traditions, rituals, habits and gestures I knew nothing of. Despite my shyness, though, the silence was overcome; even if I were only the young man Odette's daughter had met in foreign parts, that was enough to make me an honorary member of the family. And in this corner of the world family is everything – Robert's clan had done its best to make me feel part of it.

And now here they were again. Some things had changed. On that first meeting we had been dressed for an icy winter's day. Now we were garbed in a mix of straw hats and shorts and summer frocks, bright shirts and rope-soled *espadrilles*. And we all a little bit older. In the meantime I had moved on to new countries and new travel stories. The Chauvins had moved on to new houses, new babies, new farming techniques. And Robert had moved on altogether. Nonetheless there was something essentially changeless about this family – its dependability. Each Chauvin knew he or she could rely on the other Chauvins. No matter how the world spun about around them, the family remained a central and fixed point of reference.

It was the kind of solidarity that often comes from rural hardship. Electricity only came to Le Marronnier in 1938. Indoor plumbing arrived after the war. Robert continued ploughing his fields with horses into the Fifties. Their adversity had made dedicated communists of the Chauvins, as it did of most small farmers in these hills. But Robert's children were as ambitious and hard-working as they were politically idealistic. They went on to university, and most of them now lived in town or city and had busy professional lives of their own. The horses disappeared. French Communism now barely staggered on. Le Marronnier was still there, however, and still the centre of a universe – few were the weekends when at least a couple of the six children did not show up. With them they brought their own children in tow, renewing ties to family and land for yet one more generation.

Here in front of me was Robert's youngest son Frederic with his small brood. We hugged. Frederic was less bear-like and more athletic than Gérard. When he was not teaching farmers the utility of computer programs in agricultural management – a real revolution in this conservative countryside – he was out cycling. A spin over nearby 6,000-foot Mont Ventoux, the most challenging obstacle in the annual Tour de France, was a pleasant outing for Frederic. Neither he nor his wife Emilie thought a thing of cycling fifty hilly miles in a single day. Emilie was a softer kiss, though.

I continued mingling. I greeted lean, wiry Rolland, permanently sun-browned by years in the fields; Robert's oldest son had taken over Le Marronnier and with vast effort was converting to *agriculture raisonnée*, a system of natural farming methods that aimed at the highest-quality niche in the market. I hugged Marie-Noëlle, Robert's youngest daughter and the rebel of the family – after years of bumping around the African interior and the islands of the Indian Ocean she had recently settled down, less exotically, in a village less than an hour from Le Marronnier. I chatted with Jean-Jacques, Robert's son-in-law, owner of a flamboyant pair of curling moustaches. Jean-Jacques had spent his entire career as an agronomist researching tomato cultivation. His big news now: he had moved into an entirely new field of study, green peppers. Such were the rhythms that rang the changes of life in the steep little Dôa Valley behind Apt.

When people began moving to long trestle tables ranged under the big red tent I realised I was not going to make my 600-kiss quota. All around, mothers and family cooks were emptying bags and bundles. Soon the tables were groaning with a hundred fragrant things. It was time to eat.

There was little of the heavy fare the Chauvins ate at Christmas. With Jany on one side of me and Robert's oldest daughter, Monique, on the other, I gazed at a lighter feast of Provençal summer specialities. Odette's savoury *tomates farcies* were just the start. We moved on to duck paté on crusty bread, stuffed courgettes, spinach *caillettes*, tomato omelettes, *crème d'aubergines*, marinated mushrooms, olive *tapenade*. There were bottles of red wine and chilled rosé throughout, slices of Cavaillon melon and bowls of cherries to follow. Exuding the rich odours of rural kitchens and old family recipes, almost everything came from Chauvin fields and farmyards.

Just how rich those odours were I realised when we moved on to the cheese. Gérard never let a fête go by without laying on some of his prized goats' cheeses. With a loaded tray in his arms he moved from table to table, offering everyone a choice. Some cheeses were soft and fresh and mild – fat, white pucks hardly more than a few hours old. Others, hard, blackened little discs reduced to a quarter of their original size, had been dried over time. But the most breathtaking cheese was Gérard's *cachat*.

'It's nothing,' Monique said to me as she filled a small glass from a bottle of home-made *eau-de-vie*. For I must have looked dubious. The *cachat*, a thick white paste in an earthenware jar, was so smelly it almost audibly hummed.

'First, you spoon a bit of *cachat* onto a piece of bread and pop it into your mouth, like this ... Then you take a good bite of spring onion, like this ... You chew, and finally you wash it down with a big gulp of *eau-de-vie*, like this ... '

Gérard was watching us closely. Well, if his cousin Monique, a dainty little thing about half his size, could eat *cachat* so nonchalantly, so could I. I imitated her every gesture, and almost passed out. I had trouble breathing. The veins swelled in my throat, my forehead broke into a sweat, and the scene about me danced before my eyes.

When I finally came to my senses Gérard was laughing hard. 'That cheese has been closed up tight in its jar for more than six years. It's so strong not even maggots would look at it. You have to be a real Provençal to eat *cachat*.'

'Do you know,' I said to Monique as Gérard moved on, 'I'm not a real Provençal at all — if I hadn't drunk a large amount of rosé first I don't think I could have done that.'

'Don't worry,' she replied, smiling, her own forehead beaded with perspiration. 'Nobody could do that without drinking a large amount of rosé first. That's why we save it for fêtes.'

A few minutes before lunch broke up a distant cousin made the rounds drawing up lists. It was time for the annual Chauvin *boules* competition, an event hotly contested and rewarded each year with a large trophy cup.

There were some very good players present, but which team they were eventually assigned to was unimportant. What really counts in *boules* is not so much technical excellence as fervour and bravado. And in the fervour-and-bravado department almost everyone present was at championship level. Groups were formed and soon, to the afternoon buzzing of cicadas and the gentle snores of older Chauvins already deep in their siestas, was added the noise of half a dozen *boules* games.

Thwack! went the heavy steel balls as they flew through the air and crashed into other steel balls already lying on the ground. In its general objectives *boules* vaguely resembles that subtle Anglo game of the north, lawn-bowling. But *boules* is a Latin game, a Mediterranean melodrama. It produces large amounts of emotion. There is no polite and gentle applause, no quiet conferring over strategy in this exchange. *Boules* is all theatre, a show requiring as much verbosity as dexterity – it demands of its actors continuous joking, ribaldry, innuendo and destabilising verbal subterfuge.

'*Ô pauvre couillon!*' The words rose loud and strong above chortles of glee and groans of despair as one particularly crucial ploy failed miserably. And this was between members of the same team. But when one *boules*-player calls another *boules*-player a pathetic testicle it is not to be taken amiss. It is an essential part of the game.

I had decided not to play. Overwhelmed by *cachat*, I needed fresh air and a walk. So I joined a children's expedition being organised by Gérard. It seemed odd on this warm, bright day to see children arming themselves with electric torches and pullovers. But ten minutes later, up a dirt track towards the hill behind Les Jean-Jean, it all became clear. After the glare of the overhead sun the deep galleries of the farm's abandoned ochre mine were deliciously dark and cool.

Half an hour on the other side of Apt the village of Roussillon, built over a ravine of brilliant red and yellow ochre, attracts tens of thousands of tourists every year. Here Gérard had a whole hillside of the stuff to himself. Outside a large iron gate sunk into a vermilion-coloured bank of earth he took a head-count of a score or so of small Chauvins, and warned them not to wander off on their own. Then we marched into the hillside, the children delighting in the reverberating atmosphere with high-pitched yodels and express-train whistles.

As we walked, Gérard swept a high-powered beam down aisle after aisle of transverse galleries. They were twenty feet wide, forty feet high, and as red as blood. The walls were ruler-straight, the corners and edges cut in precise right angles. All of them had been painstakingly carved by hand. It was like walking in a Technicolor cathedral.

'One hundred and fifty years ago,' Gérard told me as we gazed upwards, 'there were enough miners here to keep half a dozen bars busy in Les Jean-Jean. Ochre was part of the local economy – it added to paint and coloured half the houses in southern Europe. Today, of course, paint is synthetic and mines like this are worthless.'

Not entirely, at least not in Gérard's case. He could find his entertainment anywhere. At an intersection I saw one wall marked by a long, deep gouge. 'Car rally, couple of years ago,' he explained. 'I took the corner too wide.' Further on, deep in the heart of the hill, we came to the highest, widest gallery of all. There, bordered by benches and generator-powered lights strung along the walls, stretched a forty-foot-long table.

'My banquet project,' Gérard said fondly. It was a bit of work to organise, he admitted, but when he was feeling particularly festive he threw big dinners in the mine, with cooks, scurrying waiters and musicians attending to the pleasure of his guests. 'Last time we had a small orchestra and a rather good opera singer from one of the local summer festivals. The acoustics,' he added modestly, 'are not bad at all.'

By the time we returned to Les Jean-Jean, all children accounted for, the *boules* competition was over. A winning team had been announced. Speeches had been made and cups presented. Gérard now threw himself into preparing an outdoor fire that would burn down to make coals for the evening *grillade*. There were piles of lamb cutlets and spicy

36

North African *merguez* sausages, and already Gérard was warming round wooden boxes of Camembert in the declining afternoon sun. Placed near the edge of the coals until they were scorched and smoking, they would yield up another of Gérard's favourite courses – Camemberts with slightly charred crusts which, once broken open, would reveal hot and steaming cheese so liquefied it had to be soaked up with bread. How could one create any discipline at all, General de Gaulle once lamented, in a country of 365 cheeses? De Gaulle, of course, had never counted on Gérard Chauvin's additional undisciplined innovations.

Odette, René, Jany and I did not stay on for the meal and the fireworks that followed. For Odette had a visit to make before evening fell and we returned to Aix-en-Provence.

On the edge of Apt we parked the car and walked through high iron gates into the town cemetery. We made our way over crunching gravel, past the crosses of the war-dead and the polished grey granite of bulky family mausoleums. Near a row of tall cypress trees we collected water from a tap in a small, battered green bucket and proceeded to Robert's grave. On a flat tablet of black marble there stood a small doubled-armed Cross of Lorraine, symbol of wartime resistance, and on either side of it a pot of flowers.

Odette stooped to carefully water the flowers. She righted herself, and stood silently in front of the grave with tears coursing down her cheeks.

'We can go now,' she said after for a minute or two.

We returned the watering bucket to its place beneath the cypresses. Then, with arms linked, saying nothing, we went slowly back to the car. Her second reunion of the day over, Odette was ready to go home.

∽

A couple of weeks later, sometime towards the end of May, I returned to Les Jean-Jean. One day there had not been enough. Celebrations are exceptional things, full of colour and emotion, but they say little about the real life of a place. If you want to get to know Trinidad, Venice or Rio de Janeiro you do not go there at Carnival time. The same, presumably, applied to Les Jean-Jean – I wanted to see the little hamlet just being itself. I had no doubt I would only be getting in the way, but over the telephone Gérard had been gracious enough to pretend along with me that I might be useful. In return for bed and board I would become, for a few days at any rate, a Provençal poultry-producer's apprentice.

I brought hot weather with me. Normally the fearful heatwaves of Provence – the *canicules*, or dog days – occur in high summer. But now an early *canicule*, its breath dry and panting, was hot on our heels. The windows of houses remained shuttered all day. Laundry no sooner hung on lines grew dry as parchment. Village streets remained silent and deserted between noon and four. And although the sky remained clear and achingly blue above the narrow valley of the Dôa, eyes were upcast more often than one might have thought necessary. For there never seemed to be a time of year when there was not some threat or other hovering just over the horizon. If it stayed too hot too long this early in the year, heavy storms would build and break. And that would threaten the wheat harvest, now just days away.

There was no red tent on the grounds beside Gérard's farmhouse when I arrived at noontime – just a dazzling overhead sun and tall clumps of grass leaning limply in the heat. The shade beneath the trees where I parked was so dark that, like a black hole in space, it seemed to possess solid, material properties of its own.

Nor were there any hula-dancers swaying seductively around Gérard's ample midriff when I located him in the little abattoir at the back of his farmyard. He was in work mode – despite the heat he was dressed in heavy boots and a white rubber apron. Any bright red about him at the moment was not Hawaiian hibiscus, but gouts of spattered blood. It was Monday, the day before Tuesday's Farmers' Market in Apt. On Mondays Gérard killed chickens.

Most of the morning's work had already been done – Gérard's industrial refrigerator was already full of plucked and hanging birds, their wings and legs neatly trussed against their bodies with elastic bands. They already looked familiar; not like the birds which clucked and pecked just outside, but like the chickens you buy at the butcher's. All around, though, was the evidence of the minor, violent struggles that had accompanied the transformation – buckets of blood, tubs of guts and heads, piles of claws, great heaps of sodden feathers.

Gérard was not alone in the little room. While he held down and bled briefly-flapping birds half a dozen helpers were busy over the less gory task of plucking. When there was a rush on, manpower was short and everyone in the family pitched in. I donned an apron myself and joined them.

Plucking chickens is not much fun. Heads down, they hang from a hook in front of you. Grasping a few damp feathers between thumb and forefinger close to the chicken's skin, you give a short, sharp tug. If the just-killed fowl has been submerged in near-boiling water for the right amount of time the feathers come away easily. If it has not you have a bothersome time ahead. What makes it all bearable, chicken after chicken, is the chatter.

On one side of me Sylviane was talking and plucking away at high speed. She and Gérard made an unlikely couple – where he was vast and lumbering, she was tiny, blonde, and quick on her feet. They were like Asterix and Obelix. But she was indispensable – slight as she was, she had a stabilising, down-to-earth influence on Les Jean-Jean. She ran the school kitchen in Rustrel, the village down the road, ensuring a second and steady income. With her two children from a previous marriage, she provided Gérard with a family he adored. And just as important, she kept Gérard in line when his Obelix-sized enthusiasms and projects became overlarge, which they sometimes did.

Behind me were Gérard's parents. Denis, now at least officially retired, was also an indispensable part of the enterprise – he was the chief feeder of hundreds of birds, and spent long afternoons grinding, mixing and distributing grain. In front of me was Gérard's sister, Magalie. Some years ago Magalie discovered she had a gift, a form of greater-than-ordinary physical sensitivity to illness, and began practising as a *guérisseuse*, or traditional country healer. Such arcane arts are old in rural France, and still command respect. These days Magalie was busy up and down the valley, and spent more time laying hands on humans than on chickens.

That left, crouched beneath the aluminium table where Gérard was busy removing last wisps of body-feathers with an acetylene torch, Sylviane's two little boys. Like any sensible children they were more interested in play than work – at the moment they were busy opening and closing chicken's claws by pulling at protruding tendons.

When the last gizzard was cleaned and the final liver de-veined, when the offal was binned and tables and floors hosed down, Gérard shut down for the morning. Off we trooped to lunch, his parents to their house on one side of the lane, Gérard and his family to their own house on the other. Neither old stone building had been altered in at least half a century. Like all genuine Provençal farmhouses not yet in the hands of well-heeled northern expatriates, they were striking in their sparse and utilitarian simplicity. The only decadent touch in Gérard's kitchen was an ancient stuffed

41

peacock, its dusty fan-tail spread over a sideboard and a rack of favourite hunting guns.

As a neophyte to the world of blood and feathers my own appetite was a little light that afternoon. No one else seemed bothered in the slightest.

'Ah, where's my *drap?*' Gérard sighed with satisfaction as he poured himself an aperitif of cold white wine. What, I wondered as he made for the sideboard, would he want with a sheet? Then I saw him tuck into his shirtfront the largest napkin I had ever seen.

'Couldn't eat without my *drap*, wouldn't be happy,' he said, arranging its folds around his knees before draining off his glass. And then, despite the wilting heat and the morning's sanguine proceedings, he settled down to lunch.

It must be said that under Sylviane's influence Gérard had cut down on food a lot. In his younger days, he told me as he sliced a couple of tomatoes from the garden, he could really put it away – he had once eaten 250 snails at a sitting before concerned friends had finally removed his plate. And then there was the memorable birthday party when he downed six litres of ice cream. But all that was over now, he assured me as he judiciously added a little olive oil and salt to the tomato slices. One had to be reasonable.

So, reasonably, we worked our way through an enormous mid-day meal – a freshly-roast duck, thick slices of smoked breast of ham, a coil of blood sausage, a gratin of courgettes, some cheese and fruit, the whole washed down with copious quantities of wine. It might as well have been dinner for Gérard – he had been up and working, as he was up and working every morning in summer, since four o'clock. And it might as well have been bedtime, too – by the time I left the house five minutes after lunch was over Gérard was fast asleep upstairs. A two-hour siesta was part of Les Jean-Jean's daily regime.

With keys jingling in my pocket, I made my way up to the little stone-built house lent to me for the duration. Empty for much of the year, it was a small jewel. Perched in woods high up on the valleyside, its delightful stone terrace looked out over the fields, vineyards and red-tiled roofs of the little Dôa Valley, and to the rugged slopes of the Grand Luberon beyond.

I tried for a while to sleep. No matter how uncreative it might look, the Mediterranean siesta is an art, and a noble one. It invigorates, renews and restores. Nor is it unproductive. It is reserved for that part of the day when strenuous effort in the hottest hours would only reduce total daily output. It is a practical and obvious solution, an adaptation of the body to the limits imposed by environment. That, at least, is what I told myself. But my Anglo body was not having any of it. The siesta has to be assiduously worked at by non-Mediterraneans – any activity carried out horizontally and with the eyes closed does not come easily to those brought up on the work ethic of the North. I couldn't sleep at all.

So instead I sat in the shade on the terrace of the house and simply enjoyed the place – the heavy, hypnotising *tzee-tzee-tzee* of cicadas singing in the surrounding pine trees; the velvety, light-green skin of the almonds growing on the tree below the terrace; the equally velvety feel of warm air on my own skin whenever the slightest breeze moved across the sun-heated hillside. I savoured the peace and tranquillity of it all. Provençal chicken-killing did not have quite the same emotional drama as, say, Spanish bull-fighting. But *frisson* or no *frisson*, I'd had enough blood for one day.

The sun was lower but hardly any cooler when I rejoined Gérard around four o'clock. He was starting his day for the second time with a small, strong cigar and a cup of coffee blacker even than the shade beneath the trees outside. All his tastes veered towards the keen, the vivid and the concentrated. Things got a little more vivid than I might have liked, though, when we headed over to the abattoir again. At Gérard's, death in the afternoon had nothing to do with bulls. The creatures we confronted instead were rabbits.

In the language of the French highways a *coup du lapin* is the equivalent of the Anglo driver's whiplash – violent trauma to the back of the neck that accompanies a rear-end collision. In Gerard's abattoir I discovered the origins of the expression. With a rabbit held upside down by the legs, Gérard delivered an abrupt, open-handed clout to the base of the animal's skull. It was all over in seconds, the vertebrae broken, the nerves of the stunned animal quivering, the knife sliding efficiently into the side of the throat and around.

Skinning a rabbit is like peeling off a glove. From a shallow incision around the midriff the fur is simply pulled away, right down the lower body to the top of the not-so-lucky rabbit's foot. The same happens to the upper half, right up to the once-wiggley nose.

Now none of this appeared to bother Sylviane's younger son at all. He was playing under the table, humming a song as one little bunny after another was turned inside out. He was not insensitive; he was one of the sweetest little children I have ever met. But at five years old he had seen it all before.

I hadn't, and it bothered me. The pulling-away of clean, white fluffy fur to reveal naked pink flesh beneath reminded me, obscenely, of changing a baby's diaper. I stood there for a while with my hand held defensively to my own throat, trying not to show my alarm. Somewhere around the fourth rabbit, though, it all became too much, and I made for the door.

Outside the sun was still shining and the world turning unperturbed. I wandered down to the other end of the farmyard, where Gérard's father was pouring maize seed into the rumbling, funnel-like mouth of a battered old electrically-powered mill. It was making a great din, and every now and then emitted a strange pinging noise from somewhere deep inside its steel casing.

45

'This mill's like me. At our age we've both got dodgy digestion,' Denis chuckled when he finally turned the machine off. 'You know, I've been pouring grain down this poor machine's throat for over sixty years. I began on days-off from school when I was ten. The motor's not so good now. But we're old friends and we stick together. If its magneto doesn't go first, then mine will.'

Denis was an inveterate *raconteur*, a funny, irrepressible teller of pungent stories and improbable conceits. He always had the saving jest – in his ability to make light, to amuse, to smooth over the rough spots of life, he was equal to any situation. Behind the broad banter lay kindness.

I imagined Denis could see I was looking a little pale in the bright sunlight. Apart from the occasional plate of *civet de lapin* – another of Odette's Provençal specialities – the only rabbits I had ever encountered were the funny ones in cartoons. I certainly had not seen them having their faces pulled off. I told Denis I feared I hadn't much of a stomach for blood.

'Oh, you'll get over it,' he said as he began pouring milled grain into the clattering, revolving paddles of an ancient baker's kneading machine that stood beside the mill. 'It's different out in the country. You live with animals. First you feed them, then they feed you.' He added water and chunks of old baguette that Gérard picked up from local bakeries. The machine began churning the mixture into a thick mash.

'When I was a boy I was mad about ortolans,' he said. 'They are a tiny bird, but they used to fill the skies, millions of them. I used to shoot a couple of thousand a year, sometimes a hundred or so in a single morning. You hang them until they are very soft, about a week, then skewer half a dozen on a spit in front of a fire. The heat bursts them, and you put pieces of bread below to catch the insides. You eat the bread and guts first, then the entire bird, bones and all. You just crunch it up. There's nothing left but the beak and claws. That, plus a salad from the garden and omelettes from eggs in the hen-house would feed a whole family. Sometimes we'd find truffles on the hillsides and slice them into the omelettes. The whole lot cost us nothing. We used to call those meals *les festins des pauvres*. They were delicious.' Remembering his poor man's feasts, Denis' eyes lit up.

He began pouring out the mash into buckets. 'Of course, I don't hunt ortolans anymore. It's illegal. There aren't very many left. But Gérard and I still hunt thrush. We lime the tree branches and lure the birds in with *appelants* – singing thrush we keep in cages. It's much more difficult than catching chickens. But we've always done it – hunting's part of life here.'

If Denis was trying to offer some sort of comfort it didn't seem to me he was doing much of a job. Shooting small songbirds is the kind of southern habit that is almost guaranteed to arouse northern ire. But as I followed him round various runs, carrying buckets and helping feed animals all eventually headed for the knife and the pot, I thought I saw what he was getting at.

He was right. It *was* different out in the country, at least out in this country. In Burgundy the French peasantry had been eating snails long before they became a sought-after delicacy of *haute cuisine*. In the Lyonnais marshlands frogs were being hunted before Auguste Escoffier ever thought of turning them into *cuisses de nymphes aurore* – dawn nymph's legs – for the Prince of Wales' dinner at the Carlton Hotel. Wherever the French peasantry has made a living from the land it has hunted and killed small wild animals. For centuries it wasn't a question of taste at all, but a strategy for survival. If getting extra meat meant putting tiny birds on spits, well then, on spits they were put, and their bones and bodies crunched up for every last gram of protein.

Nothing was overlooked then, and nothing is overlooked now – when a pig is killed in a French rural farmyard there is no part of it left unused but the squeal. When food has become that important there is a less fastidious division between killing it and consuming it than in the world I had grown up in. Of course I could pretend that the supermarket chicken I usually ate had never been anything other than a piece of food neatly wrapped in plastic and styrofoam. But seen from a farmyard, Denis was saying, raising, slaughtering and eating animals was all part of the same process. It was hardly worth denying.

⇛

It was still dark and cool the next morning when, at a little before six o'clock, I arrived back in the farmyard. Gérard had already been up for a couple of hours, enough time to carefully weigh, wrap and load freshly-plucked birds into his old Peugeot van. He had spruced himself up for the Farmer's Market in Apt. The blood-spattered apron was gone. The unruly beard was neatly combed. This was not a Hawaiian shirt day but, just a grade lower on Gérard's scale of formal social accoutrements, a Provençal shirt day. Bright yellow with diamond patterns, the shirt was added to boots, old shorts and a battered straw hat. Together they made up what Gérard considered to be one of his nattier outfits.

He spruced the van up too. After twenty-two years of farm service his Peugeot J-9 needed it. I couldn't understand how the French, who design sleek machines like the Concorde and the *Train à Grande Vitesse*, could also come up with the J-9. It was a right-angled box of corrugated iron on wheels, so breathtakingly styleless and utilitarian that it had a certain *je ne sais quoi* of its own. But the sliding side-panel door was held closed with a bungee cord and the passenger door could not be opened at all. The radiator was badly dented and there were deep scratches along one side. However, once we had driven the six miles into town and parked beside other farmer's vans on the Cours Lauze-de-Perret the J-9 underwent radical transformation.

With the back doors swung open Gérard slid an electrically-cooled, glass-covered display case into position overhanging the van's rear end. Like delicate little skirts, lengths of cheerful blue and yellow Provençal cloth were clothes-pegged to doors and bumpers. A large, café-style parasol was set up over the display case, providing shade for customers. A colourful hand-painted wooden panel featuring waddling ducks and rabbits hopping over streams was put in place on the sidewalk. Neatly labelled, it proclaimed to the world at large the existence of *La Basse Cour des Jean-Jean* – The Jean-Jean Farmyard. Dressed and decorated, the van had become a poultryman's showpiece. By the time a dozen birds had been neatly laid out behind glass, their heads and long necks draped artistically backwards over their shoulders, I felt this was a conspicuously superior operation.

So did the customers who began showing up as the sun climbed the sky. The men and women selling produce here were not the practised professionals who made their living selling wholesale-purchased goods day after day in an endless circuit of Provençal towns. These were local farmers. But in drumming up custom they, too, had that rapid patter, the quick wit and jocular repartee which has always been the hallmark of any meeting of Provençal people.

'Ô Madame, buy a few bunches of my spinach!' one burly farmer to our right would inveigle a passing shopper. 'It will give your husband extra vigour!'

'Never mind your husband, Madame; forget the spinach!' rejoined another on our left, with a suggestive nod and wink. 'Look at my cucumbers. Now that's vigour! Buy them instead!'

Gérard, though, stayed above this good-humoured, often salty banter. He would trade jokes and mock-invective with his fellow farmers, but when it came to customers, he simply stood by silently, letting his produce and his own imposing presence speak for him. And speak it did. All sorts of people came to buy a goose breast, half a duck perhaps, or maybe a whole chicken to roast for dinner. Some were first-time customers. Others had sampled Gérard's poultry before, and were coming back for more.

'It's nothing like a store-bought chicken,' they would say. 'It's got texture. It tastes the way my grandfather's chickens used to taste.' In answer to these compliments Gérard would smile with keen pleasure, and tell them how best to baste the beast, how long to cook it, what wine to serve it with. It made him genuinely happy to see others made happy by what he did. The morning ended when he gave his last chicken as a present to the young farming couple parked beside us. In return they gave us a crate of small, juicy Cavaillon melons, the first of which we devoured, their hollowed centres filled with muscat wine, the moment we sat down to lunch at Les Jean-Jean. It had been a satisfying morning.

～

Gérard was not so sweetly disposed when he confronted that afternoon's task. For years he had been fulminating against the encroachments into his life by distant, invisible, but powerful opponents – the agricultural commissioners of the

51

European Union in faraway Brussels. He took their ever-tighter restraints on traditional peasant farming methods as a personal attack. As I followed him out into his farmyard he seemed to be searching for something. But as he walked Gérard maintained a running diatribe.

It was the EU and their ridiculous regulations that were ruining the chances of good food ever being produced, he muttered as he gazed left and right. With rules that suited vast economies of scale, Brussels was handing the future to industrial food giants. Monstrous multinationals were making synthetic food with long shelf-life and no soul. Small producers of genuine, high-quality food, producers like himself, were being squeezed out, he growled, now striding purposefully towards the distant end of the yard. EU rules were not just impoverishing consumers' tastes – they were doing the same thing to peasant-producers' wallets.

What Gérard was gnashing his teeth over was an upgrading to his abattoir. It was not enough that he had put in a drained floor, electricity, refrigeration and running water. If he wanted to stay on the right side of those bastards up north, he said, he was now going to have to cover the building's interior with insulated siding as well. Luckily, he had just the thing, if only he could only put his hands on it.

Far beyond his bird-runs, we made our way deep into the nether reaches of an uncharted territory where few but Gérard knew their way. For here lay an astounding collection of objects given, bartered, inherited, bought cheap, hauled from the dump or recovered from the side of the road. We picked our way between old cars, hydraulic pumps and hoses, pneumatic wood-splitters, outsize plastic tanks and fibreglass containers, rusty metal bins and wooden palettes, shopping carts, old refrigerator motors, metal sinks, coils of wire, iron railing, superannuated hotel kitchen equipment, pipes and plumbing, stained bath tubs and outdated toilet cisterns.

'Aha!' Gérard finally shouted triumphantly, pulling at a pile covered with tin sheeting. 'I always say you never know when you might need something.' And there it lay, a stack of aluminium siding, only slightly damaged, recuperated from a supermarket building site years before. It was not perhaps going to make the hearts of the hygiene-hysteric Brussels' commissioners swell with pride, Gérard admitted. But it might just get him through the next inspection. We spent the rest of the afternoon dragging it over to the abattoir, and stayed up long after dark, cursing, cutting and fitting it.

⌒

It was still dark as, early in the morning, we drove the loaded J-9 up the winding valley road to the pretty little hillside village of Rustrel. When the French military interred their nuclear missile arsenal in underground silos on the Albion Plateau above the village, Rustrel had been a popular billet for military families – the place had bustled with men in khaki and housewives happy to spend their husband's military pay cheques. In these post-cold-war days, though, with Albion

53

wound down and the military families transferred elsewhere, Rustrel had reverted to what it had always been – a sleepy little place with an even sleepier once-a-week morning market.

Nonetheless, Gérard was offering it the full *Basse Cour* treatment. Up went the blue and yellow Provençal cloth on the van parked beneath plane trees on the village square; out came the display case, the parasol, the panel with the waddling ducks and leaping rabbits. Out, too, came, all sorts of things Gérard had not put on sale in Apt. Roasted in the kitchen oven by Sylviane the night before, there were golden-brown, ready-to-eat ducks and chickens. There were cases of fresh goats' cheeses; baskets of strawberry jelly Gérard had made in his transport-truck field-kitchen; stacked pots of watermelon preserves spiked with sticks of vanilla; tins of paté flavoured with sprigs of sage; jars of lavender honey collected from hives in the fields behind Les Jean-Jean. There was even a miniature wooden wheelbarrow filled with lollipops of hardened honey. There was so much that while Gérard manned the poultry case at the back of the van I was put in charge of a heavily-loaded table beside it.

Other vendors who arrived on the square were no less busy setting up. A wine merchant constructed towering pyramids of Côtes du Ventoux bottles on his stand. A vegetable-lady built tall piles of purple-black aubergines and shiny red peppers on hers. The local baker's wife laid out dainty croissants, fresh baguettes and large rounds of thick-crusted country bread. The *escargotier* of Rustrel, a man with a flair for drama, assembled an elaborate sort of miniature theatrical stage, complete with red velvet curtains, to highlight his stock of snails. A flower-seller filled buckets with water and set out fresh-cut flowers, making bright explosions of colour on a square now growing dappled beneath a fast-rising sun.

The only things missing were customers. For all the charm of the shady little square, for all the care given to the display of good rural produce, there was barely anyone to appreciate it. Except for two or three small children on bicycles who regarded it as their private raceground, the surrounding streets, the whole village appeared almost deserted. So when everything was set up the stallholders decamped *en masse* to a large terrace table at the nearby Bistrot de la Place, and called for café au lait. We were hungry, too – it was a little early for snails, but for a long time the only business conducted that morning were our own personal trading transactions involving croissants, jam and pain au chocolat.

No one minded. The morning, the pastries, and the gossip were all fresh and invigorating. Every now and then one of us would wander back to the stalls to shoo away a leg-lifting dog or pick up a small, wailing cyclist who had collided with a plane tree. Occasionally a potential customer would wander onto the square and stroll about, sniffing at this and prodding at that. Then the table would empty, each stallholder heading to his or her post. Sometimes there would be a sale. More often than not it would prove a false alarm, and we would drift back to the café and desultory conversation.

I was getting worried we wouldn't sell any chickens. At this rate not even a single lollipop was going to change hands. The Soviet empire had not been all evil, I remarked to Gérard – it had, at least, been good for Rustrel.

But he had kept his equanimity. '*Vas doucement le matin, et pas trop fort l'après-midi*,' he said, smiling as he stretched back in his chair. Go easy in the morning, and not too hard in the afternoon. 'Yes, that's my motto. One needs a little patience. We weren't going to get rich today anyway. We might get rich tomorrow, but I doubt it. In the meantime we can enjoy things just as they are at the moment.'

I sat back, too, and tried not to think about not selling chickens. I knew that Gérard did not have any such motto at all – when there were things to do he worked harder and more enthusiastically than the next three people put together. But I also knew that when there was nothing to be done he was much better at sitting back and enjoying life than I was. In Italy it is a recognised activity with a name of its own: *il dolce far niente* – literally, 'the sweetness of doing nothing'. The Provencaux happily pursue the same activity. Like the siesta, the ability to simply enjoy the surrounding world is a skill, very close to the Mediterranean heart, that takes practice – it certainly doesn't come naturally to those who fret over selling chickens when there are no buyers of chickens about.

And so I relaxed. Mid-morning came and went. The day grew warmer. Large glasses of cold beer began replacing small cups of hot coffee. The wine merchant got a game of *boules* going. Nobody seemed in the slightest way upset that the market had been a wash-out. Eventually I did sell some lollipops and jam, and Gérard a couple of chickens. He seemed entirely satisfied. I suppose we might have just covered our costs, but I didn't have my mind on the maths of it. It was too hot.

As we drove back to Les Jean-Jean over narrow back-roads I asked Gérard how he had got started chicken-farming in the first place. It was easy, he told me. Before he kept poultry he had kept a large herd of goats and made cheese. But it was too much – he had stopped when he woke up one morning and realised he had not had a single holiday in five years.

And before that, I asked?

Eh bien, before that things were a little more difficult. He had come very close to dying. In his late twenties, he said as we rolled along through a coloured patchwork of fields, he had taken a job driving an electric fork-lift in an Apt fruit-packing plant. One day, pushed for time and paying less attention than he should have, he had gone around a corner with a heavy load raised too high on the lift. Four tons of machine had toppled over on him. The last thing he heard before he lost consciousness was the sound of bones snapping. When he woke up there was not a single one of his ribs left intact. His lungs were punctured, his spinal cord displaced, some vertebrae split, his scapula fractured and his legs broken. If he had not been such a big man in the first place he would certainly have been killed.

'It was well over a year before I was up and about. I rather lost confidence in myself. I thought I would never have a life again. But I do. And that is wonderful.' He smiled. 'And that is why I don't worry if I sell fewer chickens today than I did yesterday.'

We came to a halt at a stop sign by an intersection. And for one brief moment, without any help from Gérard, I knew I felt what he felt about enjoying the surrounding world just as it was.

Four different fields met here, one at each corner of the crossroads. This was not a country where farmers grew vast acres of anything. Instead, they grew a little bit of this and some of that, so spreading the risk – if one crop failed, another might succeed. From the stop sign each direction I looked in made the world seem a different place. Together they made it delightful.

Ahead of me, to my left, rows of gnarled grapevines were coming up fresh and green, their leaves still new and soft, their growing tendrils curling out into the air in search of support. Off to my right a tawny-golden carpet of ripe wheat rustled in the breeze, the top of each whispering stalk bent with the weight of a full head of grain. To one side behind me lay the dark, lush green of a cherry orchard; here and there, wherever they had been missed by the pickers, small, bursting globes of now overripe fruit glinted a deep, rich red through the leaves. To the other side grew a field of lavender, greeny-purple at its thinly growing edges, a dense, saturated

58

colour at its heart. Lavender's clean, sharp, astringent smell blew hot through the open window.

It was only one panorama among the thousand to be found along every summer road in Provence. But it stayed in my mind, so rich and varied and alive was it, so complex and so simple. And so fleeting, too – when I returned the next day to look at the four fields again the wheat had been cut and the symmetry was gone. Which is why Gérard was right. The only way to enjoy things is at the very moment, now and just as they are.

〜

That afternoon Gérard hitched a flat-bed wagon to the back of his Massey Ferguson tractor. Ahead of us lay a little task that couldn't have been a pleasant chore even in the dead of winter. In the middle of a summer heat wave it took everything I had not to gag as we loaded a large tub of chicken guts and hauled it up the hill for disposal.

Gérard was all right – driving the tractor, he stayed upwind. But no matter where I stood on the wagon I could not get far enough away from the fermenting bouillon of intestines that was slopping about in an open 120-litre plastic container. If there is anything smellier than *cachat* this was it.

There was worse. As the tractor began climbing a steep and rutted track up into the hills I could see danger – already one of the lengths of baling twine holding the tub to the wagon floor had given way. The rest might snap at any moment. The whole stinking, jiggling, agitated mess would go flying. Taking a last, deep lungful of relatively uncontaminated air I advanced on the fly-swarming offal, holding my breath and the violently bouncing tub of guts at the same time. By the time we had risen into forests high above the valley floor I was red-faced and swooning.

In a small glade Gérard backed the tractor to the edge of a deep hole, and together we tipped the heavy tub from the rear end of the wagon. Down the contents went with a loud, wet, sucking sound. It could not disappear fast enough for me. Who needed missiles in underground silos? In the panoply of chemical and biological agents available to the world, Gérard's subterranean cache of chicken guts surely rated among the mightier deterrents.

We had not finished with the tractor yet. In an hour we were back up the hill again, not with another 120 litres of fermenting intestines, but with a much bigger tank sitting astride the wagon. It was time to water Gérard's other animals.

For Gérard took it upon himself not only to care for the hundreds of domestic animals flapping about his farmyard; in the summer months when rain was scarce he worried about pheasants, hares, deer, wild boar and the other wild beasts of the woods and hills. When heat and sun had dried up the last remaining water in streams and puddles, he made the rounds, filling the little concrete ponds he had constructed in the forest.

I will not, of course, pretend Gérard was some sort of
Provençal Saint Francis, a sprout-eating, animal-rights paci-
fist offering protection to all creatures great and small. He
liked having wild animals around because he liked shooting
them. Hunting was one his great passions, and whenever he
had a few free hours he would walk off into the hills with a
gun and his dogs. Even he wasn't sure which he liked best,
eating food or hunting it. It amounted to the same thing,
anyway – half the pâtés, hams, smoked meats and sausages
hanging in the cool obscurity of his cellar came from the hills
rather than the farmyard.

But as we trundled through the woods, filling one watering hole after another, I could also see Gérard's love of the
outdoors and its inhabitants. He knew every path, every rise
and fall in the terrain, every tree along the way. When we
came to one tree looking particularly poorly, it roots exposed
and its leaves drooping, we stopped and watered that, too.

There was even a rough field up here which Gérard
ploughed and sowed every year with oats for the birds to
feed on. Beside it was a small hunting blind he had built,
its interior complete with stone seats and a miniature fireplace for waiting out long, cold winter hours. As we now
crouched for a moment in its summer shade Gérard grew
lyrical describing the chase: the rising in the pre-dawn dark;
the trudging across frozen fields and forests, the frenzy of the
dogs, noses to the ground, when they came across a scent; the
pulse-rate climbing as the tracks were pursued; the sighting

of the quarry; and finally, the shot fired and a limp body, still warm beneath soft fur or feathers, being gently, almost lovingly, slid into a game-bag.

I am not a hunter. Such pictures failed to raise in me any primal, deep-rooted instincts. But later, as I sat on the terrace of my little house on the hill enjoying the day's slow transition into night, the images returned.

It was an evening of blue and gold. The sky, the land beneath it, the air between the terrace and valley below – all were filled with a bright luminescence. Halfway between warmth and coolness, light and darkness, the whole country glowed with a mysterious amalgam of two hues, blended and separate at the same time. As the day slowly died, its gilded tints bled from the atmosphere. As twilight came on, a serene blue grew in the same proportion as the gold diminished. It settled on the wheat fields, in the spaces between the nearby trees, in the ridges furrowing the slopes of the distant Luberon. It grew deeper and richer by the moment until it, too, peaked and gradually began to fade away. Eventually it was night and there was no colour left at all.

I watched the light fade thinking that this was as beautiful and peaceful a place as I had ever been. And yet at the same time there were equally strong and opposite impressions – naked, quivering bunnies, tubs of innards, sudden, lethal gunshots by peacefully waving fields of oats. It definitely wasn't the Provence I had gazed at in the glossy coffee-table picture books. This was a different world, sensuous certainly, but not the fashionable and sterilised sensuality we are normally given to peruse. It had something to do with that larger, more complete Mediterranean life I had been thinking about ever since my return from London. It all made for a curious mix, and I turned it over repeatedly in my mind. If I had not been quite so worn out, I might not have gone to sleep for a long time that evening.

෴

Next morning Gérard got an emergency phone call. A friend's freezer had broken down and an entire hunting-season's worth of wild boar – two or three hundred kilos of livers, loins and chops – was rapidly thawing out. By this point I was quite capable of forming a vision of the kind of chaotic and meaty mess Gérard was likely to get himself involved in, and I declined to go along for the ride. Instead I took up his father Denis' invitation to help him look after the shop.

This was not quite the dull duty it might have seemed. The 'shop' was a small room off Gérard's house, and gave onto a wide spot in the lane that ran through the hamlet of Les Jean-Jean. Inside there were fresh eggs for sale, and shelves of the home-made jams, pâtés and other produce Gérard sold from his van. Just outside the shop's lavender-blue door, protected from the sun by tall, broad, shade trees, sat benches and a table. This was Denis' *quartier-géneral*, the place from which he kept an eye out for customers. As there were only two or three of these a morning, and anyone who came after eleven o'clock was invited to stay for a pre-lunch aperitif, minding the shop was a relaxed affair.

I found Denis in a contemplative mood, sitting and gazing up at one of the trees stretching over our heads – a large, broad-leafed chestnut.

'I know this tree very well,' he told me. 'I've been looking at it almost every day of my life since I planted it with my father. I was eighteen. I like to watch the way it changes from day to day.'

Not long after he planted the tree, Denis said, he was conscripted. It was the time of France's war against Algerian independence and he spent two years languishing in a French desert-camp on the Libyan border. He was supposed to be on the lookout for camel-borne gun-running. He saw nothing at all, sometimes not even his own tent, he claimed – he'd spent most of his time out there in sandstorms. Apart from that period under canvas he had never lived anywhere but Les Jean-Jean.

'In all my life I've lived in just three houses,' he said. 'Every one of them is within fifty metres of where we're sitting – there's the house Gérard lives in now; there's the school-teacher's house, where I lived after I married the new teacher and where Gérard was born; and then there's my parents' house, to which we returned. I sleep in the same upstairs room I was born in.'

From the main road it looked uninspiring, just another small collection of old houses. But in Les Jean-Jean Denis had nonetheless created an entire universe, complete with its own rhythms and crowded with its own significance. He knew a thousand stories. He knew the little place's history, its inhabitants, its dramas and tragedies. He could tell you about the fabulous ochre-mining days or the miseries of the German occupation. He could show you the place where, before his great-great-grandfather put in pipes and a stone fountain, Les Jean-Jean's restorative water sprang from between the living roots of an oak tree.

Here there were all sorts of wonderful things, near-magical things, he told me, if only one had the time and the patience, and the eyes to look. Why, said Denis, in this very hamlet there was even a plant whose flowers opened at the precisely the same time every evening and then dropped off, only to be replaced the next evening by fresh buds that in their own turn bloomed and died.

I was doubtful. Denis was not above pulling the leg of an innocent foreigner. It sounded a little too miraculous, I replied, even for Les Jean-Jean.

'But it's true!' he insisted. 'Come, and I'll show you.'

So off we trotted down the lane, dodging from one cool patch of shade to the other, until we arrived at the family garden. It was a vast plot, furrow after furrow of lush vegetables growing beneath the hot sun. Leading me past beans on runners and tomato plants carefully tied to bamboo stakes, Denis took me to a far corner of the garden. There, planted in a neat row, half a dozen leafy bushes grew chest-high.

'*Voilà!*' he said proudly. 'I found them a few years ago growing down by the Dôa and dug a few up. Do you see these tightly rolled flowers? Well, at nine o'clock every evening they unfold and open. Pop! Just like that, they unfurl in front of you, all at the same time. It's a big yellow flower the bees go crazy for. They only bloom once and die the same night. It's a spectacle. Sometimes I pull a chair over here, sit down with a glass of pastis, and wait. You'll have to see it. It's better than television.'

The whole notion of watching flowers come and go before your eyes sounded improbable but attractive. I agreed I would have to see it. But before that happened there were a few necessary and rather less attractive chores to undertake.

Among his animals Gérard had four or five sheep. He got them as lambs but, as will happen, they had grown. They would soon reach the point where their meat would too tough and scrappy to eat, and it was time to slaughter them.

Sheep are large animals, and together this little flock made too big a job for Gérard alone. He had invited in a professional colleague. Pierre had worked for years at the Apt municipal abattoir. He was brawny, small, feisty, and as full of energy as an alkaline battery. You could feel the nervous discharge in the air around him when he turned up after the siesta that afternoon. As I watched him getting suited up for work I could see he meant business.

He wore the same white rubber apron and high rubber

boots that Gérard did, but in addition carried four thin knives in a belted holster on his waist. He also wore a sort of chain-mail glove on his left hand, protection against his own blade, made of very fine steel mesh. No matter that his knives were already razor-sharp; before the first sheep was hauled in he walked about the abattoir in small, tight circles sharpening them on a steel; *shkk-shkk, shkk-shkk, shkk-shkk*, they went, the bright blades flashing at lightning speed under the ceiling's fluorescent glare.

Then it was down to work. Up into the air went a bleating sheep, its hind legs attached to a block and tackle hanging from a beam. Pierre's knife flashed just once, so quickly that I did not realise the animal's throat had been slashed. Suddenly, with the same splashing sound as a large tap suddenly opened full-bore, there was blood all over the floor. At the same time there was a dreadful squeaking and gurgling, the noise of the sheep drawing breath through its gaping throat. Barely had both sounds subsided – it lasted only seconds but seemed forever to me – when Pierre quite literally threw himself into his work.

I had never seen anyone go so hard at anything. As it is most everywhere else, time in big commercial slaughter-houses is money. But even by professional standards Pierre had developed a whirlwind style. He was everywhere at once, boots splattered, apron dripping, hands gummy with blood. His knife was fast and tireless as he sliced skin, snapped shinbones, popped testicles from scrotums, peeled off heavy woollen fleeces like so many winter jackets. When fat or sinews opposed his progress he would hurl himself sideways against the sheep's body, seeking leverage by pulling the resisting pelt downward over his raised shoulder with both hands. When he got down to red meat his pace picked up even further. Pierre went at the hanging carcass with maniacal intensity. He hacked, he sawed, he chopped and cleaved. He sweated, he cursed, he joked, he grunted. When there was nothing left of one sheep he moved straight onto the next.

'Pierre's a little bit crazy,' Gérard whispered to me as I stood there, goggle-eyed at the performance. I think even he was impressed. 'He'd been in that abattoir too long. It's the smell of the blood that does it, you know.'

All I knew was that I wanted out. It did not matter that I enjoyed meat as much as the next non-vegetarian. It didn't matter that if people were going to enjoy their *Rognons d'agneau à la moutarde* this kind of thing had to happen in a thousand places a thousand times a day. Muttering a quick goodbye, I made my way outside and up the hill for a long walk in the forest.

That night at dinner, after a steadying glass or two of wine, I asked Gérard how he coped with all the blood. I knew he was proud of the fine food he produced, I said. And so he should be. But what did he feel about the chickens and rabbits and sheep that became meat? Didn't their deaths bother him?

He did not answer me; at least, he did not answer me directly. Instead, after a long moment's thought, he told me a hunting story.

A few days after a particularly festive Christmas some winters before, he said, he had felt like being on his own for a while. Taking his favourite dog, he climbed high onto a rough plateau several miles up the valley. There was an isolated hunting cabin up there where Gérard knew he could find a quiet three or four days.

Early on New Year's morning he went out with his gun and dog and soon found the spoor of a large deer. It was easy enough for his dog to follow, for there was blood in the tracks. Nonetheless, Gérard pursued the traces for a long way until, some six hours later, he finally came across his prey. It was a magnificent animal, a stag with a broad rack of horns. Exhausted and unable to go any farther, it was sitting upright on a rocky shelf. There was a deep wound in its foreleg.

No distance away, Gérard dropped down, so as not to frighten the animal, and simply sat there. For maybe half an hour he looked unwaveringly at the stag. And the stag looked back unwaveringly at him.

'There was something that passed between us,' Gérard said, his voice gone husky, his dinner in front of him forgotten. 'I don't know what it was, but it was important.'

The animal was no longer afraid, and understood Gérard would not hurt it. Gérard finally got up and approached the stag, stroking its coat and talking to it. For a long time they sat together in perfect peace. Then Gérard, with no option to being caught outdoors on a freezing winter's night, headed back to the cabin. When he went back to the rock early the next morning the stag was gone.

What was just as remarkable as the story was the obvious effect it had on Gérard. As he recounted the tale it assumed an almost mythological quality, and he an almost dream-like state. When he finished he seemed to come back to himself from a long way away.

'I still don't understand it,' he said simply. 'But it was one of the most powerful moments of my life.'

I did not understand it either, but I think I knew why he had answered my question with his story. Animals were part of Gérard's existence, so much a part that he could not separate their lives from his own, their violent and sudden deaths from the death that, equally violent and sudden, had come so close to him. They shared the same world, and he saw them as he saw himself. When things are that close, that integral a part of life, they are too near to judge or answer to.

The days passed, the heat remained, and I fell into a kind of sun-dazed rhythm. I got up before light and went to bed after dark. In my after-lunch siestas I learned to sleep deeply but not long, and felt I was getting double value, two days for the price of one. I helped Gérard make paté in his transport-truck kitchen. I went to markets in the old Peugeot van. I sold jam and jelly in the shop. I paddled in a plastic garden-pool with the children. I put up more siding. I drank pastis and ate gargantuan meals. I played *boules* with Gérard and Magalie in the rutted lanes of Les Jean-Jean by day, and alone watched the stars wheel above the Luberon hills late at night.

More important, I became a competent plucker of feathers. I also came some way to accepting the struggles, human and animal, that go into making good food and a good life in the Provençal countryside. In short, by the time of my departure I had made a little progress in my education as a poultry-producer's apprentice.

I had arrived in Les Jean-Jean with a heatwave and, curiously, left the little hamlet on the day it broke. The morning had started clear enough, but there was a pronounced sultriness in the air, and by noon dark and heavy clouds had started building. The long-feared storm was on its way, but it did not matter now. The wheat harvest was behind us and the grain safely stored in sheds and barns.

I was sitting in the kitchen with Gérard and his family, stupefied by one last, vast, lavish lunch, when Gérard's father burst in through the door.

'Quick, quick!' Denis shouted. 'They are opening! The flowers are opening! They think the night is coming. It's the clouds making the sky dark. The flowers think it's nine o'clock! Follow me!'

We all leapt from the table and rushed off down the lane

after Denis. Off course I had forgotten all about the story of the nine o'clock flowers, and was going to leave without ever seeing if it was true. But the clouds had changed that.

When we arrived in front of the flowers – I think now they were some sort of evening primrose – Denis already had a big grin on his face. It was just as he said. Triggered by a suddenly darker sky, scores of tightly closed flowers were unfurling. It was like watching a piece of speeded-up film. One moment the flowers were long, narrow cylinders, the next they were spreading outwards, like butterflies opening their wings, into brilliant yellow blooms.

We all broke into applause. I was cheering not only because this was so unexpected and visually startling. I was cheering because the others were cheering, because these delicate, short-lived flowers seemed as important to the inhabitants of Les Jean-Jean as anything else. Their sudden emergence in the family's garden was as vital to them, as much a part of life, as the equally sudden exit of the chickens, rabbits, and sheep around the corner in Gérard's abattoir. Both were part of that larger Mediterranean life, that older existence – immediate, profound and compelling – that I had been looking for.

I gazed on, spellbound. A few fat drops of rain began falling. We all looked skyward, then scattered.

Three

The Micheline, the blocky little four-carriage commuter train that trundles south from Aix-en-Provence several times a day, is nothing like the *Train à Grande Vitesse*. The TGV barrels down from Paris in just over three hours, its aerodynamically-raked body howling along a modern high-speed rail link at 160 miles an hour. The tired and unwashed Micheline, on the other hand, slowly sways and clatters its way over a spur-line built more than a century ago. There are no public announcements offered for the long delays that often hold the train up *en route*. But the people of the Midi are even better at talking as they are at listening – conversation rattles along at a good clip even if the little train doesn't. Eventually, delays barely noticed, passengers arrive in the Mediterranean waterfront city of Marseilles.

For Jany and me the Micheline's slow crawl towards Marseilles' St Charles station on this still and airless afternoon was as dramatic as any arrival by sleek, long-haul TGV. Although Aix sits just twenty short miles away, the two cities are so dissimilar that to disembark in the station's cavernous and echoing interior is to step down into another country.

In the past there had been brief visits when, finding Aix just a little too self-consciously fashionable, its nose just a little too high in the air, I had taken to strolling the down-to-earth streets of Marseilles. Christmas, for example, was a perfect time to escape the faux yuletide cheer of Aix's luxury shops and shoppers for the grittier pleasures of the Old Port. The Micheline would drop me off in the morning and have me back, feet cold but faith in humanity restored, by evening.

Now, even with the windows lowered it was stifling in the train compartment as the high-rise tenements and outer suburbs of the city rolled by. The early heat wave that had engulfed Les Jean-Jean may have passed, but as high summer approached day after day of torrid sun was baking the city as dry and pale and brittle as a biscuit. Given half a chance even the proudest, toughest Marseilles street-kid would have cleared off its hot and oppressive sidewalks, happy to have his nose in higher, cooler air elsewhere.

But to me, now beginning to relax and enjoy my search for an elusive Mediterranean world, it seemed that this was also the best season to wander about the city. Even brief excursions here in wintertime had taught me that Marseilles' reputation as a mean place was undeserved. But it had felt closed-up then. Its beaches were dank and deserted, its doors shut tight against the gusty Mistral, its streets abandoned for warmth and companionship indoors. Now things were different. Marseilles is like nowhere else on earth, but in summer it resembles every other city on the Mediterranean shore – it lives outside in the open, hoping for a bit of sea-breeze to bring some cooling relief.

It was in fact a perfect time to explore narrow streets and hidden neighbourhoods, awning-covered squares and marketplaces, the shadier nooks and crannies of a city that in all seasons remains mysterious. Twenty-six hundred years of secrets lie buried beneath the surface of daily existence in Marseilles. But in summer shutters and windows are left ajar, indoor life becomes outdoor life, private life becomes public, and the city's intimacies are bared beneath a burning Mediterranean sky.

What's more, with Jany's work-year as a teacher in Aix now over she was free; together not only could we mingle with the Marseillais, we could be Marseillais. High above the rue Paradis, one of the city's main thoroughfares, an apartment loaned by a holidaying friend awaited us on a hill over-looking the sea. In a city known by the rest of the world to be hellish, the idea of living higher than paradise was just too tempting. I felt a long way from the waving wheat fields and quiet vineyards of the Vaucluse. But maybe here, too, among the teeming crowds, I would find further reminders of the nature of those old ties that held – and perhaps still hold – the Mediterranean world together.

One emerges from the dim, diffuse atmosphere inside the St Charles station and suddenly it is clear, beyond the shadow of a doubt, that one is in the south. Outside the doors we found ourselves at the top of a broad, ceremonial stairway, and stood for a moment adjusting our eyes to the dazzling light.

Hadn't we already been in the south when we boarded the Micheline less than an hour before, I wondered? Did light not bounce at the same angle from sun-heated surfaces in Aix-en-Provence? Of course it did. But here nonetheless was a concentration of southernness, a tangible difference created by surroundings that for centuries had made the Mediterranean Sea the measure of all things. This sensation did not seem to come from the water itself, which is barely visible from the St Charles station. It rose instead from the ancient city, from the dense mass of stone, concrete, red tile and humanity which lay noisy and sprawling beneath our feet at the bottom of the stairway.

Bags in hand, we made our way down wide stone stairs built by proud city-fathers in the early 1900s. In that prosperous, optimistic age this elaborate descent into the metropolis had made for lesser, northern Frenchmen, just arrived from Paris or Lyons, a suitably grand introduction to the glories of Marseilles. Here on a series of three flights of steps the great port, already old long before a French nation was ever dreamed of, boasted its difference with the rest of the country.

Of course Lyon, the stairway bragged, might have had similar wrought-iron handrails and equally elegant lamp standards. And yes, certainly Paris had the same stone-carved lions, proper to any great European empire, that embellished the first broad landing here. Did either of those cities, though, have these tall, feathery-topped palm trees as well – not carved of stone but alive and faintly rustling in the hint of air wafting in from the sea? Marseilles, the palms seemed to say, was not a metropolis to be held back by the constraints of mere geography. France might be a temperate place, but Marseilles had one of its own feet set firmly in the tropics.

The distinctions become more pointed at the top of the second flight of steps. From each side of the landing there rose the granite-sculpted hulls of sailing ships. High above stone bow-waves infested with sea monsters, female passengers in flowing robes gave the ships an air of classical antiquity. *Marseilles – Colonie Grecque*, read the carved stone lettering beside the ship on the right. *Marseilles – Porte de l'Orient*, proclaimed the ship on the left. We are different, we are not wholly of this place – these might have been the inscriptions written there instead.

At the very bottom of the stairway lay tributes to the two continents from which the city's trading wealth had poured in for centuries, ship after loaded ship, across the Mediterranean. Asia and Africa had been given the form of women, stone statues reclining in nubile majesty.

Colonies d'Asie was shown as a languorous, almond-eyed

beauty wearing a Khmer head-dress, an inscrutable smile and not much else. Around her on her stone plinth were gathered symbols of Eastern wealth – a sinuous Chinese dragon, slender ginger-jars, tropical fruits, a young servant-boy in a turban.

Colonies d'Afrique was equally exotic, a gorgeous savage with Afro tresses, pendulous earrings and full, sensuous features. Like her sister Asia, she, too, was clad only in bangles, necklaces and feathers, and proudly offered her full breasts and upthrust stone nipples to the city at large. She also had her treasures about her – a pet monkey, pineapples, a negro slave-boy with an elephant tusk balanced on his shoulder. When it came to portraying the allure of Marseilles' colonial commerce in the great age of Suez, political correctness bowed low before barbaric splendour.

And then we were on the Boulevard d'Athènes at the bottom of the stairs. Abruptly, colonial splendour was swallowed up by the modern city. What remained before us was a tangle of traffic, a weaving, honking confusion of drivers heading down towards the water and the Old Port. Like most things Marseillais, modern city-driving has evolved its own distinctive and home-grown style here. And like the age of steam-ship commerce it, too, can lack political correctness. Sometimes you have to jump. Our jump was only onto a bus, and in no time we, too, were also swallowed up by the clamorous city.

What can be divined of a place seen through the faintly

oily, forehead-imprinted windows of a crowded bus? Little. But as we ground our way across the city's wide central avenue, the Canebière, then along the rue de Rome to the monumental fountain at the Place Castellane I noticed one thing – Marseilles was not a colourful Mediterranean town. There were no warm Italian ochres, no scintillating Spanish whites, no sublime Greek blues. Most of the city seemed to be a motley collection of buildings a century or more old, maintained in a better or worse state of repair, that might originally have been coloured grey, or chalk, or beige. But with the passage of the years and accumulated neglect, with winter storms and a blazing sun, even those tints had been bleached out of the surroundings. Marseilles was faded, a nondescript colour, no colour at all. As I was to learn later, Marseilles' real colour – for the city is decidedly a place of splendid and varied hues – springs elsewhere.

～

High above the rue Paradis, our apartment block was a great elephant of a building, a long, bulky monster, and curvilinear to take maximum advantage of views from both sides. Set at the summit of one of Marseilles' rocky hills, it wholly dominated a residential quarter of modest villas and little gardens that spilled downwards to the sea. *Le dernier cri* in modernity when it was built in the 1960s, it is tempting to say that property developers could not get away with such an eyesore these days. But this being Marseilles, a place where relations between power, money and civic authority remain as cloudy as ever, you can never be wholly sure.

All moral concerns, though, vanished the moment we set foot in our top-floor apartment and pulled the curtains wide. Light came flooding in, and along with it a bird's-eye Mediterranean view.

Through windows on one side of the building the city lay far below. Set against the high, bone-white limestone hills that ring Marseilles I could see the modern docks and cargo terminals of La Jolliette; the disused chimneys that climb the old industrial waterfront at L'Estaque; the ranks of high-rise housing that sprawl across the infamous northern suburbs of the city; the great stone forts of St Nicolas and St Jean guarding the entrance to the Old Port. Far away across town, over a swathe of red roofs cut through by 19th-century boulevards, I spied the St Charles station. All were basking in afternoon sun, visions deformed by shimmering waves of rising heat.

The only higher point around us was the towering steeple of Notre Dame de la Garde, set close by on the next hill. Topping the steeple, so close it seemed we could almost touch her, was the symbol of the city, Marseilles' golden, gleaming Virgin. You don't have to be pious to call her *la Bonne Mère*, the Good Mother. Every Marseillais – sceptic or believer, white, brown or black, Christian, Jew or Muslim – calls her that, and with genuine fondness. She is family. From all over the city she can be seen by sinners big and small.

She can also be seen by homecoming sailors far out on

the waves. On the opposite side of the apartment, the side facing open water, I stepped out onto the balcony and looked over the horizon. Abruptly, Marseilles was no longer a collection of run-down and sun-bleached buildings. The city was transformed and showing its real self. Marseilles was the sea. And I, like those homecoming sailors, was suddenly part of both.

If there was little air in the narrow and crowded city streets far below, up here it was blowing a storm. The wind moaned through the balcony railing like a gale through a ship's rigging. It whistled through the open door and crazily riffled the pages of a book left on the balcony table. If I hadn't quickly snatched the sunglasses from my face, the wind would have done the same thing for me.

No one but a blind man, though, could have missed the great blue-gold glitter of the Mediterranean spreading its way to the ends of the earth. A lively lapis inshore, its waters deepened to a rich ultramarine further out. Spanked up by the wind, creamy white seahorses raced across its surface. Seagulls, too, played over the water, rising and falling erratically in the face of buffeting gusts, then turning and running with the wind.

There were larger and more substantial creatures out there as well. White-sailed yachts tacked courses across the water, flitting as aimlessly as butterflies. Without warning, from around a high, rocky seaside massif to the south the hull of a tanker appeared, crossing the roadstead ahead of me, bound for the refineries at Fos-sur-Mer to the north-west. A big blue and white ferry of the Corsica Lines steamed along in the opposite direction, its unlovely bulk – six stories of windows as regular as any office block – slowly ploughing its way to Napoleon's hometown of Ajaccio.

There were even larger object out there, leviathans basking on the surface of the water. Looming through the spangles of golden afternoon sun that bounced off the sea I could make out the black silhouettes of Marseilles' islands – Frioul, the medieval port-city's plague quarantine site; the Château d'If, gloomy prison inhabited by the ghost of Dumas' hero, the Count of Monte Cristo; the Ile Maire, a distant, hump-backed monster guarding the southern approaches to the port.

The more I discovered out there, the more I felt myself, too, to be part of that windblown, sun-dazzled sea. This gargantuan edifice in which I stood was no longer a residential block, but a heavy-freighted coaster plying the shallows at the most cautious of speeds. This was no mere apartment I stood in, but a pilothouse high over its bows. Nor was I quite the same. The longer I stood there, the wind ballooning my lungs, the more I felt myself detached from an ancient city, a mariner afloat on an even more ancient sea.

⌒

As we set off to walk down the hill to the water next morning, Jany's eye chanced to fall on the street sign in front of our building. We were living, she pointed out, on the rue Protis.

It was a name, she told me, suddenly inspired, that reverberates deep in the furthest recess of Marseilles' past. Whether the story of Protis is literally true is, like most Marseilles stories, unverifiable and beside the point. The real truths of Marseilles are its myths, all of them – the Mafia legends, the football fables, the big-fish stories, the pastis-fuelled tales told in bars. But Jany, an incurable romantic, assured me that once long ago a beautiful Celtic princess named Gyptis really did meet and fall in love with a certain Protis, a brave Greek mariner. She liked the story because it was, a little like our own story, the tale of a local girl who meets a wandering foreigner.

'It happened in 600 BC, when the Gauls were just tangle-haired barbarians hunting wolves in the dark mists of the northern forests,' she began. If Jany was over-painting the picture a little, it was because we were walking down narrow, stepped alleyways over whose sunny walls sprigs of lemon branches and flowering bougainvillaea protruded. Like every true Provençal, Jany relished the difference between north and south, especially when it was cold and rainy up there.

'At the time, what is now the *Vieux Port* was just a marshy inlet,' she continued. 'But already it was inhabited by the Ségobridgians, a tribe of Celts led by King Nann. It happened that on the day that Nann's daughter Gyptis was to marry, the prow of a ship came nosing its way up the inlet looking for a safe harbour. It came from Phocea, a Greek island-colony far away off the coast of Asia Minor. The Celts had never met Greeks before, but this was a special day, and they invited them to the festivities.

'Now the Ségobridgians were advanced for their time. Instead of marrying off their princesses to a man chosen by their father, they let the princess do the choosing. That night, with Protis and his Greeks gathered about, Gyptis made the rounds of the assembled suitors with a silver goblet of wine in her hands – if he drank from it, the man to whom she passed the goblet would become her husband and win half her father's kingdom.'

By this point we had walked down into Roucas Blanc, one of Marseilles' most prestigious quarters, and palatial villas had now replaced simple stuccoed houses on the hillside. I would not have minded exploring, but it was impossible. Jany was in full spate. On we rushed, down the hill to the sea and the conclusion of her story.

'Well, around Gyptis went, sizing up one hopeful Ségobridgian suitor after another. None of them pleased her. Then, suddenly, on the edge of the crowd, she noticed the handsome Greek stranger, Protis. Of course you know what happened.' Jany breathed a deep mock-sigh of romance. 'Without hesitation she approached and proffered the goblet. It was an impetuous *coup de foudre* – a lightning-stroke of love. He drank, and that is how this place became Massalia, a Greek city.'

It may have been an impetuous lightning-stroke of love, I thought as we finally came down to the water, but in accepting

84

the goblet Protis might have been using a little astute calculation, too. What is certain in the story of Marseilles' founding is that, like the Phonecians, the Alexandrian Ptolemies and other Levantine peoples living at the far eastern end of this sea, the Phoceans were prodigious traders. They made their living through shrewd and aggressive maritime commerce, by buying cheap and selling dear at ports around the Mediterranean. Never yet had they settled this far west, but in making common cause with local Celts they struck a profitable, long-term business deal. Not only did the Phocean Greeks build a city that with its high coastal hills and rocky islands resembled the place they came from; they also obtained a home-port through which they could trade across the western Mediterranean from Sicily to southern Spain.

Twenty-six centuries later the inhabitants of old Massalia are still prodigious traders with a flair for a deal, buying cheap and selling dear whatever and wherever they can. The history of those centuries has been a history separate from France's, for Marseilles' mercantile interests have rarely coincided with the political interests of the hinterland, or anywhere else for that matter. Greek territory never extended very far inland, but Massalia established daughter-colonies along the coast – Antipolis became today's Antibes; Nikaia, Nice; Monoicos, Monaco. Wherever the Greeks went they transformed the landscape with those life-giving gifts, the grape and the olive. To Marseilles itself they brought another present, one just as highly valued. By the 5th century BC the city was renowned for its school of Greek rhetorical polemics. Today the tone may not be as polished as that of Aeschylus or Euripedes, but in city streets it is still in operation – the Marseillais remain among the smoothest of smooth-talkers west of Nicosia.

But none of its eloquence, though, could help Massalia when it came up against Julius Caesar. Where the Greeks, half-eastern and fatalistic, looked for their destiny to the sea and the wind, to epic poetry and to the unpredictable whims of the gods, the Romans were more down-to-earth – they trusted in the law, settlement of the land and the heavy-handed administration of man. Not long after the Romans invaded and christened their new territory *Provincia Romana* – the origin of today's word Provence – their proconsul Julius Caesar found a pretext for dispute with the Greeks. He laid siege to Massalia. Roman trenches and siege-towers encircled the city. Greek and Roman warships fought off the island of Frioul. When Caesar's forces finally breached the city walls after six months of fighting Marseilles was stripped of its independence. Greek pre-eminence in the western Mediterranean disappeared, never to return.

Ever since, Marseilles has lived a phoenix-like existence, shifting its allegiances countless times. Again and again it has risen from the ashes of pillagings, sea raids, plagues, wars and occupations. Detached, ungenerous in its loyalties, it has looked always to its own wealth and benefit. A thousand years ago the Marseillais were doing booming business with the powers on the far side of the Mediterranean. What did they care that these were Islamic powers engaged at the same time in a life-and-death struggle with the rest of Christendom? So enraged by Marseilles' perfidy was the Christian warrior Charles Martel that after he finally broke the Muslim advance into Western Europe at the Battle of Poitiers he marched straight south and sacked the city. In the modern era, too, Marseilles has known high periods and low – the heady boom-days of the Suez Canal; the plummeting decline, with no upswing in prosperity in sight even today, that followed the loss of France's overseas colonies. But the port-city, forever independent in spirit and commercial in outlook, has survived it all.

↝

The only independent commerce I could see at the moment was a couple of kids inspecting a small chunk of hashish being offered them by another kid sitting under a beach umbrella. We had emerged at the bottom of the hill at the beginning of Les Plages du Prado, a vast stretch of grassy, well-watered park and white sand beach created by landfill two decades ago. It still looked new and a little out of place on this old coast, its smooth and undulating acres more Californian than Mediterranean.

The guy selling the dope, a bare-chested Arab boy with a whisper of a moustache on his upper lip, saw me eyeing him, scowled, and wandered over. Now everybody knows that Marseilles is a sink of iniquity, a world-historical leader in vice, wickedness, and depravity of all descriptions. It is dirty and chaotic and drug-ridden. It is corrupt, a metropolis shared between brutal Mafia chiefs, bent policemen and politicians with fingers in every pie. It is, above all, a dangerous and violent place whose dingy portside streets are traps for the unwary. Marseilles may be fine for sailors and prostitutes, the accepted wisdom goes, but the uninitiated – foreigners, tourists and other innocents – should stay away.

So what could I expect now, I wondered? I'd seen 'The French Connection'. Did the boy, who'd heard me speaking English to Jany, take me for a Gene Hackman, a DEA operative far from home? Was this where I got pushed into a car, tied to a chair in a disused warehouse and pumped full of heroin until I became an gibbering addict begging for more? Somehow I doubted it.

'*Eh, bien, tu veux du shit aussi?*' the boy asked, staring me hard in the face. He was looking for a sale. I was surprised – this kind of hustling is rare in the streets of Marseilles, and I smelled a rat. Putting on my most nonchalant of airs, I shook my head.

'*C'est pas de la merde, hé?*' the boy's voice became more persuasive. '*C'est du bon shit.*' He opened his hand to show me a small bar of stuff that was hard and dark. The linguistics were getting complicated, but apparently this *shit* – a French term for what was not shit at all – was not merde, the French term for what was. What it looked suspiciously like to me in either language, though, was a piece of clumsy adulteration. I had heard of the practice before, rubber being cut with other material – sometimes even a bit of the real thing – and sold to the gullible and inexperienced. But I didn't have to be experienced. This substance looked like something out of the Michelin tyre factory. I wasn't being taken for Gene Hackman at all. I was being taken for a dumb tourist. I didn't know whether to be relieved or insulted.

We walked on. No one, of course, least of all its inhabitants themselves, says Marseilles is a city of angels. But its reputation as a bottomless pit of evil is stuff and nonsense. The Marseillais are simply mortals and their city is simply a very old port, wide open to the universal impulses that drive the entire planet. This is a place wise in all the ways of the world, and every aspect of man's condition is found here. Certainly there are drugs, murders and prostitution. Which port, which night-time alley anywhere has not got these things? Who would walk murky portside streets in Hamburg, London or San Francisco?

If Marseilles is such an eminently iniquitous place, why is the city one of the few in France that is free of violent social discord? There are no summer riots in Marseilles, no running street-battles along the Canebière. In fact, given all its deprivations, inequalities and racial differences, it is a remarkably harmonious city. As Jany and I skirted the edge of the beach and gazed out, I knew I was looking at the principal source of Marseilles' equilibrium – the sea.

Already at ten-thirty in the morning the beach was crowded. There were joggers, cyclers, windsurfers, kite-flyers, lithe young men leaping high in the air to smash volleyballs over nets. Naked children played with buckets and spades down by the water. North African teenagers kicked footballs on the sand. Muslim mothers in headscarves demurely laid out picnics in the grass behind the beach. Senegalese men covered top-to-toe in long robes hawked ice creams to French women wearing hardly anything at all. Groups of girls lay gathered on towels, all gossip and giggle, not far from prostrate gangs of watchful boys. Were ever there gazes as focussed and unabashed as these? There was even a swimmer or two in a place that each summer day becomes the city's busiest social rendezvous.

There are lots of cities in France that have small, green, cluttered parks, but not many that have a vast, blue, empty one stretching away as this place does. On the edge of the sea everyone finds the relief, the pressure-valve release, that is missing elsewhere. Just looking out to a cool and quiet stretch of water can be calming. The municipal authorities know all about the effect, and each summer, free of charge, lay on beach-bound bus services from the over-heated suburbs that surround the metropolis.

We watched crowds of city-dwellers continuing to arrive and strip down to swimsuits. In a climate like this the sun had toasted everyone the same dark tone. But here, in fact, was every race and nationality that has ever stepped off the docks in Marseilles, every group the city has ever favoured or frowned upon. Accumulated over centuries, long-acculturated or still defiantly proud of their roots, wave after wave of immigration has deposited in one port-city the peoples of three continents – Italians and Armenians, Corsicans and Comorians, North Africans, Malgasis, Malians, Spaniards, Vietnamese, Greeks and Pied-Noirs. It is not just the sea and the sun that is at work in Marseilles – here is a mixing of many bloods of the south, an endless, energetic stirring of DNA whose fusion has blurred the edges of race. Marseilles is not ochre or white or blue. It is the colour you get when you blend all other colours together. Sun-burnished over the ages, it is a lustrous, Mediterranean brown.

⌐

We had brought towels and swimsuits, but the link between sea and city so intrigued me I wanted to see more. Stretching along the waterfront in the other direction, away from the Prado beaches and towards the Old Port, was the Corniche, a broad, sinuous roadway skirting the rocks above the water.

Why didn't we walk along it, I suggested, to the Vieux Port? Jany looked at me as if I were out of my mind. There were times, I think, when she wished she had married a Ségobridgian or some other variety of sensible local tribesman. Only an Anglo, she told me, sadly shaking her head as we started off, would walk along the Corniche in the middle of the day in summer.

But the views were glorious and I couldn't help it. Why rave about Nice's Baie des Anges or the promenade in Marbella? Here in the middle of one of the Mediterranean's tougher working-class cities was a marine prospect that outclassed them both.

Forty feet below the winding road the sea gently surged, clear enough that we could see the sand and shoals and weedbeds on the bottom. The rocky slopes from which the Corniche hung were so steep that here and there fishermen sat on benches on the sidewalk, the lines from their fishing-rods hanging over the railing and straight down into the water. Away the smooth surface of the sea swept, a silvery-bright plain running from the tumbling bulk of nearby headlands, past bare, stony islands, to the vacant disc of the horizon.

Every now and then I switched my sea-view to a land-view, gazing up the slopes past pine and oak trees to vast hillside villas. Built in grand bourgeois style more than a century ago, they had housed the wealthy of Marseilles – shipbuilders, the proprietors of maritime export companies, the owners of palm-oil and sugar refineries. Here were Italianate rococo villas with elaborate facades of moulded plaster; Art Nouveau palaces with green copper roofs and curving, wrought-iron balconies; eccentric, Second Empire follies whose soaring towers and turrets competed with surrounding stands of luxuriant palms.

But luxury is not Marseilles's' predominant or most visible ethos – always my gaze was pulled away to the sea and the less opulent, more proletarian distractions that lay on its shores. At the small peninsula of Malmousque, whose sea-edges were too steep for any kind of larger road, the Corniche took a brief inland detour. We carried along the shoreline, plunging into alleys that led us into a peaceful little world of ageing concrete construction and cheap gimcrack repair. An air of gentle neglect and dilapidation reigned here. Salt, sun, humidity and sea air had slowly eaten their way into every-thing. The shutters on cottages sagged, walls peeled several layers of paint at the same time, and metal latches and grills bled long stains of rust down the house's rough facades.

But in all the city there could hardly be more glorious waterside views. From here the Château d'If was so close it seemed you could almost reach out and touch its ram-parts. Perched on flat-topped roofs, reclining on shaded balconies above foundations washed by waves, residents of modest revenue sat out over sweeping, million-dollar views. I watched old men in shorts, wispy white hairs curling on thin brown chests, drinking pre-lunch aperitifs looking out to sea. You could tell they wouldn't change their lives with anyone.

Or their lunches. Invisible in obscure kitchens, their wives cooked as smoke and rich odours floated out into the sunshine from open windows.

'Fresh sardines,' said Jany, sniffing the air appreciatively. 'Grilled not too long, and seasoned with just a sprinkling of coarse sea-salt and a squeeze of lemon.'

Malmousque, I thought as I, too, sniffed the air and watched a skinny cat eating from a twist of newspaper, was not St Tropez or Portofino. It was not quaint, or elegant, or sleek. It was more remarkable still. It was one of those impossible things, a working-class Mediterranean seaside village that had hardly changed in fifty years.

Where, I wondered, could we be? My map indicated that we were little more than half a mile from the very centre of France's second biggest city. It scarcely seemed possible. As we penetrated further into Malmousque things got more exotic still. The houses were hardly more than simple cubes, those most basic of Mediterranean forms found from Malta to Majorca. At their doors were name-plaques – l'Africaine, La Vigie Marocaine – that placed them closer to the great continent to the south than to France itself.

There was an even odder surprise waiting at the very tip of the peninsula. The manned barrier at the French Foreign Legion post there was busy with comings and goings, the checking of identities, the saluting of steel-jawed officers in white kepis. The idea of poking about a Beau Geste-style fort was appealing, but for the likes of me there was only one way in – via the post's recruitment station. Beneath a fluttering tricolour was a sign inviting me to join up, any hour, day or night.

It's one way to see the world, but there was no need – Malmousque itself was beginning to look as foreign and romantic as any far-flung Legion outpost. Down the rue Va à la Calanque, past a spreading palmetto tree casting bright zebra-stripes onto the street, a rocky inlet no more than twenty yards wide led out to sea. Rickety stairways climbed its steep sides past lines of hanging laundry to frail-looking houses. Down by the water whiskery men scraped and caulked pulled-up boats. Everything looked jerry-built, ramshackle, improvised, crooked – there was not a straight line or right angle in sight. It hardly appeared real. Malmousque was a Popeye cartoon, a distant, sun-weathered harbour that existed only in the imagination.

At the end of the inlet a narrow concrete path continued on around the rocks. We followed it until the seafront of the Foreign Legion post came into view on the other side of the peninsula. It looked like R-and-R heaven. There were bullet-headed men reclining motionless on sun-loungers, perfectly muscled bodies executing faultless dives into the water, fatigue-clad troops being served elaborate seafood meals on an awning-covered terrace beside the sea.

As we sat on the rocks contemplating warriors at their ease a young woman approached on the path. She was stunning, a slim beauty with tanned olive skin, dark eyes, silver bracelets and a thick rope of black, braided hair hanging down her back. She chose a rock and, unfurling a towel on it, gracefully disrobed until she was wearing just the skimpiest of bikini-bottoms, the kind the Brazilians call *filo dental* – dental floss.

She might have been a secretary on her lunch-hour or a

sales assistant from a dress shop beyond the Corniche. But she reminded me of those reclining odalisques on the steps below the St Charles station. So disconnected were our surroundings, and so exotic was she, that I was ready to believe anything. Sitting there, looking serenely out to sea and somehow part of it, she might have been an Alexandrian princess, the ravishing daughter of a Lampedusan fisherman, a naked pearl diver. We stayed a little longer, serene and gazing out, too, then made our way back to the Corniche along the rue de Quatre Vents. I was still thinking of the siren on the rock. Perhaps she came from closer by. Perhaps she was Gyptis herself.

⌒

We emerged from Malmousque back into the rhythms of the big city. We strolled past the Plage des Catalans, a beach where, hard up against the urban confusion of sidewalk crowds and traffic jams, bare-skinned Marseilles pursued its love affair with the sea. On the heights over the mouth of the *Vieux Port*, we skirted the Palais du Pharo, the ornate palace Napoleon III had specially built for his much loved empress, Eugénie, and which she had not loved at all – she had disliked this dirty, working port, preferring the statelier ocean surroundings of Biarritz. We walked beneath the high-walled, star-shaped bastion of Fort St Nicolas, built by Louis XIV not to defend Marseilles from foreign seaborne attack, but to repress its rebellious and independent-minded citizenry – its cannons pointed not out to sea, but inward, to the city. Distant, formal, far removed from the populism of the great unwashed, France's leaders have not generally admired Marseilles. Rounding a corner and standing before a thick forest of masts, we could finally see why. The heart and soul of the city is as plebeian as you can get. There is no port quite as lacking in social exclusivity, quite as cheerfully cheek-by-jowl, as the Old Port.

For all its size, the *Vieux Port* is almost claustrophobic in its closeness. You cannot even see the open sea from here – it is obscured behind the headland of the Pharo Palace, and sailors must make an energetic dogleg to clear its narrow mouth. From around its three quays it appears to be a lake, a self-contained body of water. But here thousands of small vessels – day-sailers and yachts, speedboats and cabin cruisers, tour boats and fishing boats – sit moored side by side. Their fenders rub the fenders of the next boat, their bows snub tightly up against long pontoon-docks protruding far out into the water. There is little room to move, and only the finest manoeuvres of mooring avoid the dentings, scrapings and fender-benders that are the daily lot of Marseilles' dry-land pilots. Tideless, opaque and greeny-grey, there is hardly a square metre of surface water in the *Vieux Port* that is not in constant use.

We walked down the Quai de Rive Neuve towards the landward end of the port, and felt a busy energy radiating outward from the water in all directions. It penetrated the various quayside *Cercles*, *Sociétés* and *Amicales*, nautical club-houses from which issued the loud, bluff voices mandatory among bantering Provençal males. The same energy slipped across the crowded road where traffic growled impatiently at red lights. It spread out across portside bars doing a lively trade in pre-lunch rounds of pastis. And then the busyness, all hustle and vitality and life, ran up the densely packed hills that climbed away from the Old Port. On one side it ended up in the Panier, on whose summit the sails of Marseilles' windmills once used to turn. On the other it ended at the Basilique de Notre Dame where, gleaming in sun and wind, the *Bonne Mère* continues to busily generate her own special brand of high-powered energy.

Pursued by a sun that now blazed down from straight overhead, we danced from one awning-covered entranceway to another. Chasing shade, we pretended interest in a shop that sold yachting sails, in a maritime bookstore, a marine-motor spare-parts depot, a dive shop, a nautical sportswear boutique, a dim and cavernous ships-chandler's where a fibreglass shark hung suspended from the ceiling. With quick stares of regret we passed Le Bistro Romain, Le Bar de La Marine, O'Malley's Irish Pub and a dozen other watering holes. They looked invitingly dark and cool inside. But we did not linger and at last arrived, hot and breathless, at the fish market on the Quai des Belges at the head of the *Vieux Port*.

Ask a Marseillais what single image conjures up for him the essence of his city and he will not, as a Parisian might, describe something *chic* or beautiful or imposing. The women who sell fish on the Vieux Port are none of these things – they are small, tough, wind-chapped and shapeless; only their voices command attention. The rockfish they sell are less beautiful still – spiny, six-inch creatures that look like miniature marine bulldogs, they are all protuberant eye and overshot jaw. Yet both fish and fishwife are cherished in Marseilles. Emotionally as well as geographically, they lie at the ancient city's very centre.

The fish market is a morning market, and now on our arrival at noon it was winding down. But the quay was still loud with the cries of the fish business.

'*Allez, Mesdames! Une belle soupe de roche! Une vraie merveille – du vivant pour le prix du mort! Allez, une soupe, une belle soupe!*'

'Come on, ladies, a beautiful soup from the rocks! It's amazing – live fish for the price of dead ones! Come on, soup, beautiful soup!' The pitch of the calls was strident, the timbre ringing, the tone defiant. Anyone with enough nerve, it seemed to challenge, was invited to say the contrary.

We poked, we sniffed, we gazed at fish on quayside trestle-tables and at the boats that had caught them that morning. But the fish-market was above all an experience of voice and ear, an ongoing exchange between the city and the fishwives who have inhabited it from the beginning. The voices were cajoling, irrepressible, raucous. At times they were friendly and intimate, at others sharp and stinging. Always they were assertive.

They were assertive especially when it came to the subject of bouillabaisse. Listen to housewives buying from fishwives – you'll quickly learn about the spiny red *rascasse*, the *galinette*, the *baudroie*, the conger eel and the other rare and ever-costlier rockfish that swim about in a bowl of the local specialty. But listen a little bit longer, and you'll discover – apart from the fact that all agree it was invented right here – that there is little accord on bouillabaisse at all.

It was time, Jany decided just a little bit mischievously, to see just where opinions parted.

'What spices,' she innocently asked a gnarled fishwife with red forearms, 'do you add with your saffron? My mother always puts a zest of orange in her bouillabaisse.'

Immediately there was an outcry, not from the vendor but, on Jany's side of the fish-laden table, from a fellow shopper.

'*Bon Dieu! Mais c'est pas possible!*' A zest of orange with the saffron? The shock of it halted the poor woman in an act of eyeball-to-eyeball *rascasse*-inspection. She plainly did not believe a word Jany said.

'You must be from out of town.' She gave Jany a going-over from head to toe. 'My family has lived here for six generations, just ten minutes from the port, and we have never,

ever done that! We add a touch of fennel, mind you. But no zest of orange, and no bay leaf, either!'

The debate over orange-zest spread, developed, deepened, grew more contentious. As they passed by, other fish-buyers, port-strollers and standers-by stopped and listened. Everybody had something to say, an ingredient to add or a technique to advise. Bouillabaisse-talk became fish-talk and fish-talk became lunch-talk. All were enjoying themselves and nobody seemed in a rush to get home. As with most things in life, the anticipation of lunch had become as pleasurable as lunch itself.

I stood there surveying the scene – the shoppers, the women behind their fish-tables, the fishermen cleaning the last of the seaweed and starfish from their nets, Jany deep in conversation. I could see what buying *rascasse* at the port demands that buying frozen fish at the supermarket does not. Like the evolution of an ancient city, it takes time.

Just how much time I realised when I looked down at my feet. Sunk into the stone where the fishing boats arrived was a bronze plaque, a commemoration of a much earlier arrival.

'Here, around the year 600 BC,' the plaque was inscribed in French, 'Greek sailors landed, coming from Phocea, a Greek city of Asia Minor. They founded Marseilles, from where civilisation spread throughout the West.'

Coming from a shrill and smelly market in a rough sea-town, the claim seemed a big one. But maybe it wasn't.

Maybe a single ship could carry an entire civilisation. Late that evening, sleepless and full of images of tiny coves and tumbledown ports and silver-bangled mermaids on rocks, I went out onto the balcony. I was restless and feeling dazed by a long day of sun. In its place a crescent moon was now riding, making a path of silver dance on the dark water.

A single, small craft, a faint outline bearing red and green running lights, crossed the water below me. It was probably a fishing boat heading out to set nets. But in its formlessness it made me think of different boats the Marseillais had built and sailed over the centuries – *barques* and *tartans*, *saetes* and *gallionetti*, *navires* and *navi*. Or was this phantom boat perhaps manned by other sailors, sailed in other times from other ports far over the Mediterranean? Was it a *polacca*, a *felucca*, a *patache*, a *marciliane*, a *vacchette*, a *trabaccoli*, a *cara-musali* … ? They were only names I had read. But in these silvery-dark shadows such boats belonged as much to this sea's present as its long past, and seemed likely at any minute to sail across the path of the moon before me.

It was not just this apartment building, I thought. Wasn't the entire city of Marseilles itself just one great boat?

After the day's walk the city seemed more than ever to belong to the Mediterranean and not to the fixed and motionless mainland stretching away behind it. Unanchored, Marseilles appeared to have drifted through the sea for centuries, skirting every shore and loading onto its decks every people and their ways. Marseilles was a human ark with no destination and no home port — it merely sailed on, a vessel in whose deep holds slopped twenty-six centuries of life. Surrounding it was blue water, heat, the sun and, right now, the blessedly cool night breeze.

It seemed enough for the city and, for the while, enough for me too. As mysteries go, Marseilles — ancient, enduring, essentially unchanging — was quite as perplexing as the night-flowers in Les Jean-Jean that had bloomed briefly before my eyes and then disappeared forever. Was there some Mediterranean quality of perception, perhaps undeveloped in northerners, capable of reconciling these things? I didn't know. I returned to bed and slept.

～

Rose essence from Aleppo, cedar wood from Lebanon, gum arabic from Abyssinia — all night long, slowly sliding up and over waves of wakefulness, I'd had confused dreams of the thousand and one goods brought to the city from the sea. When I woke in the morning I knew where we must go. Jany had no objection, but I knew she wouldn't. Show me a Provençal who doesn't love a market.

So down the hill we headed, not seaward but inland to one of Marseilles' prosperous thoroughfares, the avenue du Prado. Held on broad sidewalks beneath shady plane trees, the Marché du Prado is the biggest market in a town full of markets, a compressed, attenuated outdoor boutique almost a mile long.

Even at an early hour we found it difficult to make our way through the crowds. Descended from their cool, airy apartments, the residents of the Prado promenaded and purchased before the heat of the day sent them home again. But in stalls beneath bright, striped awnings no one was buying Abyssinian gum arabic. There were no bolts of damask, no ivory or Barbary apes. These days Marseilles buys more modern exotica – Levi knock-offs from Tunisia, porcelain tea sets from Romania, ceiling-mounted smoke detectors from Taiwan. There was anything and everything here – brassieres, kitchen carving sets, air-fresheners, six-piece screwdriver kits, nylon wigs. None of it interested me much. The only element of superlative quality here was sales technique.

It is a gift. No one, except maybe the occasional London East-end barrow boy, can push street-merchandise like a Marseillais. If he is determined to make a sale, there is not much you can do to stop a good Prado market-man. He can out-talk you, out-joke you, out-reason any objection you might be foolish enough to offer for not buying his goods. These are artists who have been honing skills of flattery and persuasion since childhood. What can you do against master-negotiators who began their careers wheedling bonbons from their grandmothers?

Resistance was useless. So, anyway, it seemed to me as I walked away from a stall with a T-shirt I had never intended buying.

Marseilles, C'est pas la France. So began the text of what was a defiant, Marseilles-style declaration of independence printed on the shirtfront. Much of it was recited in the language of the port-city's streets, an argot that is inimitable and resists translation. How do you cope with slang that allows a young man to admire a young woman's *air-bags avant* and *air-bags arrière*, especially when she's just walking, not driving, by? But a few lines give the approximate gist of the thing.

Marseille, the T-shirt boasted to the world, was an extraordinary place; it was so different it was not really part of France at all. Where ordinary Frenchmen were divided, the Marseillais were united. When it rained in France the Marseillais basked in bright sunshine. French people went to bed to sleep; the Marseillais went to bed to make babies. The French were psychologically repressed; the Marseillais were bold rebels. The French were geographically insular; the Marseillais had the sea. The French ate blandly; the Marseillais ate garlic. The French drank water; the Marseillais added it in small quantities to pastis. The French were wishy-washy; the Marseillais were men. More than men, in fact, they were true Olympians.

All this, naturally, argued for a dissolution of the artificial bond holding France and Marseilles together. *MARSEILLE INDEPENDANTE*! the declaration finished with a final flourish of oversize letters. It was so good-naturedly combative, so cheerfully megalomaniacal that by the time I'd read it through once or twice its truths seemed self-evident.

105

Marseilles was pretty well independent already. By this point we'd reached the market's food section near the Place Castellane, and on the assurance that it would one day again be a great maritime city-republic, Jany and I treated ourselves to a snack that is associated with Marseilles and nowhere else – thick slices of that deep-fried chick-pea dough known as *panisse*. Then we hopped a bus to the city centre and another very different market in the rue Longue des Capucins.

When Alice Waters named her celebrated San Francisco restaurant Chez Panisse she definitely did not have the rue Longue des Capucins in mind. Waters took Provençal food to the rest of the world. The Capucins market brings the rest of the world's food to Provence. As we stood at the bottom of the street there was little that looked familiar. This was not really even a market, at least not a market as the rest of France knew it. This was an African souk, an oriental bazaar, an Ali Baba's cave of exotic condiments and cooking. It was an odorous, grimy, ages-old alley that led away from all things Gallic, and to arrive at the furthest ends of the earth we only had to plunge down it.

The cowled monks of the Capuchin order might once have held sway in the street here. Now there were very few Europeans at all. There were gowned and hooded men about us still as we strolled, but they were Algerian, Moroccan or Malian, men concealed in cool cotton jellabas rather than monastic woollen robes. There were Senegalese women both shrouded and revealed – their heads wrapped in turbans, they wore their flowing bou-bous off the shoulder, exposing ebony arms and delicate collarbones. There were Atlas Berbers with tattooed foreheads, Chadians with tribal scars slashed on their cheeks, Malgasis in shawls and head-wrappers that made them as bright as butterflies.

You could feel age and foreignness exude from the walls. If the Marché du Prado was a market for the French middle class, this was the shopping precinct of the city's poor. Little changes here – it has always been poor. For centuries this was the quarter that housed the thousands of slaves, criminals and captured Turks who rowed Marseilles' fleet of war galleys. The buildings above are still scabrous and peeling. The sidewalks below remain greasy and refuse-strewn. And when the day's market is over and darkness approaches, there drifts through the air the same faint but unmistakable warning that has drifted through the air of this street forever. Go home, it says, before the business of the night begins. Foul things have happened here before, and will happen again. Go home now.

But for the moment all was brightness and colour and shafts of sun penetrating the street's depths from high above. We passed one stall, one stand, one open shop doorway after another. Each unloaded a different cargo onto the still air. If the portside fish market was all noise, the rue Longues des Capucins was all smells. Thick and fragrant, clouds of blue smoke rose skyward from sidewalk kebab grills. We sniffed sweet bunches of mint and basil, their leaves sprinkled with silvery pearls of water, piled high for sale on upturned cardboard boxes. We inhaled oven-odours in a sweltering Arab bakery where boys rolled discs of flatbread at lightning speed. At a place where a Moroccan corner-shop sat opposite a Vietnamese grocer's the odours of two continents waged a war of attrition – where *citron confit*, briny olives and spicy red harissa meet sliced ginger, pickled fish and sour tamarind paste there can be no clear winner. We stumbled on, confused and smell-shocked survivors.

Tiring, we took seats where the narrow street gave onto a broad market square. Like a harbour fronting busy waters, the Café Prinder sat where confused currents brought waves of humanity from different directions. We sipped coffee and watched the tide flow. The square was frantic, all energy and effort. Everywhere market-traders were jockeying dollies, heaving crates, crying their wares and serving clamorous crowds. One eye out for the police, even the sellers of smuggled cigarettes and watches of dubious provenance were plying their trade with vigour.

Marseilles, obviously, did not have time for the studied pretensions of an Aix or a Nice or a Saint-Rémy. Centuries of maritime commerce lie at its heart, and it remains busy doing what it has always done – it looks for the main chance. We were surrounded here by merchants and peddlers from a dozen nations around the Mediterranean. What else had drawn them but trade, profit, and the thousand different ways of making it?

We sat back in our chairs, enjoying what the indolent enjoy most, watching other people work. But not even that lasted very long – after a while the waiter came out, looked at our empty cups and pointed to a sign on an outside wall. *Les consommations sont renouvelables toutes les demi-heures.* Orders must be made every half-hour. The Café Prinder, like any harbour on busy sea-lanes, had its commercial imperatives. We sailed on.

⌣

The days passed and we pursued our indolence in other ways. Usually I tire of the beach, but in Marseilles the sea was so much part of the city that the place they met was endlessly captivating. It captivated the Marseillais, too – the Prado, Prophète and Catalans beaches often grew too crowded and distracting for comfort. Did there still exist, somewhere in the city, an older, more serene kind of meeting between man and Mediterranean? If it existed I resolved, despite Jany's wild-eyed protests over midday sun, to find it.

And so began a search in which heat and sunshine became a kind of relentless plague. We took a ferry from the Old Port ten minutes out to the island of Frioul. It is treeless, rocky, and exposed, an oven in midsummer. Two hours later we were back, heat-struck and half-blinded. We made expeditions to Montredon, La Madrague and Les Goudes, once small fishing villages but now swallowed up by the larger city. All were caught in the burning hourglass of the overhead sun. The further our exploration took us from the Old Port the rockier and more heat-blasted the coastline became.

One still and cloudless morning we took a bus out to the little inlet of Callelongue on the furthest edge of the city. It was a harsh and elemental place, unadorned by the slightest leaf of vegetation. Tucked into the face of a seaside massif, a rugged moonscape of bare white limestone fell steeply to the water. With the sun bouncing crazily off rock and glassy sea, we spread a blanket near the water and laid out a picnic. Jany had not been happy about our expeditions from the beginning. Now, beneath a sun that was turning her skin an angry red, she was close to open revolt. Even I had to admit that lunch wasn't much fun in heat that sweated oil out of sausages and turned baguettes to stone in minutes. And when after eating I suggested, only half-seriously, that we climb the rocky side of the massif behind us for a view of the city the end finally came.

'That's it,' she said between clenched teeth, looking at the glaring slope. Undulating waves of radiant heat were doing strange things to the rocks up there, bending and warping them, making them look even nastier than they really were. 'The Corniche wasn't enough. You want me to climb a near-vertical rock face in the middle of summer with the sun straight overhead? It's got to be fifty degrees out here! I'm getting sun stroke. I thought you were a raving Anglo lunatic. But you're worse. You've got no more sense than a heat-addled rock lizard. Go and bake your brain by yourself!'

And with that Jany stomped off to the bus stop, leaving me to grill alone on the blanket.

And so, scorched too many times by Jany's displeasure, I was forced to call an end to our noontime expeditions. Instead, I began listening to my wife. Rather than exploring the Mediterranean I began behaving as if I lived in it. We rose early and went out in the cool of the morning, returned home by midday, and spent the hot afternoon hours in the shade of the balcony high over the sea. We read and slept and daydreamed, soothed by the breeze that always blew there. In city streets far below it was only just beginning to cool off by five o'clock. By six the crowds were barely starting to move again. Still hot and woozy, Marseilles came slowly to its senses by seven.

Such rhythms invited late nights, the evening exploration of cool, dark outdoor places. Marseilles was endlessly lively in summer weather, a city too sociable, too vivacious, too warm and airless to remain housebound at night. Its inhabitants needed to stroll and commingle, to eat and drink, to revive themselves outdoors after a day spent inside.

My own preferred evening haunt was the Place de Lenche. It lay on the tattier side of the *Vieux Port* near the Panier, one of the oldest and poorest parts of immigrant Marseilles. It was on this hill that the Greeks had first chosen to build their city. They had raised their temple to Artemis, protector-goddess of sailors, where all temples should be – at the top. The bottom of the hill, site of the present Place de Lenche, they reserved for their *agora*, or assembly place. It has been a place of public gathering ever since. Where better to sit in at the end of a day, a glass of cold rosé close at hand, than the oldest meeting place in western Europe?

At the upper end of the square sat a modest little outdoor restaurant called the Pomo d'Oro. I liked it because from there you could look down between the buildings that face the Vieux Port and see a sliver of water and boats. At the same time you could look up and see the Bonne Mère rising from the hill on the far side of the port. Perhaps I was becoming a little like the Marseillais themselves, reassured by simple proximity to that statue glowing golden in the light.

One evening Jany and I went to the Place de Lenche for seafood risotto. As we ordered dinner I asked Giovanni, the talkative Italian proprietor of the Pomo d'Oro, what he thought of owning a piece of one of the most ancient talking-places on the continent. After all, I said, the great 4th-century BC Marseilles mariner, Pythias himself, had probably sat on this very spot drinking wine and holding forth on his return from Ultima Thule, ancient Iceland.

A tray of beer balanced in one hand, Giovanni examined me sideways as if I were mildly touched in the head. Then he looked around the square for a moment, glancing at the simple bars and restaurants, the sun-faded awnings of the shops, the comings and goings of less-than-elegantly-dressed locals. He was not impressed.

'You call this ancient?' he asked with a sweep of his free

hand. 'I'll tell you what's ancient: Rome, where I'm from — that's ancient.'

He turned, looking left and right, then arched his eyebrows in rhetorical question. 'Where are the old temples, the statues, the great monuments? They're all gone! There's nothing here! In Rome they're everywhere — we piss on monuments. You think the Marseillais know about the past, or care? Ultima Thule, you say? *Vacagare!* They've never been anywhere! Don't bother asking them who Pythias was. You want to know what kind of history counts on the Place de Lenche? The time between ordering and eating. It's now, everyone wants to eat now!'

With that he stumped off to fetch us dinner. We sat, watching the evening fall on Marseilles, the sky fading, the Virgin slowly losing her golden lustre. Giovanni might be right, I thought between sips of wine. Maybe Marseilles has no memory. Maybe its history is cyclical, an endless repetition of arrival and assimilation, each generation starting afresh as if it were the first. Maybe the city lives as all sensual and materially-minded places live, for the moment and its pleasures. And then I forgot the question altogether — we were too busy eating mussels and shrimp and rings of squid. Perhaps in Marseilles the time is always now.

⤳

But there was one moment in the week when there was no confusion at all about the time. Notre Dame de la Garde was so close that on Sunday mornings the air around us heaved and vibrated with the ringing of church bells. Pulled from sleep on our last Sunday in the city, we decided to obey their call. Dressing quickly, we hurried through quiet and still-drowsy morning streets to Mass.

The way to the basilica was steep. Its hilltop was higher, its sea-horizon a wider and deeper blue even than our own. And if the building's façade was heavy and colourless, a dull exercise in neo-Byzantine kitsch, it was only camouflage, a modern cover. This hilltop has been a sacred place – cave, temple, sanctuary and church – since earliest pre-Christian times. The image and name may change, the language of worship may alter, but in one form or another the *Bonne Mère*, mother and protectress, has always looked down on the city from here.

No one entering the basilica from the bright Mediterranean world outside could be prepared for the even brighter world inside. It glowed and glittered. As Kyrie Eleisons rose into the air, as silver censers wafted smoke over the packed congregation, I gazed about. There was not the tiniest corner that was not adorned with some reflective thing, not a surface that was not polished until it gleamed.

The inlaid marbles on the floor glimmered red, black and green. The patterned mosaics on walls, arches and the basilica dome were brighter still – celestial golds, airy blues, solar yellows. But what held my attention was the grand mosaic rising behind the altar. It transformed the basilica, making it as pagan in spirit for me as the statue of Artemis that long ago stood atop the hill of the Panier.

For this image, too, invoked protection from an unpredictable sea. It showed a wooden Greek ship, its ballooning, blue-and-white sail square-rigged, its curved prow rising above decks like a windvane pointing the way home. Pushed by a lively wind over the crests of foaming waves, the craft was sailing past a lighthouse on a headland and straight into the safe haven of Marseilles.

Energetic and robust, the image was full of the meeting of wind and sun and air. It seemed to have less to do with piety than with propitiation – the Good Mother, whoever she was, appeared more concerned with the elemental forces of nature than with liturgical matters. The more I looked around, the more I realised this was not so much a church as a marine temple, an ancient grotto dedicated to conciliation with the Mediterranean Sea.

There were ship's life-buoys hanging from the sides of the nave. Near the altar two flickering oil-lamps hung from chains that ended in silver anchors. Suspended over the heads of the faithful themselves was a whole mixed fleet of ships – models of lateen-rigged sailing ships and renaissance galleons, trawlers and steamships, motorboats and yachts. There was even a little seaplane with miniature pontoons floating along up there.

It was just the beginning. Most of the space on one wall of the basilica was given over to framed paintings of ships in trouble. There were horrendous tableaux of ships climbing mountainous waves in raging typhoons. There were pictures of ships ablaze, ships aground, ships colliding, ships at war. All were ex-votos, expressions of thanks by grateful sailors whose lives had been saved at sea.

But it wasn't just mariners the *Bonne Mère* looked after. All the children of the port-city were in her charge – she had terrestrial operations as well. The opposite wall of the basilica was covered with other frightening paintings of a more domestic sort. There were houses collapsing, trains derailing, cars crashing, small boys trapped on perilous ledges, nuns sitting dazed but unhurt in the smashed wreckage of aeroplanes. In each canvas, hovering high in the air in a halo of golden mist, the Virgin looked down protectively. Like the sailors, all these unfortunates, too, had been rescued from almost certain death. 'Thanks to Notre Dame de la Garde who saved us and our families from the Cholera', read one plaque in French; it was collectively signed *Les Dames Télégraphistes, 1884*.

I gazed on at one near-catastrophe after another as the hymns, the sermon, the crossings and genuflections proceeded. It was the kind of perusal that, after an hour or so, made you feel fortunate simply to be alive. If disaster could dog the steps of the virtuous members of the Marseilles' Pool of Lady Telegraphists it could dog the steps of anyone. How we had averted mishap for so long was a mystery in itself.

Jany was, of course, used to this kind of thing – all Provence, Catholic or not, wallows in mystery. As we walked

116

home after the mass she was unconcerned, busy once again analysing the odours of Sunday lunches drifting through windows – she told me she could nearly taste those piquant ratatouilles, almost see those warm gratins and fragrant gigots of lamb. Around myself I saw only accidents waiting to happen – every car, every barking dog, every set of steps along our way was a potential threat. Somehow we ascended the lift of the apartment building without incident, and while Jany made lunch I stood out on the balcony contemplating the Mediterranean. If the Virgin of Marseilles could protect a million city-dwellers from the hazards of this bright blue sea, I felt she could probably keep an eye on us for one last visit too.

⌣

And she did. Full summer was now upon us, and it was time to leave Marseilles for higher, fresher, cooler places. But first we wanted to make our farewells to the sea. On our final day in the city we took a little suburban train from the St Charles station along the coast. It trundled through the hanging laundry of the northern suburbs and past the dormant factory chimneys of L'Estaque, then proceeded on around the wide, curved face of the Bay of Marseilles. Ten minutes out of the station, with the city directly in front of us across the bay, we stepped down at the little harbour of Niolon.

I had learned my lesson. It was five o'clock in the afternoon and still hot, but the sun was now behind the limestone hills that rise above the village – the station, the steep streets, the rocky inlet with its quay and bobbing boats were all in deep shadow. Day-trippers to Niolon, slowly coming round after a sleepy afternoon beneath beach umbrellas, were yawning, folding towels and wriggling into clothing. Soon we had the water virtually to ourselves.

It was that serene meeting of man and Mediterranean I had dreamed of. The air was silky, the rock on which we perched still radiated the day's accumulated warmth, and the water that gently gurgled around us was deep and clear. There was only the slightest shock of cold when I slipped quietly into it, then exhilaration.

I swam out past the mouth of the little harbour, away from the shadows and into bright water where the sun was still shining from the tops of the hills. I had brought a pair of swimming goggles and kicked down into another world. Suddenly everything was a profound, luminescent blue and in my ears was that muffled underwater pinging and popping that is the sound of living sea reefs. Not far below me a bank of thousands of tiny fish swam, a solid, slow-moving wall that suddenly shone brilliant silver as the fish turned in unison and caught the sun.

I drifted further out from the harbour, towards rock cliffs that plunged vertically into the sea. Here there were no weed-beds, no sea urchins to examine below – just an abyss that grew bluer and darker and emptier as I swam into it. It was like floating on the edge of deep space. Rising to the surface between dives I could see Jany, a small and distant figure on the rocks, waving me back to shore. Normally all this blue emptiness would have had me a little scared. But now it did not. I am not suggesting that Marseilles' ancient divinity was doing any looking out expressly on my behalf. But when I swivelled round and gazed across the water there she was – far over on the other side of the bay, rising above the city, was the golden statue of the *Bonne Mère*.

The brilliant light faded, the air slowly cooled. At sunset we ate on a restaurant terrace overhanging Niolon harbour. This was our apartment-view reversed: instead of looking out from city to sea, we looked in at Marseilles spread along the shore. In the near-horizontal rays of the sinking sun the city rose abruptly, a bleached-white vision floating on the surface of the water. As the sun died the vision turned gold in the clear air, then blue, then grey, before it disappeared in the dusk.

Lights came on and Marseilles became what it has always been, a great drifting ship, its thousand portholes blazing with the sensuous Mediterranean life inside. Who needed anchoring, memory, an ancestral home? An immigrant in a community of immigrants, I knew I was as happy in Marseilles as I would be in any metropolis. The sea made it so. We ate small fish, drank a bottle of cold wine, and continued looking out to the port-city until it was time to catch the last train home. Was I coming any closer to understanding Provence or what it means to be Mediterranean? I was certainly coming closer to feeling like one.

Four

Where do the boundaries of Provence begin and end? It is a vexed question. Put it to a dinner table of half a dozen Provençaux and you will likely upset your host, who will suddenly find the smooth progress of the meal halted as half a dozen answers are hotly debated. The *plat de résistance* will have come and gone by the time the subject is exhausted without the party coming to any satisfactory agreement.

There is, of course, an official Provence comprising five French *départements*. But that is mere administration, and nobody pays it much attention. Everyone's 'real' Provence is an emotional Provence – an idea, based on individual outlook and temperament, rather than a geographical place. There seems to be no stitching together of opposing views. 'Naturally you love Provence,' Colette has a character muse in her novel *La Treille de Muscat*. 'But which Provence? There are several.' [1]

Lawrence Durrell, in his last bibulous ruminations on the region, attempted to cover all the bases. He recorded that in certain periods of their rule the Roman governors of

Provincia considered their domain as stretching from Toulouse clear across to Geneva. Even to Durrell that seemed an improbable territory. In a more realistic vein he went on to enumerate not only Nice and Monte Carlo as part of modern Provence, but also Nîmes, Montpellier, Béziers and Narbonne.[2]

Such a list would have the purists at dinner howling and hurling their bread-rolls. Some would say the only true Provence left today is the desolate, windswept hill-and-plateau-country of Haute Provence. There are only limited numbers of Provençaux who think of the Riviera as part of the area – it is too fast-paced and overcrowded, too celebrity-strewn and Mafia-plagued for them. For me, too.

Still fewer are those who regard the land to the west of the Rhône as part of Provence. Even though Nîmes lies only fifteen miles from the river's banks, even though the great Provençal writer Alphonse Daudet was born and grew up there, Provençal fundamentalists would never give the town a place on their maps – its separate history and traditions, its bull-fighting and great spring *feria* make Nîmes an integral part of the Languedoc. And as for Narbonne, the Provençal heartlanders would shake their heads in sad derision; it lies deep in the territory of the French Catalans, they would say – one might as well continue, up and over the Pyrenees, and straight on to Barcelona.

I do not listen too closely to any of these arguments. Durrell's case for an expanded Provence were no doubt based on residence, for he lived much of the last part of his life in a large, 19th-century house in Sommières, a small town twenty miles to the south-west of Nîmes.

My own reasons for pushing the traditional frontiers of Provence forty miles to the north-west of Nîmes are similar. Every June Jany's family moved from Aix to take up its summer seat in another large 19th-century house, this one called La Vitgère, near the village of Sainte-Croix-Vallée-Française. The Vallée Française forms a deep crease in the heart of the Cévennes, that wild and rugged country which makes up the lower edge of France's Massif Central. But it also sits on the marches of the Mediterranean world and shares many of its attributes. While the family is there, at any rate, I regard it as an forward outpost of Provence.

Enough geography for the moment, and a little climatology instead. The afternoon we left Marseilles we stopped long enough in Aix-en-Provence to pick up our car and, among other shopping items for La Vitgère, some fresh milk and a chocolate cake. The further inland we drove the warmer it got. At Nîmes, France's hottest town – the Romans used to retire their Africa legions there – the thermometer stood at forty-one degrees Celsius. Our shirts were sticking to our skins and the seats beneath us were damp with sweat. By the time we reached the town of Anduze at the foot of the Cévennes the milk had soured and the cake had melted to a shapeless blob.

Then we begin climbing. The hills of the Cévennes are

not terribly high, but they form a barrier between Atlantic and Mediterranean weather. In summer, winds rush in from the north-west, pushing cool, damp Atlantic air across the Midi. Then they run up against the Cévennes, and can go no further – the hills trap the moisture and fresh, breezy weather, while the Mediterranean coastal plain behind them remains hot and parched. After weeks of sleepless tossing and turning in the grip of a Provençal *canicule* there is nothing as wonderful on a Cévenol night as pulling a warm blanket up beneath your chin.

But it is not only the climate that changes when you climb the hill-ridges on the route known as the Crête des Cévennes. On the baking lowlands we also left behind us vineyards, orchards, market gardens, towns, motorways and large populations. The Cévennes has none of these things, the principle reason being that there is nowhere to put them. If you wanted to make a quick three-dimensional model of the Cévennes you could do worse than to simply crumple up a piece of paper on the table in front of you – there are no rectilinear planes, no stretches of flat land in this country. Horizontality is a precious commodity – it exists in tiny quantities and only where man has laboriously set out to create it. Otherwise everything is rough, and either heads up or heads down. On the winding Crête des Cévennes we were at the top of the world – below us stretched a tumbled disar-ray of valleys, ravines, ridges, crests, clefts and escarpments.

Even on this milk-curdling afternoon it was cool and

invigorating. From ridge-top to valley-bottom the entire country was heavily treed, its forests pumping oxygen and freshness across the hillsides. In the middle of a great wilderness we left the Corniche and plunged down a narrow road that skipped and skidded, this way and that, through thick forests of chestnut trees. It reminded me of diving down into the sea at Niolon, except that the colours here were brilliant green instead of blue. Deeper and deeper we sank, descending the valleyside like divers on a steep submarine wall.

In the narrow defiles at the bottom of the valley the temperatures were fresher still. Cold and clear, running fast over shallow rocks and lingering in deep pools, the little Gardon River diffused a current of refrigerated air from its surface. Invisible but delicious, it wafted sinuously along the valley floor, thrilling us as we drove with open windows around sharp curves and corners into sudden pockets of cool. If for no other reason than its glorious air we were looking forward to a week or two in the Cévennes.

But there were other reasons. One was my desire to see life on one of the roughest, remotest, least-developed edges of the Mediterranean – here, I suspected, clues lay buried no distance below the surface, indications of a truer, older nature of the place. The other reason was La Vitgère. Two or three miles on the other side of Sainte-Croix, past tiny, terraced fields and pastures, we came to a halt at a tall house perched above the river.

Built at the turn of last century, La Vitgère was a rambling place, all stairs and terraces and different levels. It had once been home to a country doctor and his family, and in a land where everything is built of rough-cut stone it had entertained pretensions. There were sculpted fireplaces and black-and-white diamond-patterned floor-tiles in the *salon*. On the terraces above the river there had been a formal garden with palm trees, a bamboo grove, and an ornamental pool with a splashing fountain. Over the decades, though, decline had set in – the doctor had left, the pretensions had been abandoned, and the wild nature of the Cévennes had slowly reasserted itself. By the time Jany's sister Mireille bought it, La Vitgère was a shadow of itself. To make it liveable renovations were required inside and out, and although the palm trees and bamboo were still there, the garden and the fountain had disappeared in an impenetrable jungle of vines and thorn bushes. It was the kind of place where vipers, frogs, lizards and other small creatures of the Cévennes thrived.

It was from this thick undergrowth that Mireille appeared, a slightly wild look in her eye, on the evening of our arrival. There was a machete in her hand and fresh thorn-scratches on her forearms.

For most of the year Mireille lived with her husband, an American diplomat, in Washington D.C., translating books and teaching French at the World Bank. I am not sure her authors and student-bankers would have recognised their *svelte* and slender French linguist now. For when she arrived at La Vitgère each summer Mireille mounted a one-woman

125

archaeological expedition. After launching herself into the Yucatan-like undergrowth she was capable of disappearing for whole days at a time. She slashed at thickets of brambles. She hacked the trunks of encroaching trees. She uprooted vast swathes of stinging nettles. From the higher garden-terrace beside the house – a reconquered area where her father René had planted marigolds and lilacs – her progress through the jungles on the terraces below could be charted by listening for the occasional expletive and watching the swaying tops of overgrown vegetation.

Inside the house Mireille was just as energetic – she built a summer kitchen, put in cupboards and shelving, decorated cavernous hallways as best she could. More admirable still, she coped courageously if not always successfully with those greatest of all French rural mysteries, pre-war plumbing and electricity.

Slowly, Mireille's annual reclamation campaigns were winning back lost ground. La Vitgère would never be a rural notable's house again. It had become something more attractive – a capacious, slightly chaotic summer rendezvous, a delightful holiday meeting-place not only for family but for unexpected and far-flung friends as well. Mireille had lived in capitals around the world, and her friends were just as varied. With the wine supply holding steady and candles flickering irregularly over the wreckage of vast meals, it was not unusual to find a dozen people sitting long into the night around the dining table in the garden. I often wondered what the ghosts of La Vitgère, earnest provincial worthies haunting an isolated rural back-of-beyond, would make of discussions ranging from the tribal rites of Bedouins to Brazilian gay politics.

Now Mireille wiped a sheen of perspiration from her upper lip and gave us both a kiss. It was close to sunset, and time to quit work. Inside the house, beside a crackling fire, René and Odette were chatting to the latest batch of visitors. A French diplomatic family on holiday from Damascus had just left, only to be replaced by Farid and Touna. They were an exotic couple – Farid's father had been Egyptian and his mother Austrian. Touna's father was English, her mother Protestant Lebanese. Farid was one of the world's top dealers in Arab antiquities and manuscripts. They lived between flats in London, Paris and Cairo, and now were driving southward to a holiday home on Ibiza. Not only were they quadrilingual, they were erudite, unstuffy and entertaining. They were part of that new class, moneyed but wholly dismissive of the conformity that usually goes with it, that the French call *Bourgeois-bohème*, or *Bo-bo* for short. In theory *Bo-bos* were just the kind of people, I thought as introductions were made, that one should be astonished to find at the bottom of a deep valley in backwoods France.

But that was only in theory, for the Cévennes is very odd in this respect. It is one of the most isolated, least populated parts of the country. It is also one of the poorest and most difficult to live in – the major challenge here has always been simple survival. Yet for centuries the Cévennes has continued to attract a surprising population of outsiders. New arrivals have never come looking for a comfortable life here, for there isn't one. They have come for something that to them is more important still – escape. These hills have always been too rugged and isolated for central authority to impose close control. For dissidents, freethinkers and non-conformists, for rebels running from entrenched social or religious convention, they have always represented a sort of freedom. Protestants fleeing murderous Catholic persecution began arriving in the Cévennes in the early 1500s, and its hidden valleys have been a place of refuge ever since.

⌐

Jany and I did not sit down with Farid, Touna and the others for a leisurely dinner at La Vitgère, for it was a special evening. Just a few miles away, on the other side of the valley, the little hillside village of Gabriac was holding its annual summer fête. We wolfed down some resolidified chocolate cake, put on heavy jackets – it had become cold and windy after dark – and drove off up the valley.

Even in daytime the hillside roads of the Cévennes resemble each other. They zig, they zag, they cut their way through mile after mile of uninhabited forest. In daylight one chestnut tree-bounded road looks much like another, and it is easy to get lost. At night, when they all become identical, it is even easier. Up and down the hill we drove in the dark, passing and repassing through the little stone and slate-roofed village of Gabriac. It appeared entirely abandoned, its shutters closed and lights out.

Nowhere did we locate the fête – each outlying road we explored took us deeper into empty woods. After a while I began to feel like Robert Louis Stevenson's companion in *Travels with a Donkey*. It was all right for Scottish 19th-century romance-writers to spend entire weeks crossing the Cévennes, living rough and camping out at night. But like Stevenson's four-footed friend Modestine, I was fast becoming reluctant to go on.

We were about to abandon our search when we spotted a house by the road with lights on. Jany got out of the car to ask directions, and in a minute or two, shrugging her shoulders at me in the beams of the headlights, returned with a man in tow. He was large, his head bald and shiny, his lower face covered by an enormous, spriggy beard that shot out from his face in all directions. He opened a rear door and got in, filling the car with a powerful odour of sweat and tobacco.

He did not speak at all, but motioned the car forward with a gesture of his hand. When I hesitated and said '*La fête de Gabriac?*' he replied with a loud '*Da! Da!*' and motioned us onwards again.

Da, Da? What was a Russian doing in the Cévennes? Was he a dissident writer, a forest hermit, a visiting Ortho-dox patriarch? I never found out. In the Cévennes one gets used to all sorts of odd fauna. His French was nearly as unintelligible as his Russian to us, but he seemed perfectly at home. He also seemed to know where the evening's festivities were being held.

He directed us up the hill, then off onto an obscure sideroad. Soon the asphalt gave out, and as we continued climbing upwards the unpaved road dwindled to a muddy track. Still our guide urged us on. Just as I was deciding he was no patriarch but an unhinged Rasputin with unspeakable designs upon us we arrived at a bottom of a steep field. There were dozens of cars parked here, and the sound of voices trailing off in the woods.

We parked too, and in the pitch black stumbled blindly along a narrow path through the woods. It led up, then down, then across a boggy stream into which I slipped and fell to my knees. Somewhere along the way we lost Rasputin. If I had not heard the music at that point I would have turned round and gone home to bed. But there it was, a high, wild trilling rising clear and distinct above the soughing of the wind in the trees. Over the next hill, in an open, brightly-lit clearing surrounded by a dark wilderness – power cables had been run up from the village far below – Gabriac was making merry.

I had been to other village fêtes in France. But in the sudden glare of lights I could see that this particular gathering did not in the vaguest way resemble any of them.

At one end of the clearing a band was playing on a spot-lit stage; it stood in front of a *magnanerie*, one of the tall stone buildings raised long ago in the Cévennes for that esoteric cottage industry, the raising of silkworms and spinning of silk. This was not the tum-tee-tum, tum-tee-tum music of the standard village *bal musette*. The group was called *Le Chauffeur est dans le Pré* – The Driver is in the Meadow – and their music was as fevered as their name. There was an accordion, a clarinet, a double bass, a saxophone and North African drums – together they produced excited, racing cadences, part Gypsy, part Slav, part free-form jazz. There was no doubt about it – culturally as well as geographically, we were well off the map and far into the woods.

Surrounding the edge of the clearing were long trestle tables, littered with used plates and empty bottles and now largely abandoned. At the glade's far end was a small stone chapel whose entrance had been converted to a bar. But what caught my eye was the crowd dancing under bright summer stars in the middle of the glade.

They shimmed and shook, gyred and gambolled, wriggled and writhed. They danced in groups, in circles, in couples and singly. Where did they come from, the girls with the rings in their noses and ears, the long skirts, the dreadlocks and tattoos, the bright, dyed feathers trailing from the lobes of their ears? How had they ended up in these hills, the men with the bristling Mohican-cuts, the shaved skulls, the barbarian forelocks and braided, beaded beards? By what route had the rainbow-coloured waistcoats, the hand-knitted

Nepalese pullovers, the Peruvian hats with bright dangling bobbles arrived here? It didn't matter that the people in this crowd ranged from barely-upright toddlers to white-haired septuagenarians. I knew where they all came from – they were straight out of 1968.

In the rest of France, of course, the *soixante-huitard* is now a rare and threatened species. Not only the young people themselves, but also the ideology they adopted on the Paris barricades had long ago gone the way of Serge Gainsbourg, *danseuses à go-go* and the *deux-chevaux*. Here, though, deep in the Cévennes, the lifestyle seemed somehow not only to have survived – it had flourished and been passed on to succeeding generations. It was not the only thing being passed on at the moment. Here and there through the glade drifted the heady odours of home-grown *herbe*.

Not everyone was getting high and thrashing about. Gathered around the chapel-front bar was an older, quieter group. Jany and I went up to say hello to two or three locals she'd met over the summers.

We greeted Jean-Pierre, the talented mason and carpenter who carried out repairs at La Vitgére. We exchanged news with Jean-Claude, who lived up the river from La Vitgère and taught art at the university in Nîmes. We asked Petit Jacques, who wove sublime modern tapestries on an ancient handloom, how this year's river-crayfish hunt had gone. We chatted with Evelyne, who raised trout in an old millpond and served them to guests at her *table d'hôte*, Le Rivet.

These were no zonked-out hippie punk-rockers. There was not a natty dreadlock, not a Celtic-rune tattoo or a silver tongue-stud between them. In fact, of all the people celebrating this evening it was the original *soixante-huitards*, the back-to-the-land counter-culturalists who'd retreated here from the cities three decades ago, who seemed the least carried away.

The difference lay partly in age – when you are fifty you are less likely to perforate the middle of your tongue with a large chunk of decorative jewellery than when you are fifteen. But it also lay in adaptation. The drop-out radicals of 1968 may have arrived in the Vallée-Française to set up communes, preach free love and practise social revolution. But they quickly discovered they couldn't survive on any of these things. Some of them abandoned life in the hills and went home to the city. Those who stayed on were forced to learn local skills and ways. It simply isn't practical to herd goats wearing beads, sandals and a batik sarong. Conventional in appearance, calm in behaviour, the *soixante-huitards* gazing on at the evening's entertainment looked pretty much like any other middle-aged rural Frenchmen.

But not quite enough, it seemed. Never mind that these newcomers now had children and grandchildren of their own here. For the largely Protestant farmers and villagers who have lived in the Cévennes for centuries the latest wave of non-conformists are still regarded as outsiders. Their values are still suspect. There is co-existence between the two communities, most of it peaceful, for tolerance and non-intervention were what brought the valley's Protestants here in the first place. But even after more than thirty years the old Cévenols still keep the more recent arrivals at arm's-length. For them they are *Néo-Cévenols*, new Cévenols. To everyone in the valleys they are known simply as Néos.

We gossiped, the crowd rocked and reeled, the band played frantically on. Ten minutes later the lights went out and the clearing was plunged into darkness. There were shrieks, laughter, loud protests. Abruptly red spotlights lit the façade of the *magnanerie*, the band launched into an even more frenetic number, and the evening's pyrotechnics began.

Thick clouds of coloured smoke ballooned out through the building's windows. Columns of livid sparks rose slowly from doorways until they were gushing and splashing like fountains. From the corners of the building balls of whirling red fire climbed ever higher into the air. They disappeared in mighty explosions that sent curtains of multi-coloured trails floating down the dark sky. The bangs grew louder, the lights flashed brighter, the music became more frenzied until the whole crowd was ecstatic and cheering.

'*Oui! Ouiiii! Ouuuiiiiiii!*' the voices shot high into the air along with the rockets. There is nothing like a fireworks display on an inky night in the middle of a French chestnut forest, especially when you are stoned out of your skull.

We left the Néos of Gabriac applauding and shouting

for more. Their party would go on into the early morning. But we were tired after a long day, and drove back down the long, leafy tree-tunnels with relief. Snuggled in bed under blankets for the first time in months, lulled by the sound of the little river softly rippling in its own bed not far below our window, we were fast asleep in minutes. In the night I dreamed strange dreams of snow-white cocoons that twirled high in the air and then exploded, turning into cascading streams of brilliant-coloured silk.

~

La Vitgère rises late. Only Odette was up earlier than we were the next morning – we found her on the balcony at the top of the garden stairs pounding basil in a mortar. She was preparing that favourite Provençal summer soup, *pistou*. But she was short of white beans, she told us. Would we mind picking up a kilo for her in Sainte-Croix? We didn't mind at all, for Sunday was market-day and the community's liveliest morning of the week.

The village is small and old. Downstream from La Vitgère, it sits perched over the narrow Gardon on high, rocky banks. Its shops and institutions are more or less equally divided on either side of the river. On one bank sits the Café du Globe, the post office, Madame Cougouluègne's butchery, and the village's two grocery shops – l'Epicerie Cévenole (good for fresh vegetables and more recent copies of *Le Monde*) and Chez Kléber (better for dry goods, cheeses, and a ripe stock of village gossip). On the other bank are Sainte-Croix's two small restaurants, an even smaller tourist office, and the indispensable village bakery run by Madame Papin, an affable woman with a vast and heaving bosom.

In winter, after a brief, light spate of morning shopping the streets of Sainte-Croix are deserted for hours at a time. In summer, with the arrival of holiday people, the pace picks up – there are booted hikers tramping along with walking sticks in hand, cyclists in spandex shorts zipping through the village on thin-tyred racing bikes, upriver campers buying cooking gas and torch batteries. There are even adventurous expeditionary parties leading pack-donkeys named, inevitably, Modestine.

But it is on the once-weekly market morning that things really come alive in Sainte-Croix. It is then that the Néos descend in number from their stone hamlets and isolated gardens hidden up the hills. They set up their stalls neither on the left bank of the village, nor on the right, but in between the two. For a few hours every week the ancient and rusty iron footbridge that spans the river becomes the teeming focus of village activity.

With shopping baskets in hand we made the tour up one side of the busy bridge and down the other. Néo produce, as one might imagine, is simple, natural, unprocessed and straight from the earth. A Néo organic carrot does not look like a supermarket carrot – it is misshapen, knobbly and full of nature's imperfections. It also tastes better than a supermarket carrot. On the stalls on the bridge there were all sorts of local products made on small homesteads by traditional methods. There was dark, pungent Cévenol honey; chestnut flour and chestnut bread; blackberry jam and dandelion jelly; home-made pâtés and goose *confits*; *pelardon* cheeses from the herds of goats that graze the slopes; free-range farmyard ducks and chickens that looked as good as Gérard Chauvin's. At the far end of the bridge we found just the thing – the little white beans called *cocos* – that Odette needed for her *pistou*.

When Jany went off to buy bread from Madame Papin I bought myself a copy of *Le Monde* and strolled over to the terrace of the Café du Globe. It is a fine place to sit in the shade on market day. From a table by the water one can survey all comings and goings in Sainte-Croix, from the shoppers at the Epicerie Cévenole, to the Néos selling nettle-leaf quiches on the bridge, to the ducks quacking their way across the crystal water below.

It did not surprise me to find Marie Duroc sitting at such a strategic location. Small, bright-eyed and amiable, as lively in her seventies as she must have been as a teenager, Marie was a one-woman intelligence operation. She knew of everything happening in the Vallée-Française from Saint-Jean-du-Gard to Barre-des-Cévennes; compared to her own gossip even the rumours at Kléber's grocery were as dry and plain as their wheat biscuits. The reason Marie was so proficient at information-gathering was simple. People liked her – she talked to everyone and everyone talked to her. While few other residents even tried to cross the line separating Néo from Cévenol, she was back and forth a dozen times a day. If the story was good she was as happy chatting to a nipple-pierced *baba-cool* in purple tie-dye as to a ham-fisted farmer chopping winter wood.

Marie was far more interesting than *Le Monde*. I abandoned my paper and over coffee fell to talking. As we sat chin-wagging about who had quit drinking, who was having whose baby and other similarly vital valley affairs, I heard a commotion. From just up the road there was a banging of hammers, a screech of sawing and the sounds of bulky material being shifted.

Like the Cévenols themselves, Sainte-Croix is traditional and not much given to change. Buildings generally remain untouched for decades at a time, so I asked Marie what was going on.

'Oh, that's Elke at the Café Populaire,' Marie replied. 'She's been renovating for quite a while now. She'll be opening some time next week.'

For a small place like Sainte-Croix the opening of a second café was an event. But there were two things that I learned from Marie that for villagers made it an occasion of more than passing interest.

First, she told me, the Café Populaire was not a new café at all. It had been empty and locked for years. But back in the 1950s it had been a busy place. Not only did the Cévenol who ran it offer the regular services of a café – for many years he also cut hair, repaired bicycles, sold hunting and fishing licences, sheared sheep, watered horses and administered injections. There were even stories, which I shall not repeat here, that the proprietor had consistently winning ways with large numbers of lonely valley widows. Suffice it to say that half a century ago the Café Populaire had lived up to its name and been the life and soul of the Vallée Française.

The second thing that Marie told me was that Elke was not a Cévenol, but a Néo. She was artistic, an Austrian who had settled down in the Vallée Française a short time before. The greatest concentration of Néos lived a mile or so away up the hill in Gabriac. There they did what they liked – after all, they held a majority of seats on the village municipal council. And, of course, Marie told me, nobody objected to the Néos holding their outdoor markets and occasional celebrations in Sainte-Croix. Or doing their shopping there either – it was good for the village economy. But for a Néo to install a hippie café in an old Cévenol institution? Now that was a different matter. Who knew what sort of clientele it would keep hanging about? The paint wasn't even dry and already there were rumblings in the village.

After a while Marie went off to do her shopping and I strolled over the bridge to see what had happened to Jany. I found her, bread long purchased, sitting on a step on the little square in front of the tourist office.

It was a lively scene. Having slept in late, dozens of

younger Néos were now straggling into town for the market. After the evening's festivities some of the hard-core merrymakers – perhaps they had not slept at all – were looking a mite bleary. Bits of straw poked out of tousled hair. Their colourful clothing was grass-stained. Their feet were dirty and bare. A few smelled as rank as billy goats. No one seemed to mind. The sun was shining on potted geraniums ranged on stone balconies and stairways, and once again there was music in the air.

It came from a trio of instruments. A bearded man in a felt hat played a violin. Another with bushy moustaches turned the crank of a droning wooden instrument, burnished with age, which might have been a hurdy-gurdy. A third musician, a woman with long grey plaits and a turquoise headband, played a concertina as she slowly turned around and around, all the while intoning in a cracked voice an old French country song.

'It's the Sixties all over again,' Jany whispered to me, rapt. Fashionable Aix-en-Provence lay less than three hours down the road. It might as well have been on the far side of the earth. Was it the music? The ancient houses perched over the riverbank? The bright and unkempt clothing? The rough forests that surrounded the village? There was something of the medieval peasant fair about the whole scene. I nodded in agreement with Jany. It could have been the 1960s, or it could have been the 1660s.

We watched for a little while and then made our way

out of the square. On the edge of the crowd I spotted Sully Rauzier, the Cévenol farmer whose neatly-kept property, Campemenard, lay just down the road from La Vitgère. He looked out of place – his shirt was ironed and immaculately white, his grizzled hair was short and trim. Like us, he too had come shopping and ended up gazing on, nonplussed by Néo life. He gave us a smile of greeting, then disappeared in the direction of the bakery.

‮‬ ⤸

Around seven o'clock that evening I left Jany reading in the garden and wandered along the road for a swim. The Cévennes is notorious for its autumn thunderstorms, deluges of such astonishing violence that they can turn even the smallest stream into a monster. These wild and raging beasts hurl boulders about with ease, throw themselves out of their beds, and sometimes bring floods, death and destruction to the wide plains below. But now in high summer the little Gardon River was a docile and well-behaved as a small domestic pet, and too shallow in most places for real swimming. If you knew where to look, though, there were clear, deep holes, well away from roads, that were wonderful – you didn't have to share them with anyone but the fish.

One such place lay just ten minutes away. A rocky little pool that was as clear and cold as vodka, it lay enclosed between a pasture of Sully Rauzier's and an open glade belonging to the art teacher, Jean-Claude. It was a beautiful spot, the stone worn over aeons into shapes that were almost human in their smooth undulation. A dozen fat chub cruised the pool, their orange dorsal fins sweeping the current as they faced upstream waiting for dinner – a careless caterpillar perhaps, or a drowned mayfly. There was a quiet presence, a certain repose and serenity about the place. If you sat there motionless for long enough, just looking at rock and water, you began to feel the power of these simple elements and the time they had taken to fashion the pool.

There were more baleful elements there, too. The snakes down at water level were brightly-banded and twisting with energy, but they weren't real – they'd been painted on the rocks. Jean-Claude had also painted more serpents and strange mask-like faces on the trees on his side of the river. These, he claimed, were the purely aesthetic endeav-ours of an artist, but I suspected deeper motives. There was something slightly fetish-like about his snakes – to me they appeared to be hexes, magical jujus intended to protect the pool. I suspect he had put them there to ward off noisy chil-dren, sun-tanning tourists and other troublesome intruders. Whether they worked or not I couldn't say, but I rarely met other bathers there.

I swam, then came to rest on rocks where tiny bubbles popped and fizzed below a small cascade at the top of the pool. Jacuzzis, as far as I am concerned, come a poor second – chill Cévennes river-water is as invigorating as any I know.

As I sat on the rocks enjoying the late afternoon sun, I

heard a tinkling of bells in the pasture above. It was a familiar sound. Every morning Sully Rauzier or his wife Claire passed by La Vitgère on their way out of the farm with their herd of 120 goats. Every evening they returned after a day's grazing high on the hillsides or here, down in the fields by the river. Over the splashing of the water I could hear Sully shouting commands to his two herd-dogs. I dressed and climbed up into the pasture. Two huge black-and-tan hounds were immediately streaking their way towards me. Once Athos and Fripou had been called off I was able to make my way through a pasture of milling nannies to Sully at their centre.

Of all the people I had met in these valleys Sully Rauzier most typified an old Cévenol way of life. Now in his mid-sixties, he stood erect and straight-backed, his body firm and compact, his blunt features ruddied by a lifetime spent outdoors. I had never seen Sully sitting or even, I think, standing still. He was always on the move, finishing one job and at the same time preparing the next. Life at Campemenard, his hillside farm, started well before dawn and did not slow down until after dark. There was never any waste of time or money or energy there. Sully calculated, accumulated, worked steadily, and reinvested the profits. He never took holidays. He was a sort of independent and fiercely self-reliant kulak, a landed peasant whose native energy and industriousness had brought him prosperity.

He enjoyed life. He was not greedy or miserly or stern.

On the contrary, he was always smiling and generously good-natured. Everyone at La Vitgère liked Sully – there was rarely a visit when he didn't present us with some honey from his hives, a hatful of prized *cepe* mushrooms gleaned from the forest, or lettuces fresh from his garden. There was a sort of quiet confidence about him. He seemed completely in, and of, his element. Although I am not sure he would know how to ask for help for himself, he was ready when others needed it. But deep down was a hard, unflinching streak of that Protestant morality brought to the Cévennes by his ancestors in the 1600s. What you sow is what you reap.

I always thought of Sully as the king of the valley. Campemenard was a large, well-kept place, its houses, barns, sheds, goat-pens, chicken-coops and extensive vegetable plots spread out over a series of high stone terraces running down to the river. But this was just the beginning of his kingdom. Sully ran a small sawmill on the other side of the Gardon. He leased a campground to summer scout and youth groups. He owned a number of *gîtes*, cottages and simple holiday homes that he rented seasonally to tourists. He owned pastures, hay-fields, riverside meadows, grazing grounds and woodlots for many miles up and down the valley. In all he held title to over one hundred different plots of land. Some of them were tiny, a few yards of narrow stone-walled terrace isolated high on the hillside. But if there was a use they could be put to Sully found it.

Now, surrounded by scores of browsing goats, we shook

hands and exchanged news. Claire, who with book in hand often herded the goats herself, was *gîte*-cleaning for new holiday arrivals. Jean-Pierre, their son, was in the midst of finishing the season's haymaking. Up in the Trabassac Valley, a long, deep ravine that ran high into the hills behind Campemenarde, Sully himself had repaired a centuries-old irrigation system that had not worked for years. It did not matter if it no longer served any vital purpose, he said; he liked to see things working as they had been intended to work.

But there was also news of the larger community. All over the valleys this summer, Sully told me, Cévenols were celebrating a 300th anniversary – in the early 1700s, after years of Catholic persecution following the revocation of the Edict of Nantes, the Protestants of the Cévennes rose in popular rebellion. The War of the Camisards had not been a glorious struggle. Guerrilla actions brought barbarous reprisal by royal troops – civilian imprisonment, the wholesale burning of farms and villages, the wreaking of economic havoc. The Cévenol memory is long, and its past a constant reminder of the hardships endured to preserve a valued way of life. This summer's celebrations were as much remembrance as fête.

In return I mentioned another fête – the previous evening's shenanigans in Gabriac. Sully laughed; Gabriac's all-night parties were famous. But he knew most of the older Néos, the ones who'd arrived decades before, and he respected them. They had energy and ideas, he said. More important, they had principles, even if they weren't his own.

And what about the younger ones, I asked, remembering Sully's bemused face at the market that morning.

He smiled and pursed his lips. '*Eh bien*,' he said with resignation, '*Ça, c'est une autre histoire.*' That's another story.

Sully was too discreet, too immersed in that Cévenol tradition of live-and-let-live, to begin a litany of grievances. I'd heard them all before anyway. The newly-arrived Néos had no energy or ideas. They came to the Cévennes for home-grown pot and cheap living. They had no interest in getting jobs – they lived on state welfare and government housing-credits. They paid no social security, but were the first to call for helicopters to ferry them to hospital in Nimes. The list went on and on – while the Cévenols had spent their entire lives in backbreaking work, young Néos were assiduously avoiding any kind of work at all.

We stood there watching Athos and Fripou head off unbidden, intent on turning half a dozen goats wandering towards the steep banks of the river. I had no response to Sully's silent head-shaking. On the face of it the critics weren't wrong. Lots of young Néos really had fled the cities with cheap dope and subsidised living in mind. My only question was what would eventually become of them.

There was no time to ask. When Athos and Fripou brought the wandering nannies back, a message seemed to spread silently through the herd. The goats grew restless, stopped browsing and began bleating. Sully whistled to his dogs and the goats started moving off, their bells clanging, their heavy udders swaying in the long grass. It was an old, practised routine that could not wait. It was time, said Sully, to head for home and the evening milking. I headed home myself, looking forward to the evening *pistou*.

〜

A day or two later Jany and I were up even earlier than Odette, for we had a rendezvous with a man named Dominic Foubert. He was a trim, fit-looking naturalist with the Cévennes National Park, and he was going to give a nature tour. I am not much on guided tours of any sort, especially ones as zippily titled as '*Beside a Stream*'. But Jany was insistent. If I could walk for hours beside a sweltering sea in Marseilles, I could walk beside a cool stream here. There was no telling what we might find out.

And she was right. When I discovered that the stream Dominic was proposing to explore was the clear brook that ran up behind Campemenard I was all for the outing. I loved the steep little Trabassac Valley. It was lush, dense, overgrown and barely populated. Not far up its course grew a great spreading tree, its ancient and crooked trunk protruding far out over a high, sheer bank of rock. Below, still and limpid in the green shade, a deep pool lay concealed. It was my favourite swimming place. Too high to dive into and too steep to climb out of, you could get there only by swimming upstream through a narrow defile. There were delicate ferns, splashing rock-cascades to climb over, and above a band of bright blue sky barely wider than your outstretched arms. It was a wonderful spot, wild and secret and about as close to the hidden heart of the Cévennes as you could get.

Dominic did not seem disappointed when just one couple showed up for his tour – if there had been no takers at all, he told me, he would still have walked the Trabassac alone for the sheer pleasure of it. This was his backyard – his house was built high on a crest here. He'd been observing the valley's trees, animals, insects, soils, plant-life, seasons, geology and thunderstorms for decades. And still, he assured me, he was discovering new things.

That morning we crept up on a stick-and-mud dam built by beavers and spied on their semi-submerged lodge. We surprised a *couleuvre de Montpellier*, a slinky, sinuous, yard-long snake, as it swam upstream hunting for frogs. We looked for trout in still pools, searched for rare crayfish beneath rocks and boulders. I learned about scarab beetles, spotted salamanders, silver gudgeons, green lizards and the mating habits of the common dragonfly.

Now all this made for a fine outing, and the hours passed unnoticed as we slowly made our way up through the valley's chestnut forests and open glades. But what really astonished me was the discovery that over the last 500 years the dominant life-form in the Trabassac was not furred, or feathered, or winged at all. Trabassac was not even vaguely untouched. Despite the wild and unspoiled look of the valley, natural history had long ago been supplanted here by human history.

Dominic led us away from the stream and upwards across a grassy meadow. On the flank of the valleyside he stopped. At his feet was a narrow channel full of smooth-flowing water. The stream below us followed the steeply descending valley floor, but here the channel pursued its own gentle, winding course along the elevated contours of the hill. There were smaller, secondary channels, connected by little gates that raised and lowered, which wandered off to lower destinations. The hillside meadows were being fed by water drawn from the stream far up the valley. Simple, ingenious, wholly transforming in its ability to support life, this was part of the old irrigation system that Sully Rauzier had recently repaired.

Sully, said Dominic, was only maintaining a practice that had been initiated six centuries earlier. Long before Sully's Protestant ancestors arrived, solitude-seeking Benedictine monks had begun a process that would eventually alter the face of the Cévennes, making an ungenerous and hostile environment at least liveable. The stream below us, Dominique said, was no ordinary stream – to tame its erratic behaviour men had smoothed out its bed, changed its course, retained its walls through years of labour. Every boulder and stone in it had been deliberated over, picked at, or modified.

On we walked up the irrigation channel, Dominic continuing to point out and explain. There was nothing here, in fact, that was not the result of human intervention. The chestnut trees that now flourished wild and untended were not native to the Cévennes. They'd been painstakingly planted because no other food crop would grow in these steep, flinty soils – the flour they produced became the staple on which an entire Cévenol society had been built. Not even the wild forests were really wild – beneath deep layers of forest detritus we found level after level of terraces built of the same grey stone that make up Cévenol houses. Centuries ago entire valleys here were highly-engineered plantations, multi-levelled and irrigated, feeding dense populations.

'You can't imagine how the Trabassac Valley looked in the 1600s,' Dominic said as he led us past a water mill that once ground dried chestnuts to flour. 'The Cévennes was ten times more populated than it is today. The pressure to produce food was terrible. The tiniest plots of land were coveted and fought over and contested in the courts. There were water rights for irrigation – they were allocated not by the day, but by the hour and around the clock. If you were in any doubt you'd stay up all night watching to make sure you got every last drop that was yours.'

Dominic pointed to some gnarled mulberry trees, their leaves broad and heavy, growing close to the water. 'Those peasants had to worry about more than just feeding them-selves. They had too feed their silkworms, too. They were their only source of cash. Of course they're tiny, but if you started with thirty grams of silkworm eggs you'd end up needing two tons of mulberry leaves to feed your worms on. And you'd have to build those vast houses, the *magnaneries*, to rear them in. It all took time and effort. Of course, the Cévenols had a different conception of such things then – they were all just part of the slow, steady rhythm of their lives.'

As we walked on I could only think of Sully Rauzier, of his self-reliance, his relentless work, the energy he put into everything he did. These days chestnut flour and natural silk were just Cévenol folklore, and all man's works were crumbling back into the ground. Sully seemed more than ever a kind of throwback, a stubborn holdout who refused to give in to the decline that lay about him. What remained strong and unbroken were his links to the past.

Tired after a long tramp, we walked back down the Trabassac, not talking but just enjoying the cool greenery. Looking at river and rock, mulberry and chestnut, mill and *magnanerie*, I couldn't help wondering. There are natural rules that govern people and the places they live. No one escapes the dictates of powerful landscapes and the kind of life they impose. Over time man might have moulded the Cévennes, reshaped it incessantly to make it part of himself. But wasn't the reverse true, too? Could the Cévennes, in its turn, do anything other than reshape man?

⌇

Over the next few days Jany and I fell into La Vitgère's rhythm of easy sociability. There were lazy swimming and picnic parties under shady trees. There were market expeditions along winding roads to the little valley-town of Florac. In the hillside village of Le Pompidou there were classical music recitals in an 800-year-old chapel dedicated to a Cévenol pope. And in the evenings, of course, there was boundless food and talk on the garden-terrace of the tall house by the river.

But it didn't matter whether I was talking with Farid about early Ottoman calligraphy or watching dragonflies, quite as graceful as any Islamic poet's pen, describing fanciful loops and arabesques over the surface of the Gardon. I found my thoughts continually returning to our walk by the stream, and to questions of ownership and belonging.

Who belongs to any given place? How is the spirit of that place transmitted to the people who live there? Is it the property only of those who observe its traditions? Is it transferable to anyone else? How long does it take? Not belonging to any place at all myself, of course, I hadn't the faintest idea of an answer.

I wondered if thirty years, for instance, would be long enough. That was the time Janine Berder had lived in an old riverside house downstream from Sainte-Croix. Janine had arrived with the first wave of Néos and not budged since. Was almost half a life enough to become part of a place? Finally, one warm afternoon when the rest of the inhabitants of La Vitgère were laid out flat and snoozing, I decided to ask her.

I found Janine working at Camparado, a traditional

Cévenol house lying in grassy pastures by the river. But there was no mistaking the woman staking tomatoes beside it for a traditional Cévenol peasant. Janine did not do her gardening any more conventionally than she did anything else. Wearing high heels and a tight green skirt, her hennaed hair glowing almost as red in the sun as her tomatoes, she might have been ready for an elegant evening saunter down the Boulevard St-Michel.

I was impressed. Janine may have looked like a seductive and sensuous Left-Bank bohemian. Even by Cévenol standards of industriousness, though, she was a force to be reckoned with. The garden I walked into was just as large and well kept as Sully Rauzier's. But it had something else – where the Rauzier acres were efficiently utilitarian, Janine's were poetic as well.

In between rows of spinach, rhubarb, beets and potatoes, Janine had grown plants purely for the pleasure of colour and form. There were bright ornamental peppers, huge sunflowers with tilted yellow heads, flowering roses, multi-hued beds of poppies. The wooden posts in Janine's garden were not just uprights from whose taut cords runner-beans grew; they were also tall masts from whose tops fluttered the bright naval standards of Brittany, her home province. But Janine's grandest achievement in her garden this year, she told me, was literary. She led me over to a corner of the garden where a bed of small blue flowers stood. They didn't look like anything special, but they obviously charmed her to bits. They were grown from seeds, she told me, collected from the garden of George Sand.

Janine was not the only exuberant and unconventional spirit at Camparado. From the edge of the garden we looked down at Joël working on a stretch of flat loamy soil close to the river. Stripped to the waist, his hair tied back in a pony-tail and his moustachioed face intent on the job before him, he was channelling water into a small flooded field retained by banks of earth.

'Joël's been reading about Chinese rice cultivation,' Janine said as we waved down at him. 'He got so interested he went out and bought forty kilos of unhusked rice and built a paddy-field. It may work or it may not – we don't think anyone has ever tried growing rice in the Cévennes before.'

On the other side of the garden we stuck our heads into a small studio of thick, whitewashed stone and said hello to Petit Jacques. A few nights before I had stood beside him watching intricate, coloured patterns of fireworks unfold in the sky above Gabriac. Now for a minute I stood watching far more intricate, even brighter patterns unfold on Petit Jacques's loom. If Jacques was slight in build his tapestries were heroic in size and conception. Back and forth he plied the shuttles with deft concentration, many months' work behind him, many more months ahead. We left him at it and climbed to Comparado's vine-shaded terrace for a glass of cool rosé.

What might Janine tell me about Néos and Cévenols and the land they shared? I had no idea. Here before me was one of the more vigorous and uninhibited characters in the Vallée Française, a creative free spirit with a penchant for provocation. She was not the type to miss a chance for dramatic statement.

This, after all, was the woman who had stolen the show at the annual Néo event known as *Un Thème*. Held each year in the streets of Sainte-Croix, it was rather like a Sixties happening, a spontaneous, free-form party organised around a single word. When the theme at the previous year's event had been announced as *'Rouge'* there had been all sorts of responses. Suddenly there was a home-made traffic light halting pedestrians at the foot of the rusty iron bridge. There were people traipsing through Sainte-Croix with scarlet capes and carmine masks and bowls of goldfish on their heads. There was a cunningly constructed catapult you loaded with ketchup and fired at your choice of photograph – George Bush, the Pope, or General de Gaulle.

Janine, though, had brought the little village to a halt when she'd shown up wearing a flaming red dress beneath which bounced huge artificial breasts. At the tip of each breast protruded a button-operated spigot. Behind it lay a five-litre reservoir. One simply accepted one of Janine's proffered plastic cups, held it out, pressed a tit, and lo! – a copious flow of red wine sprang forth. It was irresistible. Néos and Cévenols alike lined up for their share, and continued returning until the spring ran dry. There was absolutely no telling what such a woman might say to me.

But Janine, for all her daring and poetic whimsy, was entirely down-to-earth.

Of course, she agreed with me, every landscape has a special nature and a force of its own. It was what makes the identity of a place. And yes, the Cévennes had a more imposing presence than most. It expressed itself through the character of its people – in the end land and people couldn't help but became one and the same thing. Belonging to a place was a mysterious thing. But the transfer of identity, Janine insisted, was straightforward.

'There's no magic about it at all,' she laughed, 'no spiritual mantle bequeathed to one group and not another. It is something that is learned. Belonging to the Cévennes is as simple as going to school.'

For all her non-conformity, Janine was a firm believer in the benefits of learning. When she was younger, she told me, she'd taught French literature – even today she contributed to scholarly reviews. But from the moment she'd settled here the real lesson at hand had been in the regeneration of community.

'You have no idea how isolated people were, how sad life used to be in these valleys.' She shook her head. 'After the war the young people left, looking for work and easier lives. The old people who stayed on had a terrible time. They lived far apart. They had no telephones or transportation.

There was no social contact, no communication at all. It was dismal.

'When the Néos arrived in the late Sixties they didn't have much money, and they had no experience of rural life at all. But the far-sighted Cévenol mayor of Sainte-Croix – not everyone saw him as a man of vision – encouraged them to settle down. He could see that they brought something more important than either money or experience. The men had virility. The women had fertility. They made babies. And it was babies, not adults called Cévenols and adults called Néos, who were the future. It was they who stopped the schools, the building blocks of valley life, from closing down. It's the children and the schools that keep this place going.'

Janine poured more wine and we sat watching the sun slide down the sky towards the forested ridge above us. It was not just school that brought a sense of belonging, she added. Perhaps she looked silly with wine gushing in streams from five-litre breasts. But the fêtes and celebrations the Néos organised had serious purpose – they kept people together. Over the years the Néos had laid on more and more elaborate events. There had been a weekly newspaper, a pirate radio station, art exhibitions, carnivals, sound-and-light shows, dramatic performances that took over the entire village. Once Petit Jacques had spent months organising a *grand spectacle aquatique* on the water beneath the iron bridge at Sainte-Croix. It had been such a magnificent spectacle, Janine recalled, that its reputation was still growing – it was the equal these days, by Néo accounts anyway, of the great naval dramas mounted by the Romans in the flooded Coliseum.

And what of the old-style Cévenols, suspicious and slow to accept change? Had they merely stood by? Perhaps not completely, Jannine said as we watched the afternoon draw on. The really vast and generous bosom in the valley served not wine, but bread, and belonged to Madame Papin. The village bakery, the vital heart of village life, was no longer run as a private business. Seen as too important to village well-being, it was now collectively financed and operated. If Néo children were learning Cévenol ways, perhaps Cévenols were becoming a little bit like Néos.

～

On July 13, the eve of Bastille Day, there was some doubt as to whether the fête of Sainte-Croix could proceed. All day long brief, heavy showers had passed over the area, darkening the skies, drenching the forests and swelling clear streams into muddy torrents. Sainte-Croix's giant outdoor paella party, the village's answer to Gabriac's hippie dinner-dance, was in dire risk of being washed out.

But as afternoon drew on the clouds dissipated. The sun emerged and in the woods surrounding the village newly-washed chestnut trees glistened from every dripping leaf. In the courtyard of the stone-built Sainte-Croix school, perched on a hillside on the edge of the village, brisk and efficient teams of Cévenol housewives launched themselves into action. Trestle tables and school chairs were set out in parallel rows, long paper tablecloths were expertly unrolled, knives, forks and spoons were set down rapidly but precisely in their place. By seven o'clock, the hour at which the first celebrant walked through the school gate, every last detail had been attended to.

The most demanding job of all went to a small and unassuming man, the merchant who in everyday guise made the round of Cévenol village markets in his refrigerated fish-van. It was only now that his real worth, the true extent of his competence, was at last revealed. A growing crowd of admirers gathered round as he set up a huge gas-burner in a corner of the schoolyard. On it he placed the largest pan available in the valley, a deep metal dish six feet across. Cooking paella for 200 hungry Cévenols is not a task taken lightly.

Stripping down to his undershirt, he disappeared into enveloping clouds of steam. From time to time he could be half-seen stirring vigorously away with a wooden spoon the size of a canoe paddle. Vast quantities of ingredients went into the mix – bags of rice, sacks of chopped onion and peppers, boxes of mussels, scoops of chicken, handfuls of shrimp, a chopped squid or two, broadcast scatterings of chorizo sausage. Like the afternoon's rain clouds, the steam over the paëlla eventually dissipated too. Then the sunny, round brightness of the dish emerged into the open air, and the whole concoction was left to slowly simmer to perfection.

In the meantime the crowd grew thick around the make-shift bar, and from the table where René, Odette, Jany and I were installed I cast a glance over the gathering.

This was no hairy assembly from the outer margins of French society. There was not a rainbow-coloured waist-coat, not a silver tongue-stud, not a Néo in sight. Everyone, without exception, wore shoes. These were solid Protestant valley folk, entire families from Sainte-Croix, Pompidou, Molezon and other surrounding villages. Scrubbed and spruced up after a day's work, anticipating dinner and the *bal musette* that followed, they positively glowed with pink health and sociability as they sipped aperitifs and talked to friends not seen for weeks or months.

René spotted Sully, Claire and Jean-Pierre Rauzier in the crowd and waved them over – we had been saving them seats. Sitting beside Claire, I asked her what she would be cooking in the kitchen right now if she weren't eating paella.

What else? she replied. Soup. Her family had eaten soup twice a day, every day, all through their lives. Leek and potato soups; onion and celery soups; soups enlivened with mushrooms from the forest; soups thickened with the trotter of a farmyard pig – these were the basis of Cévenol existence. No real Cévenol, she told me, could happily see himself through each day without at least a bowl or two of the stuff. Sully's ageing mother even had it every morning for breakfast. We were still talking soup as dinner was finally pronounced ready and we joined a long line of diners slowly snaking their way to the giant dish in the courtyard.

An hour later the able ladies of Sainte-Croix were clearing tables and bringing on cheese, dessert and coffee. The sun was down now, and strings of lights in the courtyard trees were switched on. I was only half-listening to the conversations around me. I was thinking instead of the Café Populaire – Elke had finally opened her new establishment. And when the tables and chairs were removed and the band struck up a lively little waltz number I was still thinking of it. Tum-tee-tum, tum-tee-tum, thumped accordion, drums and guitar. For a few minutes Jany dragged me through a medley of cha-chas, rumbas and paso-dobles. Then it was my turn. I dragged her off the crowded dance-floor, down the hill and over the iron bridge.

Elke was indeed artistic and Austrian, a tall, willowy creature in patchwork leather and jewellery that softly tinkled. Her café could not possibly have looked this way half a century ago. It aimed at cool, gallery-like minimalism, and its brightly-lit white walls were decorated with modern paintings. There were candles on the bar and a soft jazz saxophone on the stereo. On one low table stood a slender brass water-pipe. On a second table two tiny kittens lay fast asleep in a bread-basket. At a third we found Mireille, Farid and Touna finishing dinner and a bottle of wine.

They were in fine and mellow mettle, chatting with Elke about café décor, vegetarian cooking and the ways in which

161

Nordic women end up in hill-valleys deep in the south of France.

'Coming across Sainte-Croix the first time was easy,' Elke said in her Teutonic-accented French. 'It was a long time ago. It was whirlwind trip, and I didn't pay much attention to maps, names or anything else. How could I, roaring along at seventy miles an hour on the back of a boyfriend's motorcycle?'

But even at that speed she had fallen in love with Sainte-Croix. It was finding the village a second time, she said, that had been difficult. It had taken twenty years. Once she'd relocated it, though, Elke had known that this was the place for her.

We all congratulated Elke on her rediscovery of Sainte-Croix, and on her re-opening of an old village institution. It was a perfect story for the new Café Populaire – romantic, fanciful and very Néo. We ordered a pot of verbena tea to celebrate.

Farid and Touna also had a story. Over the last few days they, too, they announced, had fallen in love with the Cévennes. If they had arrived too late that evening for Sainte-Croix's *fête du village* it was because Mireille had taken them to an estate agent's in Florac. They had looked at pictures of an old Cévenol stone house on a hillside not far away. Of course it would need fixing up, they said. But the peace …! The tranquillity … ! The view … ! Ibiza was beautiful, but of course too crowded now and, frankly, getting a little *passé* – the Cévennes was real escape. Farid and Touna had an appointment with the agent to look the property over first thing next week.

And this, too, was another perfect story – romantic, fanciful and very *Bo-bo*. I stirred honey into my tea and watched Elke serving a tofu-and-alfalfa-sprout salad to two young women in flowery skirts.

One generation of newcomers was replacing the other. The wheel had turned once again, the gates been raised, the spate set flowing. Who, I wondered, were the Néos now, and who the Cevenols? In this rough country such gentle transition was not just natural – it was as inevitable as the flow of water from a winding hillside irrigation channel to the valley-floor below.

Five

There are arrivals in the Cévennes, and there are departures. Not long after Bastille Day still other global gypsies pitched up at La Vitgère. Now the house by the river reverberated not only with Middle Eastern rhythms but Latin American ones as well. Our Brazilian visitors were a lively and exuberant import to the Cévennes, and so were the teenage offspring they brought with them. You couldn't expect teenagers raised on samba to become any more excited by the bleating of nanny-goats on the hill above the house than by the soft whispering of the stream below. Such children brought their own restless excitement – to say nothing of a large music CD collection – to the once-quiet Cévenol hills.

From the moment of their arrival La Vitgère, for all its rambling size, began to seem the slightest bit small. Bedroom allocation was a complex exercise in logistics. Meal preparation was converted to a production-line process, shopping expeditions into military-style convoys. Bathrooms were occupied from breakfast on towards lunch. Lazy afternoon siestas became a thing of the past. Simply moving a parked car in the narrow, now-cluttered driveway required multi-party conferences in several languages. For all La Vitgère's cosmopolitan pleasures the time had come, Jany and I decided, to beat a strategic retreat to Aix-en-Provence.

In the day that remained before our departure I undertook a small task. For among the numerous books that were left at La Vitgère by roving visitors I had found one that intrigued me. Most of these volumes were of the long-haul, short-attention-span variety: sex-and-shopping, spy-thrillers and who-done-its picked haphazardly from airport book-racks around the world. Abandoned by their owners on bedside shelves they joined the kind of small but junky library you'd feel a little guilty reading anywhere else. I'd already spent half a dozen long, languid afternoons on this holiday fodder, beginning with a Dan Brown blockbuster. Then, exploring the top shelf in the cramped and little-used bedroom to which we had recently been relegated, I came across *The Birth of Tragedy*.

It was a challenge I hesitated over. For *The Birth of Tragedy* was no sizzling pulp-romance. Mired deep in trash as I already was, the title at first suggested to me an explosive drama involving a powerful politician, an aspiring starlet and the shocking tabloid revelation of their love-child. But the slim volume lay much further out in the orbit of exotic reads than that – it was a serious philosophical work by Friedrich Nietzsche.

Heaven knows who had surreptitiously introduced a

German 19th-century philosopher into La Vitgère. And, to be honest, if it had been Agatha Christie in his place I would have been just as happy. But the house was crowded and noisy and I needed escape. Jany had bravely volunteered to stay around and help with lunch. But I was determined on this last day to hide myself away in a quiet, secluded spot. On the bright morning that I packed a blanket and a picnic to take up the Trabassac Valley, I carried *The Birth of Tragedy* along as well.

With a towel over my shoulder, I walked out into the sun and down the road. At Campemenard I waved to Claire Rauzier as she stood in her vegetable plot with an armful of freshly-picked courgettes. No more paella for another year, I thought – it would be courgette-and-something soup tonight. At the bridge where the stream from the Trabassac joined the Gardon River I left the road and headed uphill into the steep little valley.

Fifteen minutes later I was installed on my blanket beneath the giant oak that overhung my favourite swimming place. Lying on springy grass in deep, cool shade, I had only to glance downwards into even deeper, cooler darkness to see the pool that lay below. Surrounded by sheer rocks, inaccessible to wind, humans, and other disturbances, its surface was calm, its depths still and untroubled. It was a relief to gaze at from time to time, for the reading I now started in on was anything but untroubled.

Friedrich Nietzsche may have found writing *The Birth*

of Tragedy suitable entertainment for a debutant philosopher just embarking on his career. But from the very first pages I could see that for this reader, at least, it was going to be a trial. Brilliant, mercurial, the youngest man ever to be appointed a seat as Extraordinary Professor of Classical Philology at the University of Basle, Nietzsche wrote his treatise on classical Greek drama at the age of twenty-eight. The book was radical in its views. Its propositions were not backed up by conventional procedural argument. Its terminology was obscure, its style at the same time intellectually dense and emotionally passionate. Earning the academic establishment's immediate disapproval, the book in fact signalled an early end to Nietzsche's university career. He set off instead on a lonely if milestone-setting path of enquiry in which, before his commitment to a mental asylum seventeen years later, he vigorously attacked the philosophical basis of everything from Christianity to bourgeois German nationalism. In short, Nietzsche is a tough proposition and *The Birth of Tragedy* a bitch to read.

The sun wheeled across the sky, leafy shadows shifted over my blanket, and every now and then I had to break off to reposition myself in the shade. Small black ants sometimes raced their way toward me, requiring time out for brief counter-offensive campaigns. Once I jumped to my feet, thinking I'd heard the rustle of a snake in the grass near by. All things considered, though, the Trabassac Valley wasn't a bad place to be confronted by the fundamental questions of human existence. I kept at it, and after a little while it began to seem to me that Nietzsche was talking of something of real interest. A man driven, he wanted to explain not only why the old life of the Mediterranean was attractive, but also why it was vitally important. Here, if I understood him, is what the philosopher says.

Nietzsche's concern is for origins – the beginnings of man's spiritual consciousness, his creation of culture, his inborn drive to express himself aesthetically. And to examine these origins he looks to the earliest examples of creative drama we still have, the classical Greek tragedies of the 5th century BC. More than simple entertainment, closer to a collective religious experience than to the mere acting out of an unhappy tale, Nietzsche sees in these dramas a mirror held up to the most profound and telling of human impulses.

What interests Nietzsche is not just the myths of Greek tragedy, those stories which in dramatic fashion reveal much of that part of the human psyche that remains hidden or subconscious. His specific interest is in the *way* these myths are presented. At a certain point in the development of Greek drama, he says, there was a major shift in the tragic style. The music of the chorus, until then a principal channel for dramatic delivery, was made to give way to the spoken word and the elaboration of plot. And with that change, says Nietzsche, came a great loss – access to the deepest meaning we are able to tap from our own souls.

The philosopher divided those souls and their impulses

into two twinned and competing categories. One he named after Apollo, patron of the arts, the Greek god of light and dreams. Apollo is associated with humanity in all its rational intelligence, with reason and logic, with moderation, with man as a thinking, creative individual. Apollo is the god of visible form, of material beauty, of plastic arts like architecture and painting. In Apollo's world, even if inspiration comes from dreams, it all leads towards to a world illuminated by sweet reason.

Nietzsche's second category makes up an altogether more obscure side of man's nature. Dionysus is the god of rapturous intoxication – he represents excess, irrationality, the intuitive and instinctive. He is the patron of that materially formless and insubstantial art, music. The Dionysian impulse does not promote individualism, but the dissolution of identity into a unified and undifferentiated whole. For Dionysus man is not separate from nature; under his influence man fuses with and become part of it. The Dionysian world is not a comfortable, ego-bolstering place. It is not even a separate world, but part of the primeval, swirling cosmos, an unidentifiable nothingness in which man can lose his sense of self altogether. Dionysus is the external face of that deepest, most hidden part of man, his age-old desire to find his own completion in something outside himself.

There seems to be no contest. To contemporary man, at least, the Apollonian side of existence is its attractive and positive side. It is the part of our make-up that has allowed us to develop art and culture, to establish sensible human relations, to evolve the technology that makes life something other than brutish. Most important, it has given us what we treasure above all else, our sense of individual being and our power of free will. In short, it has given us civilisation. Dionysus, on the other hand, seems only to offer us a descent into the unknown, the inexplicable and at times terrifying. The mystic urge, the desire to merge with the sublime, seems mere superstition at best. At worst, an advance too close to the edge of the infinite can become a leap over the brink of sanity. Why risk this secure existence, says the sensible man, by wandering into realms over which we have no control? Best left well enough alone.

So far, so good. Every now and then I would look up from *The Birth of Tragedy* to make sure the world, Apollo and Dionysus notwithstanding, was in the same state I had left it. The rocks below remained steep, the pool unchanged and as clear as ever. And that was fine by me, for it is at this point in his argument that Nietzsche begins objecting that the material world is not, in fact, as simple as it might appear on the surface.

Hang on a moment, Nietzsche says to his readers, looking sceptically at modern man's conventional wisdom. You might think that mere rationality is the answer to everything. But the ancient Greeks saw the world very differently. And then he takes us – not exactly by the hand, for Nietzsche makes no concessions to simplicity – and shows us what he has found in the early Greek tragic chorus. There in full force are both Apollo and Dionysus. But they are not battling it out with each other, civilisation against darkness, as one might expect. They are complimentary and balanced forces, both working together towards the full realisation of man's nature.

It is the Dionysian element, music, Nietzsche insists, and not words and story, that lay at the origin of Greek drama. The music he had in mind was not the soothing Apollonian lilt of the lyre. In the kind of sacred ceremony that made up the earliest dramas there was another sort of music. It was the wild and primitive beat of the drum, the pounding, rolling ecstatic rhythms that fire the blood and unleash the passions. Such music was the key to everything, Nietzsche maintains, because it unlocked man's great psychic blockage.

It is at this stage in his reasoning that the philosopher begins ascending into the rarefied upper stratosphere of Germanic thought, and here I sometimes had to read the same pages several times over. It wasn't easy, for at the heart of Nietzsche's vision of the nature of being he perceives a disparity between phenomena and reality. In the philosophic tradition of Schopenhauer and Kant, Nietzsche believed that the world we perceive through our senses is just that, mere sensory phenomenon. Meanwhile, the true essence of being – will, the German philosophers called it – lies beyond our ability to apprehend it. In other words the world we see, smell or touch is only a representation of things, not the real world itself.

It seemed to me as I lay there reading that the ants on the blanket were real enough – a few had run up my shorts and bitten me where it hurts. But that, apparently, was not reality enough for Nietzsche. The entire surrounding world was deception. And things only got worse when it came to art, he said – if the world around us was mere representation, then things like paintings and sculpture were representations of representations. They were double deceptions, and in our artistic efforts to depict the true nature of reality we were only getting further away from it.

Now comes Nietzsche's triumphant dénouement. There is only one art that can possibly rescue us from our dilemma, he proclaims. It is music. For music alone has no form. Unlike words or paint or sculpted marble, it is *sui generis*, of itself, and represents nothing else. Yet it has the power to move us to our core. Why? The German thinker says that because music is non-representational it wholly bypasses the world of representation in which we live – it gives us a direct and unimpeded channel to the very essence of things. Music, Nietzsche declares, is an aural conduit leading straight to the heart of reality.

The early Greeks knew this, he says, and made it an essential component of their dramatic art. Where Apollonian words gave tragedy its artistically beautiful form, Dionysian music gave it profound sacred content. It was this complementary balance that gave Greek tragedy its force and the kind of perfection that has rarely been achieved since. The classical Greek serenity we so much admire today, claims Nietzsche, is no product of some limp and neutral acquiescence to life – rather it was the result of a long, hard struggle between the Dionysian and Apollonian elements in a human existence that is often painful.

The tragic Dionysian realisation that life can end only in death is horrifying, Nietzsche admits. But it also brings, he says, the 'metaphysical consolation that life at the bottom of things, in spite of the passing of phenomena, remains indestructibly powerful and pleasurable.'[3] Equally important, the whole Dionysian world of suffering is vitally necessary for the individual. Without it, he would not have the necessary desire for the 'redeeming vision'. Why do we undertake creative individual acts, why do we strive to make works of art and beauty, if it is not that their achievement alone makes life's suffering bearable? So do Dionysus and Apollo create and feed off each other's energy, placing man at the centre of an endless cycle of tragic destruction and creative redemption. Only when he acknowledges both sides of his nature does a man become a whole man – a complete and balanced being.

The hours had passed without my noticing. My picnic lunch had come and gone, the ants had remained and thrived on crumbs. It was only by late afternoon, when I had moved my blanket to a newly shady site on the far side of the oak tree, that I discovered how ancient tragedy had finally suffered its own tragic demise. In the end, after centuries of life lived balanced between Apollo and Dionysus, a disruptive current had entered Greek life. It arrived with Socrates, the creator of empirical rationalism, and a figure usually much revered in Greek philosophy. Nietzsche, though, saw him as nothing less than a brutal destroyer.

For under his influence the old harmony was dissolved – reason and logic quickly grew to outweigh the old intuitive insight. In drama the role of the musical chorus, vehicle for Dionysian liberation, was pre-empted by realism in plot and dialogue. Dionysus was eclipsed by Apollo and access to man's deepest mysteries through the myths was cut off. Where the search for wisdom had once stood as man's highest goal, Socratic thought went on to form the basis for the dry enquiries of science and technology – tools for material improvement only. The sense of wonder brought to the most ordinary existence was dead and the marvellous achievement of classical Greece, true equilibrium in life, was gone forever.

The hiring department at Basle University had certainly got one thing right – Nietzsche was a most extraordinary professor. It was all mysterious, wonderful, arcane stuff, much of it too opaque to get any clear view of. But by the time the sun had sunk low enough to touch the western rim of the Trabassac Valley I had finished it.

Setting *The Birth of Tragedy* down in the grass, I rose and made my way a hundred yards downstream from the pool. Here the banks of the little Trabassac were less steep and I descended a grassy bank to the water. I stepped out of my clothes and into warm water where tiny black tadpoles lashed their way about the shallows. Quickly the water grew deeper and icy cold and the tadpoles were left behind. The grassy banks were gone, too, and I was swimming through a narrow gorge, sheer and rocky, barely wider than my out-spread arms. Overhead I could see a band of bright, hot-blue sky. It was cool and damp down here. When I shouted my voice echoed against smooth walls of stone, and came back to me cool and damp too.

The passage snaked ahead to an even narrower place and a steep stone ledge. Clear water cascaded over its top and into my face. I groped for a toehold in spongy, moss-covered stone, slipped back twice and then was up and over into another watery passage. There was a second cascade to climb, higher and steeper than the first. And finally I was there, in the deep pool directly beneath my picnic place and the overhanging oak.

I lay buoyant in the green shade, gazing up at branches spread high and wide above me. I wasn't a Cévenol, and I wasn't a Néo either. I wasn't even a *Bo-bo* looking for escape. It didn't matter – I felt at ease here, as if I fitted precisely into this dim, quiet spot. With just a bit of stillness even a passer-by could feel the spirit of the place. But Nietzsche, I had to admit, had left me mystified. Again and again I turned his ideas over in my head.

I had spent half a summer plucking chickens with Gérard

in the Provençal hills, walking the age-grimed back-streets of immigrant Marseilles, following leafy forest paths in the Cévennes. All these places existed at some remove from the modern world, certainly. But it was just as certain they no longer belonged to Nietzsche's ancient, pagan, Mediterranean world. Even he had admitted that it had disappeared long ago. Why, then, did these out-of-the way spots still feel special, as if an older state of things persisted – largely obscured, perhaps, but still alive? I lay back and listened. All I could hear was a gentle echo of water flowing into the pool from the valley upstream.

There were no answers. Slowly I swam back through the narrow passage of rock, dressed, picked up my book and picnic things, and trudged down though the forest to La Vitgère.

∽

We left the Cévennes for Aix early the next morning on Jany's insistence because, she informed me, she had a surprise in store *en route*. It was only as we were approaching the Rhône River at Arles that she revealed more. Instructing me to leave the motorway, she got us on a highway heading south across the Camargue to the sea. We were on our way, Jany disclosed at last, to Saintes-Maries-de-la-Mer and a blow-out lunch of *telines*.

'I've been dreaming of *telines* for months,' she said as we sped across a landscape as flat as a Dutch polder. After the rugged, all-up, all-down topography of the Cévennes it was a little disconcerting. Disconcerting, too, was the only really remarkable feature in these flatlands – the deep and yawning gap that stretched between the myth of the Camargue and the banal reality that surrounded us.

The Michelin Green Guide that lay in our glove compartment rated few places in the country quite as highly – the Camargue was, it enthused, 'the most original and romantic region of Provence and possibly of France'. Scratching my head in puzzlement, I looked around me once again. Had the good people at Michelin finally taste-tested one glass of Côte du Rhône too many?

In theory I might agree with them – any place that could produce black bulls, white horses and pink flamingos all at the same time was worthy of some wonder, especially when that place was a river delta mostly lying under several inches of brackish water.

But where were they, these legendary creatures of the Rhône marshlands? To the Provençal poet Frederique Mistral, the semi-wild white horses of the Camargue, thundering free and untrammelled over the delta waters, harkened back to an earlier, mythic age. 'A savage race unbent,' he'd called them. And what of the heroic men, the *gardians*, those rare, tough-as-nails Mediterranean cowboys who in riding them had half-tamed this land? On the highway leading to Saintes-Maries-de-la-Mer all I could see of this epic world – when I found time to take my eyes off the bumper-to-bumper traffic streaming into town – was a series of roadside riding stables. There, waiting patiently for the next fifteen-minute group-hire, their eyelids drooping in hot morning sunshine, rows of tired, much-used hacks stood tethered and saddled. They were white, admittedly, but hardly unbent – some were decidedly sway-backed. Jany thought she also got a brief glimpse of a black Camargue bull in a field by the roadside, but there were so many people pulled over for the photo opportunity I only saw a mass of cars.

And that is the problem with travel guides: call a place possibly the most romantic in France and you can be certain that shortly after it will no longer be so. In the circumstances I was happy to know that there was another myth, one concerning that epicurean wonder, the *teline*, of which there was little doubt.

The *teline* is a bivalve, a type of tiny, violet-coloured clam, which is found only in the sands of the Golfe du Lion in southern France. When lightly sautéed in olive oil, garlic and parsley the *teline*, no bigger than your little fingernail, becomes entirely irresistible. There are dozens of restaurants in Saintes-Maries that serve the dish, for these molluscs are much harvested on the sandy beaches that stretch away on either side of the town. I enjoyed *telines* a good deal, but Jany had an almost spiritual relationship with the little creatures. Each winter, long after the crowds had gone and the Camargue was quiet once again, she was in the habit of making a kind of pilgrimage to Saintes-Maries-de-la-Mer. This time, evidently, she couldn't wait that long.

But Jany, I could see as we circled around the town, might soon be regretting her impatience. In this tourist high-season the town's pay-parking lots were full and violators were losing fortunes to the police and tow-truck companies. Finally we had no choice but to leave the car a sweaty twenty-minute trudge from the centre. The place was jam-packed.

We could only thank heaven we hadn't arrived during one of Saintes-Maries' monster spring or autumn religious festivals. As the name Holy-Marys-of-the-Sea suggests, the town had sacred beginnings. Since then, though, it's been adapted to more contemporary needs. Mont-Saint-Michel aside, these days there are few places in France where the search for the spiritual has been more thoroughly harnessed to a naked quest for tourist lucre. The pilgrims now winding their way through Saintes-Maries' streets were the more common, summertime variety, intent on spending money and having fun.

Locals appeared to be thin on the ground. Did genuine *gardians* really splash out €750 for the fancy stitched cowboy boots displayed in Saintes-Maries' boutique windows, I wondered? Did Camargue horse-trainers, rice-farmers and shellfish-gatherers indulge themselves in the exotic *glaces* on offer? I might have been stereotyping, but somehow I found it difficult to imagine a heroic breeder of Camargue bulls licking a cone of chocolate chip cookie-dough ice-cream. All of us, I got the feeling, were out-of-towners.

Oddly enough, the real temptations for tourists in Saintes-Maries remain religious. Like iron filings to a magnet, we were all drawn, past revolving racks of postcards, past beachwear window-displays and exhibits of cheesy art-gallery sunsets, to the town's pulsing heart. No one comes to Saintes-Maries without visiting the Church of the Holy Marys itself.

On the square outside the church a five-man band of copper-skinned gypsies was playing exuberant Romany music. A hat lay upturned on the flagstones in front of them. Two vigorous trumpet players, their sleeves rolled up, their instruments describing wide, unpredictable arcs from their feet to the skies above, led the proceedings. Their clothing was threadbare but their notes were sharp and crisp, their syncopations spot-on. I wanted to ask them if they'd consider playing a Néo-Cévenol forest-fête. Not even their wildest gypsy tune, however, could stop me gazing up at the building that rose behind them.

More impressive than the nearby bullfighting arena, the church towered above every structure for miles around. It was foursquare and solid, built of large, rough-hewn blocks of stone. Its entranceways were small, it walls windowless. Topped with defensive towers and crenellated battlements, it looked more like a crusader fortress than a place of worship. Nowadays a couple of bazookas could probably do the job, but when North African Moors threatened these coasts in the medieval age not even massed siege catapults would have guaranteed access. The Church of Les Saintes-Maries was built to protect a priceless treasure, and for believers in the Holy Marys story it was still doing the same job seven centuries later. The ladies in question, or at least what remained of them, were still inside.

Even the vault housing their bones was designed to be as inaccessible as possible – almost invisible in the church's cavern-like gloom, it was built into a wall forty feet above the altar. Along with hundreds of other visitors we shuffled around the edges of the church, half blind after the brightness outside. We came upon a raised niche in the wall where a heavenly pair stood in painted, carved effigy. No expert on long-deceased female saints, it seemed to me that with their long robes and blissful faces they looked pretty much like others of their kind. The only odd thing was the wooden rowboat they were standing in.

In front of them a small, neat, grey-haired women was crossing herself and praying. When she had finished I asked her about the boat.

'And why are there *two* Marys?' I added in the hushed whisper one can't help using in such places. 'Most churches only have one.'

The woman seemed astonished that such a famous biblical episode had escaped my attention. Wasn't I aware, she whispered back in a strong Provençal accent, that the town was named not after just two Marys, but three? Didn't I know that it was founded on the very spot where the three

Marys' small boat had come ashore after drifting all the way from the Holy Land? Had I never heard of the processions with which the town regularly honoured its saints?

It was a glory to behold, she assured me: the lowering of their mortal remains on ropes from the high vault, the exposure of said relics to tumultuous crowds, the shoulder-high carrying of the saint's effigies through the town to the sea, their launching onto the waves in watery commemoration. What we were remembering here, my elderly informant finally reminded me just the slightest bit severely, I thought, as she glanced up at the saints one last time, was nothing less than the seaborne arrival of Christianity in Europe.

It was becoming a little much, these milestone events concentrated in one small area. Here in the Camargue, a tourist-infested beach-town proclaimed itself the first home of Christianity on the continent. Not far down the coast, with barely a tourist in sight, the run-down city of Marseilles congratulated itself on being the very node of Western civilization itself. But by the time I'd found an adequately polite formula to express my reservations the devout little lady with the grey hair was gone.

We continued stumbling around in semi-obscurity. Ahead lay a bright glowing, a golden light that emerged from a crypt below the altar. We descended a set of stairs into an intense heat generated by hundreds of flickering candles. At the far end of a low, barrel-vaulted chamber, surrounded by a dense, neck-craning crowd, stood yet another

182

female effigy. She was about four feet high and dressed in thick layers of multi-coloured silks and shawls. Carved from a trunk of particularly dark, lustrous wood, her face, touched by a wistful smile, was the colour of baker's chocolate. But nobody was treating her as a mere piece of sculpted and decorated wood. Supplicants were kissing the hem of her dress, caressing her cheek, talking to her with the low whisper of intimate confidants. She might have been living and breathing, the real thing.

This, surely, could only be the third Mary. But no, I discovered; had the third Mary remained in Saintes-Maries her bones would be upstairs with the relics of the other two. This was Sarah. Sarah was a black servant girl, and had also been aboard that same drifting boat with the other ladies. But if she hadn't been their social equal, and now found herself sequestered and alone down in the crypt, it didn't mean she was short of admirers. On the contrary; precisely because of what she was she'd been adopted as a patron by the gypsies, and become the object of their own cult of adoration. Every August, with tens of thousands of European gypsies making their way across the continent to celebrate Sarah, the little town in the Camargue sands became a gypsy world capital.

We lingered on. The bodies of incoming celebrants pressed closer and the banks of burning candles continued to suck oxygen from the air. Jany felt faint; she said that saints had nothing to do with seafood. Driven up and out of the church at last, we emerged into bright daylight blinking and confused. I was lost in thought. An open boatload of female evangelists drifting all the way from the distant Holy Land to disembark here in Provence? It sounded very peculiar. Then on the far side of the square I glimpsed a figure through a window of the church presbytery. I glanced at my watch. There was still a little time before lunch. Jany sat down on a bench to rest, and I walked over and knocked on the presbytery door.

A minute later Father Thierry-François de Vregille had escorted me into his study. Could it be, I asked the energetic young priest, that the congregation on the far side of the square was working from some off-the-wall breviary entirely unknown to the rest of Christendom?

Not at all, Father Thierry-François assured me; the tradition had grown out of a well-known biblical story. Following the crucifixion of Jesus an angry, anti-Christian crowd in the coastal town of Caeseria in Palestine had pushed some of the church's most notable women out to sea in a small boat. The little vessel departed without benefit of oars or sails. Apart from Sarah, it contained Mary Jacobé, the Virgin's sister; Mary Salomé, mother of the apostles James and John; and Mary Magdalene, the prostitute whose seven evil spirits had been cast out by Jesus. After completing their miraculous sea-journey the first two Marys had remained in the Camargue to spread the word. The third, Mary Magdalene, had travelled on to the port of Marseilles, where she preached the gospel to its citizens before a pagan temple. The last years of her life were spent in meditation in an isolated grotto high in the hills above the city – a place where pilgrims come to pay homage to this day.

Frowning, I gazed out through the presbytery window. There could be no doubt about it – the church building that honoured the two Marys loomed as it had loomed for 700 years, solid, substantial and well fortified. It was no mere figment of historical imagination. But what about the story that inspired it? It seemed unlikely that a boat would float more than two thousand miles westward through the Mediterranean, evading every coast, circumnavigating every land-mass, before finally drifting ashore here. And what sailor, to say nothing of four frail female saints, could survive such an ordeal? It was too much to credit.

Perhaps I overdid the frowning. Father Thierry-François spoke my doubts for me.

'You are unconvinced,' he said with a smile. 'Is this journey a matter of fact? Did these women really sail here from the Holy Land? Or is this simply popular interpretation, a way of explaining what historians have learned through study – that the new cult of Christianity gradually filtered into the heart of Europe by way of the Rhône River Valley.' He halted for a second or two, as if considering the options himself. 'I cannot say,' he finally opined. 'Perhaps both are true.'

Father Thierry-François seemed to be willing to take a scholarly, tolerant approach to biblical history, to admit that facts in themselves are not important. What counted, in

185

this view, was not the past. What counted was what people believed the past to be. He glanced, as I had, through the study window at his battlemented church, and his tone became more forceful. 'What I do know is that this building, which for so long successfully defended this town against real and substantial threat, was not built by historians. It was built by faith. And that is an uncontested fact.'

There was no time for theological debate. Jany's seafood restaurant was now open and I could see her pacing the flagstones outside. When I told him of our plans Father Thierry-François was all in favour of *telines*, too, and sped me on my way. He suggested we might also try the local fish soup, served the way bouillabaisse is served, with grated cheese, croutons rubbed with raw garlic, and a spicy *rouille*.

It was an inspired recommendation. An hour and a half later Jany and I drove out of Saintes-Maries with gladness in our hearts and garlic on our lips. We had sampled both *telines* and fish soup, and decided that either dish alone made the trip to the Camargue worthwhile. But there was something else. Perhaps it was the bottle of Cassis *blanc* '98 that we also consumed, or perhaps it was finally getting away from the crowds. One way or another, the Camargue countryside that we were passing through looked altogether more appealing than it had that morning.

We were not driving back to Aix through Arles, although that was the first town upstream where a bridge crossed the Rhône River. Instead, I'd suggested while poring over a soup-stained map, we could head east across the Camargue, running more or less parallel to the coast. We would cross the Rhône close to its mouth at Salin de Giraud. There, the map indicated, was a little car-ferry that shuttled its way back and forth across the river.

Looking at the network of routes that wound their way about the lagoon-pocked Camargue, Jany had not been convinced – most of them were marked on the map with unfamiliar colours in broken lines and intermittent dots. When she consulted the map's legend she was even less certain. 'Look,' she'd objected. 'This symbol means 'unsurfaced'. That one indicates 'difficult or dangerous', and the other one 'subject to restrictions'. And what about these double-dashed red routes? That means 'prohibited road'. There are lots of them out there.'

'Nonsense,' I'd simply replied, sucking on a *teline*, not because I didn't believe Jany, but because the prospect of returning home via the marshes rather than motorways sounded so much more attractive. We had plenty of time. It was still early afternoon. The summer evenings were long. And now, with lunch over, the further we drove into the marshlands the more alluring the Camargue became.

Soon Saintes-Maries and the main highway were far behind us and we were following narrow roads deep in the Camargue Regional Park. And there, astonishingly, modern man and all his works suddenly ceased to exist. The horizons were endless and empty, the heavens above vast. There were no buildings, no villages, none of the permanent human presence you find in even the most rural parts of France. It was neither water nor land nor sky that spread itself out before us, but a *terra infirma* suspended somewhere between them all. This was a strange world of wetland and salt-marshes, mud-flats and water channels, bogs of salt-loving glasswort and wind-bent banks of feathery-topped reeds.

It was also a world of living creatures. There were no tired and hard-mouthed ponies tethered out here, but free-ranging herds of horses. Unhindered by either fences or tourists, black, lyre-horned bulls grazed over the plains. There were even flocks of pink flamingos feeding no distance away in the shallow lagoons. To me they still looked surprisingly tasteless – like gaudy suburban garden-accessories or the kind of thing you find on the top of swizzle-sticks in sleazy cocktail lounges. It was only when they rose into the sky by their dozens, their outstretched necks and legs perfectly balancing each other at either end of their bodies, that I realised what graceful animals they were. The Michelin Guide wasn't all wrong – if you got far enough away the Camargue really did seem original and romantic.

But sometimes you can get altogether too far away. Jany has always blamed me for the unhappy end to our Camargue trip. But I blame Nanou, the spare, tough Arlesian, sundried and brown as a nut, whom we met at a lonely crossroads somewhere on the far side of the Etang de Vaccares. He and his equally weathered wife were sitting on the protected, lee-side of their car as we drove by, their mahogany-tanned legs stretched out on folding aluminium *chaises-longues*. I came to a halt, got out of our own car, and began to talk to them. What we needed, I explained, was to get some of this fresh salt air in our lungs. Did they know a nice short walk, possibly one with some birdlife, that we might take?

To be heard I actually had to shout the question, for once out I was out of the car door I found the salt air a good deal fresher than we really needed. It whipped my words away. When the couple stood up, rising above the level of their car-roof, they had to hold on to their hats and sunglasses. It was, we all agreed, a fine, blustery day.

Nanou was just the man to talk to, his wife bawled back to me in the same voice. They'd been coming here from Arles since they were married. Nanou liked surf-fishing and she liked digging in the sand for *telines*. But sometimes they drove down just for the pleasure of sitting in the sun and the wind.

'They're both plagues, of course,' Nanou said in a quieter voice when we'd moved back into the shelter of his car. 'Down here you've got two choices. It's either sun with wind, or sun without wind. One's almost as bad as the other.' Nanou seemed proud to have survived such a long-standing and familiar relationship with the forces of nature.

I looked at the wind kicking up whitecaps on the lagoon across the road. It seemed to be getting stronger by the minute. The reed beds were flattening and the flamingos no longer had their heads below the water's surface – they had given up feeding. Surely a calm, sunny day, I suggested, was the preferable option?

Nanou laughed at my innocence. The wind, he admitted, wasn't good. The Mistral, in fact, was a *veritable putain*, a real whore of a wind. As it came funnelling down the Rhône Valley it gathered speed as it went. 'By the time it gets this far it can be demented,' he said. 'It is like a wild beast hunting you down with fingers and nails. If it doesn't rip you to pieces it can blow for so long it makes you half-crazy.'

But, asked Nanou, did I have any idea of the alternative? 'When there is no wind there is sun and heat alone,' he said. 'It is terrible heat, the heat of the swamp. And with it come the *arabis*.' The *arabis* were an especially vicious kind of wetland midge. They were microscopic. They bit anything with blood in it. They rose off the marshes in clouds and they filled your ears, your eyes, nose and mouth. There was no getting away, warned Nanou. If the Mistral could test the nerves of even the calmest man, the *arabis* could drive him stark raving mad.

'Ah no, my friend,' Nanou concluded. 'Today you are lucky – those filthy insects are being blown all the way to Africa, where they belong. You must learn to like the wind. This is just the day for a walk, and I can tell you where to find more birds than you ever dreamed of. There is nothing simpler.'

And so Nanou proceeded to provide the kind of detailed

190

directions no one can remember. About two kilometres further on we would find an unpaved *piste* off to the right. We weren't to mind that there were no signs or road-markers down there – the track was private, and belonged to the Salins du Midi, the company that made salt on the flats near the sea. All we had to do was park at the third dyke, follow the sluice channel to the spillway on the right, then turn left 200 metres after the second bridge we crossed. This kind of direction went on endlessly, and ten minutes down the road the wind had blown it all completely from my head.

We were not usually so hopeless about finding our way around unfamiliar parts of France. But the further we got out into the marshes, the stronger the shrieking gale became. First we lost the feeling we were in familiar France, and then we lost the feeling we were in France at all.

The great sweeps of barren, empty landscape disoriented us. The normal rules of perspective ceased to apply. The planet's solid, liquid and aerial elements, normally separate and distinct, mingled and became inseparable. The wind was so strong now it was driving long, angry trails of foam across the water. Blobs of it were scudding past our feet and vanishing into the boggy distance. Nanou was right – the wind had fingers that tore at our hair and tried to get under our clothes. We were not in the middle of some dark, confusing, midnight storm; it was a bright and sunny afternoon. And yet the effect was the same. In full daylight the Camargue was not only un-French – it was unearthly.

Jany was even more distressed than I was. We walked on for some time, our eyes slitted and our bodies crouched against the wind. Finally she refused to go on, or even to go back. Desperate to get out of the wind, we crawled into the middle of a thicket of low, tangled bush and, hoping that the wind would eventually blow itself out, lay down.

↜

We emerged from a half-conscious stupor, a sort of dizzy, waking coma, some time around sunset. The wind had stopped completely. There were still twigs and little leaves in our hair, but the branches over our heads were no longer thrashing and the air's manic whistle and howl had stopped. Our little shelter lay a few yards from the end of a large, brackish lagoon – from where we lay we could see an unruffled surface polished to a chrome-like gleam. The sky over the Camargue was dead calm and its western end had turned a magnificent, hard-to-believe fuchsia-pink. I had never seen anything like it. But Jany and I had become distrustful of nature's wonders. The slightest stirring out from our thicket, I had the suspicion, would result in the heavens bringing another nasty surprise hard down upon us.

But there was something else that kept us prone on the ground in that tangle of bush. It started softly enough, but as the sun sank it swelled, grew louder and more insistent. There were hundreds, maybe thousands of birds preparing to roost for the night, and they were singing.

I don't know any more about ornithology than I do about saints, and I couldn't have named more than a couple of the birds that spend time in the marshes of the Camargue. But the area is unique in Europe, and has some of the richest birdlife, both migratory and sedentary, on the continent. So it was no problem, as I did afterwards, to look up lists of local summer birds in the French bird guides.

What was it we were listening to as the sun hit the flat rim of the horizon and the sky grew even gaudier than the sleaziest cocktail-lounge neon? There were chirps, squawks, screeches, twitters, hoots, croaks, quacks, cackles and trillings out there. I don't think there were flamingos — we would have seen them out in the water of the lagoon. These birds were gathering somewhere in the surrounding reed-beds and low-lying, scrubby vegetation. Were they marsh harriers or egrets? Storks or crakes? Curlews, owls, avocets, stilts, bee-eaters, hoopoes or night herons? Perhaps they were all present, perhaps none. But one thing I am sure of – somewhere out there was a great bittern.

The great bittern is a bird that lives only in marshes. You won't find it in city parks and ponds – in human environments it doesn't do well even with water. It is an animal that thrives only in wild and unspoiled wetlands, where it lives in reed-beds on small fish and amphibians. It is a large bird with a three-foot wingspan, but its plumage is unexciting, a camouflaged blend of tawny browns. Neither is its behaviour terribly flamboyant. It is a shy, solitary bird which, when it senses itself being watched, holds its head and neck vertical and blends, immobile, into the surrounding rushes.

But it is at dawn and sunset that the great bittern, outdoing the pink flamingo entirely, becomes an almost supernatural creature. Its call is one of the eeriest noises in the marshes, a cry so far below the register of ordinary noise it doesn't belong to the human world at all. I have returned to the Camargue to listen to it since. It is an eerie, evocative sound, a low, vibrating boom that holds steady for a few seconds, stops, and then picks up again in regular, repeated, plaintive rhythm. The call is primitive and ethereal and quite literally disembodied, for the bird's voice has astounding carrying property – on still nights it can be heard from a distance of two miles and more. Like the equally mysterious will-o'-the-wisp of marsh legends, the cry has been the source of endless superstitious tales. Heard out in the lonely and desolate marshes it is a sound that can raise goose-bumps on your arms.

It certainly gave us the chills. Immobile as bitterns ourselves, we lay listening to the sublime, ghostly orchestra for a long moment, then scrambled to our knees. It was time to get out of the marshes.

We weren't as far from the car as I imagined, nor as lost as I feared – the wind has a capacity to suck even the simplest reasoning power right out of you. The twilight was fading when we reached the car, and it was pitch black by the time we arrived in the little riverside town of Salin de Giraud.

But the ferry that plies the river there runs until well after midnight, and by eleven we were first on and waiting for other cars to load.

We were standing at the railing near the captain's bridge, watching the dark Rhône roll away in the night, when it came to me.

'I've got it,' I said.

'Got what?' There was something in Jany's voice, an apprehensive, here-we-go-again tone that told me she was preparing herself to be less than enthusiastic about whatever I was going to say next. I'd heard it before.

'No, really,' I said. 'That bird, whatever it was. I know its call.'

'What is it?'

'It's Nietzsche's tragic chorus.'

'It's *what*?' Jany had turned from the railing and even in the dark I could feel her eyes on me.

'It's the music Nietzsche wrote about. The book I was telling you about last night; you remember what I was saying about Apollo and Dionysus?'

'Yeees,' said Jany hesitantly. 'So?'

'So, I admit that bird wasn't a Greek tragic chorus. But that singing tonight came straight from Dionysus. It's Nietzsche's chorus. It's all in there – the primitive, the excessive, the elusive, the irrational … Just think of that call we heard.'

We thought. And for once Jany didn't tell me, as she

usually did when I tried to explain some idea I'd had, that I was losing my mind.

'Well … ?' she said.

'Well, we all know that the Greek classical world is finished, that Nietzsche's fusion of Apollo and Dionysus fell apart long ago. If perfect equilibrium ever existed in the first place – and somehow I doubt it did – it's gone from life for good. The old Mediterranean is dead. So why is it that more than two thousand years later we can get caught in a Mistral in the Camargue swamps, lie in a bush listening to some birds, and still recognise that music?

'So why is it, then?'

Because deep inside those things never left – they are still with us. Sometimes the inner myth is more real than the fact. It's like the pilgrims in Saintes-Maries-de-la-Mer. Do you really think that 2,000 years ago three women and their servant-girl drifted twenty-five hundred miles to safety in an open boat? But it doesn't matter. Their arrival still counts. It's a way for people to understand who they are. It's the same with Nietzsche's Mediterranean balance and sense of wonder – I think it still lives in the Mediterranean places we've been this summer.'

The last car clanged off the loading ramp and onto the ferry. The ferry-engine's growl grew louder, the metal deck below us vibrated, and the boat nosed out into the current.

Look at Gérard and Sylviane and Denis in the back-country at Les Jean-Jean,' I said. 'Look at Marseilles – those immigrants and the sea they live by. Look at Sully Rauzier and Janine Berder up in the hills in the Cévennes. None of their lives are easy or self-indulgent. But there is a kind of balance and proportion, something that holds those lives together. Their attachments are strong and simple. I wouldn't use terms like Apollonian and Dionysian, but they seem to have some sort of immediate connection to the world around them, some tie that makes what they do vital and have meaning for them. But what's that connection made of? That's my question.'

Jany watched the ferry's square-ended bow push into the waves ahead of us. Not far to the south the Rhône was losing itself in a warm, salty sea. 'Perhaps the thing you're talking about isn't only found in places,' she said.

'What do you mean?'

'Well, you said Nietzsche wrote about creativity. What was it? Something about making art to compensate for life's suffering? Maybe the balance and proportion you're talking about isn't just connected to special places. Maybe it's found in special people, too. Creative people, people like musicians or sculptors or painters. Why has Provence produced so many painters?'

The lights at the landing on the far side of the river grew brighter. A dozen drivers gunned their engines, impatient to get away down the highway and home. I said little as we rolled off the ferry and into the industrial hinterland that stretched down the road to Marseilles. I'd talked more than enough. Back in Aix it was a while before I settled down. I lay in bed thinking about what Jany had said. Aix was full of painters. Loaded with speculation like a bird-watcher hung about with binoculars, cameras and checklists, it was late before I finally came to the shore of that smooth, unruffled lagoon, sleep.

Six

Mont Sainte-Victoire is not a tall mountain – at just over 3,000 feet it is scarcely a record-breaker at all. Mont Ventoux, the highest peak in Provence, is twice its height. Nor is Sainte-Victoire easily visible from the town it has been linked to since Roman times. Its bare limestone mass begins to rise from rolling countryside some eight miles outside Aix-en-Provence, and from the old part of town it can only be seen from certain rooftops, high balconies and east-facing windows. Although it is undeniably a good-sized chunk of stone, in shape the mountain is narrow and elongated. Even residents in the more elevated quarters surrounding the old town see it end-on, from which perspective its real bulk – thirteen miles of rocky flanks rising steeply to a scallop-edged ridge – cannot be appreciated. Foreshortened, Sainte-Victoire from Aix looks like a squat and lop-sided pyramid.

These were some of the reasons why Jany and I decided to celebrate our return from the Cévennes with dinner at the Petite Auberge. For we were both great admirers of the mountain, and from here you could sit smack in front of it, get the full broadside view, and linger over a Provençal meal at the same time.

The restaurant lay in hilly country not far off the Route du Tholonet, the road that runs from Aix, past the pretty little village of the same name, and along the foot of the mountain. On tourist maps it is also known as the Route de Cézanne. Beyond undulating folds of red earth covered in patchwork fields and stands of feathery pine and cypress, the mountain suddenly reared its pearly-grey mass. Close-up, unobstructed and seen in its full length and volume, the rocky wedge of Sainte-Victoire seemed to sit on the very edge of the auberge's outdoor terrace. If I could reach out a little further, I thought, I just might be able to touch it.

It was only an illusion, but Mont Sainte-Victoire has that kind of effect on people. It impresses itself on outsiders during even the briefest of visits. Long imprinted on the sub-conscious of generations of Aixois, the effect is even stronger. Never mind that it is not constantly in plain view – the mountain claims a looming and predominant place nonetheless. For what it lacks in overwhelming size it makes up for with the living presence of its personality. That, at least, Jany said, was the way she saw it.

We ordered. I asked for a cold ratatouille followed by a *daube* of baby boar. Jany chose a hot goats' cheese on salad, and *supions* – tiny squid in a herby tomato sauce. Could a mountain really have a living personality, I wondered? For the sake of peace I don't usually take Jany up on this sort of discussion, especially not before dinner. So far New Age mystery has entirely failed to take hold in this part of the world – its old secrets are more than enough. But here, hovering on the fuzzy edges of the metaphysical, I felt I should register a little scepticism.

'Explain, please,' I said as a waiter brought some *crudités* to tide us over, and I began dipping a carrot stick into a bowl of anchovy cream.

'I cannot speak directly for all mountains,' Jany admitted. 'But I know a thing or two about the one in front of us, and it most definitely has a personality.'

And why shouldn't it? she continued. Mount Olympus, Mount Sinai, Mount Ararat – throughout history such mountains have held an undeniable power over the people who live around them. What else but personality could you call a specific inner energy, an influence exercised not just on the people of Aix, but on the plains, the valleys and villages for many miles around? There was something especially solid, a kind of inevitable, profoundly-anchored *thereness* about Sainte-Victoire's presence, she maintained – even when you couldn't see it you could feel it.

A bottle of chilled rosé arrived. 'Not everyone appreciates the feeling,' Jany said as I filled her glass. 'I once met a man who lived directly beneath the mountain near Puyloubier. Like just about everyone else in the village he was a winegrower. For him Sainte-Victoire was a gloomy and baleful thing. No matter what he was doing – pruning his vines, washing his car, eating his dinner – the mountain was inescapable, always there over his shoulder. He felt he was constantly being watched. Eventually the sensation of being spied upon day and night grew to be too much. He came from a family that had grown grapes around Puyloubier forever. It didn't matter; he finally sold up and moved away.'

But most Provençal people, she went on, regard the mountain as beneficent. The Celtic tribes who first lived around it called it Ventour, after their god of the winds. They'd used its caves and grottoes for their cults' spiritual ceremonies for centuries before the Romans arrived. The Romans, too, regarded the mountain as a suitable place for the joining of destiny. It was here their first settlers took root in Provence. In the 2nd century BC Sextius Calvinus established a thriving garrison settlement no distance away beside the thermal springs that soon became known as *Aquae Sextiae*, the waters of Sextius.

Every Aixois knew the story of the founding of *Aquae Sextiae* – it was their own town, after all, the awkward Latin name not yet neatly contracted to its present three letters. But what, I said to Jany just the slightest bit impatiently, did that have to do with the mountain? By this point our entrées had arrived and I was interested in getting down to eating mine.

But Jany was equally interested in getting to the point of her story. Like many of her more emotive countrymen, she was a great talker with her hands. Watching her gesticulating with broad sweeps of her forearms and making the finer points with elegant little finger-arabesques, I have often thought that she might be totally silenced by simply tying her hands. Now, not even possession of a knife, fork and *salade au chèvre chaud* could stop her enthusing. After a harrowing day in the Camargue marshlands she was, after all, back in her own element.

'It has everything to do with the mountain,' Jany said. 'Between them, Aix and Sainte-Victoire probably saved the Roman Empire.'

What happened, she explained, was that after twenty years of peacefully enjoying their spa-water the town's garrison were given the fright of their lives. Over the horizon came rumbling the largest threat to western civilisation ever assembled – a vast army of 200,000 Teutonic barbarians bound for an invasion of Rome. But they had not reckoned on Provence's wily Roman general, Marius, who set a trap for them. Permitted to bypass his outlying defences at Glanum near the Rhône River, the barbarians marched straight into the bulk of his Aix legions lying in wait at the foot of the mountain.

'It was total annihilation,' Jany recounted with some satisfaction. 'The invaders were boxed in against the mountain. They had nowhere to go. Dead Teutons lay piled high across the plain – at least a hundred thousand were slaughtered. Marius was said to have climbed to the summit, where the tall iron Cross of Provence now stands, the better to look down on the battle and his enemy's destruction. To celebrate he had 300 captured chieftains brought up the mountain and hurled into the Garagaï, the deep chasm that lies at the top.'

Jany paused in her eating and sighed in a showy, non-chalant way. She is a sensitive thing – she was obviously relieved to find that she could talk about bloody slaughter and at the same time eat, all without betraying by any signs of distress.

'The victory,' she said, 'was so great that it remains with us even today, at least in our choice of local names. The mountain, of course, was renamed Sainte-Victoire, holy victory. The name Marius has become a favourite for the christening of Provençal baby boys. And the soil became so fertilised with the bodies of dead Teutons that there is another wine-village – it's not far from Puyloubier – still called Pourrières. It was taken from the post-battle name, *Campi Putridi*, the fields of putrefaction, and is a deformation of the French verb *pourrir*, to rot. There were bumper crops there for years after the fight. The farmers used to build their vine trellises from human bones.'

If my *daube*, chunks of baby wild boar swimming in a sauce made of red wine and its own blood, had not been quite so good I am not sure I would have carried on eating. But it was and I did. And I continued listening.

Sainte-Victoire, Jany went on, has never ceased being an object of curiosity, fascination and veneration. By the

Christianised 5th century hermits had settled on the mountain, by then considered a dwelling place of the saints. Camaldolesian monks built a refuge for pilgrims, a building which still stands near the summit beside the present-day priory. From the 12th century onward mothers were bringing marriageable daughters and unwell children up the mountain to pray for divine intervention. Shepherds, too, got in on the act – they would lower sick animals on ropes down the gaping mouth of the Garagaï, where far below, it was thought, the Golden Goat of Provence grazed in therapeutic meadows beside an enchanted lake.

And so dinner continued, story after story of strange beliefs and miraculous occurrences. In the history of Provence Mont Sainte-Victoire was plainly a larger-than-life phenomenon. Once she got going on Provence Jany was a phenomenon herself.

By the 1600s, she was telling me as dessert arrived, the mountain had become so thoroughly invested with spiritual legend that the parliament of Provence in Aix could no longer hold its burning curiosity – it finally offered a condemned prisoner his life if he agreed to descend the Garagaï on ropes and tell them what it was really like down there.

And was it, I asked Jany, all it had been cracked up to be by the seers and holy men? She shrugged her shoulders. Unfortunately the poor fellow had became so tangled in his ropes he was strangled before he could get back up to make his report.

'So there,' Jany said as she finally ran out of stories and

I was scraping the last traces of *fromage frais avec son coulis de framboise* from my dessert bowl. 'Don't tell me a mountain can't have personality.'

And I didn't. For a while we said nothing at all, but simply watched the great stone hulk in front of us fade into invisibility as the evening light fell. As it did so I found myself thinking of the man who had felt Mont Sainte-Victoire such a compelling presence that he spent much of his time giving it life on canvas. By some subtle magic he had made it his own forever, and in doing so turned it from a religious icon into an artistic one. I had decided to take up Jany's suggestion that the Mediterranean was rooted as much in people as it was in places. I couldn't look deep into the Garagaï, I reflected. But I could at least try looking into the life of Paul Cézanne – no one had ever given the mountain more penetrating thought.

⮜

To be perfectly honest, I have always felt more comfortable with the countryside that surrounds Aix than with the little city itself.

It is, without a doubt, one of the most attractive cities in Provence. With their penchant for the ordering and top-ten listing of all things superlative, American travel magazines have gone much further – they often rate the Cours Mirabeau, the broad central avenue that cuts a leafy swathe through Aix's narrow streets, among the most beautiful thoroughfares in the world. And as I walked down the Cours towards the Aix tourist office the day after our meal by the mountain I had to admit that the place did look pretty good.

Who wouldn't admire the tall double-rows of plane trees that rose high on either side of the Cours, their branches so pruned that they fitted smoothly and precisely overhead, filtering bright sun and casting an even and flattering glow on the prospect below? And who could criticise the harmonious proportions of the *hôtels particuliers*, former family palaces, which lined both sides of the street? Sober and discreet in their baroque decoration, their facades sculpted in warm, honey-coloured sandstone, they set the tone for the entire avenue. Just large enough to give the Cours an air of grandiose nobility, they were also small enough to leave it feeling intimate and comfortable.

But the Cours Mirabeau was not just an ornate 17th-century assemblage. The manicured trees, sculpted stone and the splashing fountains that graced the length of the Cours were a mere backdrop. What brought the whole sun-dappled scene to life were the crowds. On one side of the thoroughfare, banks, pâtisseries and expensive clothing boutiques had taken up residence in venerable premises. The other side was occupied by a score of café terraces stretching from one end of the long flag-stoned promenade to the other. Each was equipped with its own bright awning, matching tables and chairs, and waiters in colour-coordinated waistcoats. Today, as every day in summer, the parade here had began early in the morning. It would thicken progressively through the afternoon and by evening reach rib-prodding proportions. Only in the early hours, well after the end of music-festival performances, would the crowds begin to dwindle.

Even at ten o'clock in the morning I found it hard going. On the far side of the Café Grillon I got caught behind a large, slow-moving Japanese tour party. Like off-duty nurses who just hadn't had the time to remove their surgical scrubs, some of the women in the group were wearing face-masks and white gloves. As they proceeded along the Cours the group-leader at their head held aloft a little white flag.

But he wasn't surrendering a mobile medical unit – he was leading his party on a determined assault of Aix cafés. Half the reason foreign tourists surged onto this street in such numbers was simply to gaze at the city taking its leisure. On the Cours Mirabeau fashionable Aix either sits at café tables and negligently watches the crowds pass by, or strolls blithely along eyeing the talkers at the tables. In either case it's all display. This is a world of *far niente*, of professional lounging, stylish posing and frothy conversation. There are, in fact, a good number of things to see and to do in Aix. But none is as important as to be seen to be doing nothing.

I decided to wait for the tour group to move on and sat down on a bench. A trio of cello, flute and violin players set up on the sidewalk in front of me, primed an open violin-case on the ground with a few euro coins, and launched into the opening bars of Vivaldi's Four Seasons.

So what is wrong with sophistication, leisure, culture and urbanity? Nothing, if that's what it really is. But I am always a bit suspicious of this elegant little city's motives. Aix is a place of a thousand exquisite boutiques and shop-fronts, and sometimes its cultivation of the stylish and fashionable seems as superficial as its window-dressing. The city's renowned festivals, its cafés, baroque facades and colour-filled markets are all part of a splendid and carefully-calculated visual presentation. In Aix image is everything. Once the festivals are over, the cafés closed, and the market squares swept clean, one wonders if there is anything of substance left at all. Sometimes the mask slips and the town's self-proclaimed mastery in the art of living resembles little more than an exercise in that other, slyer art of commercial branding. Like an elegant call-girl who professes taste and refinement, at the end of the evening Aix is prepared to jump into bed with whoever has the ready wherewithal.

Vivaldi done with, the trio moved with *brio* on to Mozart's Enchanted Flute. The silver notes trilled upwards like small, fast birds aiming to settle in the lower branches of the plane trees. Perhaps, I considered, it was not surprising that Aix pandered so unashamedly to notions of prestige and status. Long ago Aix was a place that had had real power and social standing.

Under Good King René – the name still retains its fairy-tale inflections and the man is still loved – Aix had been a capital. It was a city famous for its troubadours, its patronage of the arts and its traditions of courtly love. When the kingdom of Provence was absorbed into the French realm it remained the provincial capital, home of the Estates, the governor, and the royally-appointed *Parlement*. Not only was Aix a political power whose tax-raising parliament became notorious for soaking the peasantry; its resulting wealth attracted a social elite which enjoyed its waters, its baroque architecture and its decorous manners. Swanning about has a long and distinguished history in Aix-en-Provence.

Only with the Revolution did the city's golden age come to an end. Parliament was dissolved, nobility divested of title, and Aix's administrative machinery whisked off to Marseilles. Even the main rail-line that eventually connected the great port to points north bypassed Aix, and the little city, its inhabitants humbled, resentful, and looking ever backwards, declined into provincial somnolence. Nor did Aix's mid-20th-century marketing of itself as France's most prestigious opera festival do anything to efface its deep conservatism. Marseilles' heart and soul might be poor, rough things, I thought as the music ended and I continued on down the Cours. But the port-city wears them on its sleeve. If Aix has a soul at all it is well hidden, locked up safely somewhere behind those elegant and exclusive facades.

⤳

Ville d'Eau, *Ville d'Art*, read the signs on the roads leading into the city. And from the bustling and noisy Aix tourist office just off the splashing fountain on the Rotonde one could hardly doubt it. Inside the door long queues ran forward to a series of desks. From the back of one of them I watched teams of smiling young ladies, pink with heat and exertion, dispensing information to ardent holidaymakers. It was like watching a reservoir-sluice opened wide. Inundated by a vast and unending gush, Aix was drowning in culture.

Opera in the palaces, dance in the courtyards, chamber music by the fountains – there were brochures and leaflets galore. The entire city appeared to have been commandeered to satisfy an unquenchable summer thirst for highbrow entertainment. Here any building more significant than a fruit-and-vegetable stand seemed capable of producing its very own baton-waving conductor or bosom-heaving diva. But when my turn in the queue finally came it was not a live performance I enquired about. Paul Cézanne had been dead since 1906.

The woman behind the desk was willing enough, but there was little time for pleasantries. Already there were half a dozen people waiting behind me.

'In French, English or German?' she asked.

On the cover of the brochure she handed me were two photographs. One was a colour image of Mont Sainte-Victoire. The other, in grainy black and white, showed a man standing outdoors in front of an easel. He was slight, bearded and elderly, and dressed in a long, paint-spattered coat and a *chapeau melon* – a bowler hat. In English the handout was titled *In Cézanne's Footsteps*.

'It's got everything you need,' the brochure-lady said. She seemed so assured, so efficiently cut-and-dried about this tricky business of seeking out long-dead artists. 'There is a map and a numbered itinerary showing all the places Cézanne frequented in and around the city. All you have to do is follow the route indicated on the sidewalks. You cannot go wrong.'

No sooner had she handed it over than the man behind me was making his own enquiries and I was out the door. I found myself gazing downward at a series of yellow brass studs sunk into the tarmac. They lead away in a trail up the street. Each was embossed with the city's coat of arms and a large raised letter 'C', for Cézanne.

The tourist office might be glibly reassuring, but I wasn't at all confident about not going wrong. Why should I be? In a sustained act of cowardice I had in fact been avoiding Paul Cézanne's footsteps for years.

Not all painters of the south made me quite so uncertain. I was quite happy gazing at pictures of starry nights or sunflowers in glazed pots. For me, as for just about everyone else, Vincent Van Gogh was non-threatening. He could make an object like a pair of old shoes or a worn-out cane-bottomed chair seem familiar and valued. You did not have to study Van Gogh. He simply invited you to look – in his extraordinary love of ordinary things and people he was accessible.

So, more or less, were a dozen other painters of this bright and luminous countryside. Matisse, Renoir, Signac, Bonnard, Dufy, Braque, Picasso – all had painted here and created vibrant Mediterranean canvases radiant with light and colour. Cézanne had too, of course. To me, though, he was different, of another order of difficulty.

In our living room Jany and I had had a framed print of one of Cézanne's Sainte-Victoires hanging for years. It fascinated me – in the painting there was the same inevitability, the same dignified and monumental presence that permeated the mountain itself. But things got more mysterious than that. In our kitchen was another Cézanne print, a still life of onions lying on a table. They were not even especially handsome onions; they had been left sitting too long and were sprouting long green stalks. They sat beside some other everyday things – a kitchen knife, a glass and wine bottle, a rumpled tablecloth.

Yet, somehow, these onions, too, had precisely the same inevitability as the mountain – they could hardly be called monumental, but there was a rightness in the way they sat, a quality of solidness that gave them a kind of serene dignity. In a strange way they had a more substantial existence than the real onions that sometimes sat beneath them on our kitchen table.

It was inexplicable – how could anyone make you think that an onion had serene dignity? But there it was. I could look long and hard at Cézanne and not understand what the man had done or how he had done it. His work was too cerebral, his methods too subtle, his aims too complex to be simply enjoyed. Apart from prints, I had read the art books on Cézanne and perused learned abstracts full of painterly analysis. They had only made it worse. There had been so much else that was bright and colourful and uncomplicated all around that eventually I had taken the easy option, and turned away. To casual callers like me Cézanne, it seemed, was not at home.

But now I was hoping there might be another way in. Before the critics, before artistic technique, before the artist's transformation of the world into paint, was the place itself – Provence. There were still many spots where I could stand where the artist had stood and see the same things he saw. If I was lucky, if time hadn't worked too many changes, the painter, the painting and the thing painted might all come into some sort of alignment.

That, at least, is what I was hoping. My brochure safely clutched in my hand, I headed back up the Cours Mirabeau. I would tour these city sites – the buildings, the streets and views that had surrounded Cézanne all his life – that very afternoon. In the meantime lunch waited at home.

～

If I said that Jany and I lived on the banks of a river in Aix-en-Provence it wouldn't be a lie, but it would be stretching it. The River Torse, whose burbling course ran just beneath the kitchen window where we sat eating, was barely six feet wide. And that was on a good day in autumn, after a heavy downpour.

Yet the Torse also provided us with calm, or at least with a level of calm that is becoming increasingly rare in Aix. When René and Odette moved there after the war barely 40,000 people lived in the little city, and the pace was leisurely – Jany and Mireille could play on roller-skates in the street outside their parent's shop in the rue Matheron with little fear of traffic. Now 150,000 lived in the old Roman city. Life was faster, parking had become a nightmare that would scare even today's Romans, and urban spill-over pushed the edges of city outwards from one day to the next.

Our own home, in a modest little building of six apartments, lay only ten minutes walk from the old town off the Route du Tholonet. Before the 1960s, when our street was built, this had been open countryside; even then residents used to walk 200 yards to the bottom of our cul-de-sac to buy goat's cheese from a farmhouse there. The farm was long gone now, but we were lucky; while Aix continued its noisy expansion all about us, the little ravine through which the Torse flowed was too steep for any more building. Its thickly-wooded bank outside our windows was a small haven of peace. On it thrived oak and purple-flowering judas trees, yellow forsythia and lilac gone wild. There were thrushes, nightingales and red squirrels with tufted ears who hurled themselves with high-wire daring from one tree to another. There were owls that hooted in winter and frogs that croaked in summer. Occasionally hungry wild boar would come night-raiding down the ravine from the hills above

– we would only know about it the next morning, when we discovered the flower-beds below our windows savagely ploughed-up and plundered of tulip bulbs.

Against all odds, something of the original river had survived. It was not impossible, then, as we sat in the kitchen over quiche that lunchtime, to imagine a young Paul Cézanne and his best friend Emile Zola lounging about on the banks of the Torse a century and a half ago. As I ate I looked through one of my Cézanne books, dipping here and there into his early life. In the 1850s the Torse, and the River Arc into which it flows, had been among Cézanne's favourite escapes from town.

Neither boy, of course, had had the faintest inkling of the future – the literary celebrity that awaited Zola in Paris as a popular novelist and pamphleteer, the obscurity reserved for Cézanne as a failed painter in his home town. Even in their youth the pair had harboured literary and artistic ambitions; it was Cézanne, though, who dreamed of becoming a writer and Zola who hankered to paint. But both were of a romantic cast of mind and shared a deep love of nature – for the time-being their greatest satisfactions were the simple physical pleasures of the Aix countryside.

I flipped to a reproduction of a rough ink sketch sent in a letter from Cézanne to Zola when they were still young. It showed three happy and carefree boys, one in a straw hat, cavorting in the water beneath a tree on a shady riverbank. Cézanne had drawn it in an amateur hand sometime in the

1850s, too early for him to owe anything to either French impressionism or his own talent. Instead, in its sunny and youthful exuberance the sketch immediately reminded me of the adventures of Huckleberry Finn. On the opposite page of the art-book sat an excerpt from Zola's autobiographical novel, *L'Oeuvre* – The Masterpiece – in which he relived his early days with Cézanne and Jean-Baptiste Baille, the other friend in the sketch, tramping about the Aix countryside.

'While they were still in elementary school', I read, 'the three inseparables had developed a passion for long walks ... They could swim when they were scarcely twelve, and they loved to splash about in the deeper parts of the stream; they would spend whole days, stark naked, lying on the burning sand, then diving back into the water, endlessly grubbing for water-plants or watching for eels.' [4]

If that wasn't Huckleberryesque I didn't know what was. It may have taken Cézanne an entire lifetime of slow and painstaking effort to turn his observation of nature into an art form, but he seemed to have started out delighting entirely spontaneously in everything to be found under the blue Provençal sky. On a following page I came across a passage by another school friend who had accompanied the trio on one of their country walks.

'At three o'clock in the morning' he wrote, 'the first one to wake went and threw pebbles at the shutters of the others. We left right away, provisions having been prepared the night

217

before and stuffed into game-bags. By sunrise we had already covered several kilometres. Around nine o'clock when the day had warmed we found some shade in a wooded ravine. Lunch was cooked in the open air. Baille lit a fire of dead wood. Suspended on a string above it twirled a leg of lamb studded with garlic, which every now and then Zola would flick with his finger to keep going. Cézanne seasoned the salad in a damp napkin. After lunch we all had a siesta.'[5]

Here was a *dejeuner sur l'herbe* with a difference. I read the passage to Jany, and the idea of a French literary giant flicking a leg of garlicky lamb with his finger while the father of modern art made salad-dressing brought a fit of giggles on her.

As mid-19th century visions of escape go, it was really not so different from Mark Twain's. Change the *gigot a l'ail* for a hickory-cured ham, substitute the names Huck and Tom for Cézanne and Zola, and you had life on the Mississippi with *vinaigrette* thrown in for free. Joyfully present in both, too, was a sense of irksome restrictions finally evaded, of liberation achieved. Somewhere in both scenes a sleepy and conservative town lay off in the distance.

But already I had picked up from random quotes and passages the principal tenor of Paul Cézanne's relationship with his home-town. As far as I knew, Hannibal, the river-town where Mark Twain grew up, had from the very beginning made much of its son's creative talents. The difference with Aix, I thought as we finished lunch, was its stiff-necked circumspection. No town in Missouri was ever as reluctant to recognise homegrown creative genius.

⌒

Off we set on foot, Jany acting as guide in Aix's narrow streets. Site number one in my brochure map was 28, rue de l'Opera – the house where the painter was born. It seemed a sensible place to begin.

I was not sure what to expect as we strolled up narrow streets, the trail of brass studs in the sidewalk now glinting in shafts of afternoon sunlight. Did my quest for a creative Mediterranean spirit make any sense here? Are there places, when you are hunting elusive prey, where you can actually sense something, register some sort of presence made up of more than what you are actually looking at? Perhaps there are, if that presence belongs to something as massive and undeniably concrete as a mountain. In the case of one frail-looking man now long dead I had my doubts. I'd have been pleased to have bumped into the painter's ghost right then and there in the cluttered jam of cars parked two-wheels-up on the sidewalk.

But Number 28 left me feeling little of anything at all. A heavy, shuttered building stained with age, it seemed to have gone through several incarnations. High on the wall on one corner a niche was occupied by an exhaust-fume-eroded Virgin and Child. Had the building once been a convent or religious institution? Certainly at some point it had been a school – over the stone-lintelled doorway was painted the sign *Entrée de la classe enfantine*. Cut into the wall beside it in smaller letters was an inscription in French: *The painter Paul Cézanne was born in this house 19 January, 1839.* The door was covered in spray-painted graffiti and looked as if it hadn't been opened for years. Of the painter himself there was not the slightest sign. I felt let down.

It was just the beginning of a long afternoon of disappointments. Site number two in my brochure was on the Cours itself at Number 55, once a hat-shop belonging to Louis-August Cézanne, the painter's father. Between the hubbub of two cafés the faded words *Chapellerie du Cours Mirabeau, Gros et Detail* – The Cours Mirabeau Hatshop, Wholesale and Retail – still floated on an ochre-coloured wall. It was from this shop that Cézanne *père* had begun his ambitious jump upwards from the *petite bourgeoisie* – rabbit-fur hats made him so prosperous he was eventually able to buy Aix's only bank, move into a nearby country estate, and become one of the richest men in town. But here it was far too crowded even to stand still without being jostled, much less think about Cézanne's difficult relationship with his father.

Site number three, the Café Deux Garçons, was just a few steps away at 53, Cours Mirabeau. It should be easier to get a feel for Cézanne here, I thought as we made our way across the table-strewn terrace. The Deux Garçons, in local mythology at any rate, was reputed as the haunt of Aix artists, writers and intellectuals. But once we were inside and had ordered coffee there was no sign of any of these – the place was packed with holidaymakers looking for artists, writers and intellectuals. We sipped, gazed at an astronomically-priced menu, and watched imperious waiters in black waistcoats and white aprons bully foreign tourists. In a hall at the rear I spotted a copy of a Cézanne self-portrait on the wall. But if the painter had once frequented the Deux Garcons he had long ago finished his coffee and slipped quietly out. We did, too.

This was looking much less rewarding than I'd hoped. I cast my eye over the next few sites in the brochure. There were more cafés, the church where Cézanne was christened, an early home of his parents, the apartment his mother had died in. None of them seemed to offer any real entrance into the painter's world. Then I saw site number fifteen, the College Mignet, where Cézanne and Zola had gone to school together. Immediately I had Jany by the sleeve and was towing her down the Cours.

The school, of course, was now closed for the summer, and inaccessible to the public anyway. But that did not matter, because the Collège Mignet was where Jany taught Spanish. It was from this imposing 17th-century building, once an Ursuline convent, that she returned home daily in the school-year, looking distraught and muttering vaguely about adolescent waywardness. But just imagine, I thought – perhaps Jany taught in the very classroom where two towering figures of late French civilisation had once studied the classics and laid scratchy pen-nibs to paper.

The grand entrance hallway was silent and empty of students. But by the glassed-in cubicle that she inhabited through much of the year, the off-duty school *concierge* showed us a wall-plaque dedicated to an honoured alumnus, Emile Zola. Of Paul Cézanne, though, there were no reminders. After much racking of brains and pursing of lips the concierge said she had a vague memory of a staircase being named after the man, but she couldn't remember which. We tramped three floors of covered arcades and crossed vast treed courtyards, former cloisters where demure nuns had long ago strolled. The whole place was empty and echoing, and if a timid spirit had wanted to come forth and show itself it could have. But not even repeated wanderings up and down every set of stairs in the place evoked the faintest emanation.

I hadn't given up. Back outside, I thought we might carry on up the street to site number sixteen. What better place for a painterly presence than the Musée Granet, a museum that in the mid-1800s had also been the *Ecole Spéciale et Gratuite de Dessin*, Aix's municipal art institute? It was here that Cézanne, then 18 years old, took his first modelling classes. Like his school, the museum was an imposing, stone-sculpted building of ecclesiastic origins, a former grand priory of the Order of the Knights of Malta. What better place to house the fine collection of Cézanne paintings one would have expected to find in the painter's home-town?

But I already knew that no such collection existed. By the

time Cézanne had begun painting mountains and onions he had gone far beyond the city's understanding of what a painting should be. In this, Aix was no different than any other place – when art is new and different it fails the public's expectations and is seldom liked. But it wasn't simply that Cézanne had ignored the rigid academic conventions of the 19th century. Just as bad, he came from an upstart hatter's family which had gate-crashed Aix society; over the years the painter had proved himself to be increasingly reclusive and socially inept. Today in Aix you still hear tales of small boys throwing stones at the artist as, easel and oils strapped to his back, he trudged his way out of town to paint. Perhaps they took him for a tramp. Perhaps the story is just fanciful. But the truth is that if Aix didn't actively shun the painter it did its outright best to ignore him.

Even in the year of Cézanne's death, when the artist had begun to achieve some sort of reputation in the larger world, Henri Pontier, curator of the Musée Granet, called Cézanne a 'dirty boor'[6] and promised that in his, Pontier's, lifetime not a single one of Cézanne's works would enter the museum. The curator kept his word, and by the time he died two decades later the price of Cézannes was so high they were far beyond the reach of the municipal budget.

We wandered about the museum, and at last came upon a meagre collection of Cézanne drawings and lithographs. There was even a handful of oil-paintings on loan to the city by the French state. But was the painter's presence to be found devotedly hovering about a place that had so firmly rejected him? Of course it wasn't.

By now I was properly discouraged. In all there were thirty-four Cézannian sites on my Aix tourist-office itinerary. But I knew that none of them – neither the bank where Cézanne had once worked for his father, nor his one-time homes in the rue Matheron and rue Boulegon, nor the Saint-Sauveur Cathedral where his funeral was held – would ever reveal Paul Cézanne.

We made one final visit anyway. Less than 500 yards from where we lived the painter lay buried in the Saint-Pierre cemetery. We searched for the grave for a long time, and found it only after asking two men digging chest-deep in bright red soil. Compared to some of the ornate tombs in the same row Cézanne's was simple. There was a cross, a pot of grubby plastic flowers, and at the foot of a raised and polished family gravestone the small, chiselled sign, *Ici repose Paul Cézanne.*

Was it by chance that the grave was sited at the extreme upper end of the cemetery, the only place from which the tip of Sainte-Victoire could be seen? Scintillating in the evening light, as massive and serene as ever, it was the only cheering thing in sight. Tired, we finally trudged home around sunset. Whether I looked out of the window at the Torse or up at the painted onions on the wall, there was more of Cézanne to be seen from our small kitchen than in all the town of Aix-en-Provence.

Cézanne's old haunts were unhaunted, the city abandoned by his spirit. But still I had hope. Could I have simply been looking in the wrong places, I wondered? Should I have gone straight to the motifs instead, to the very spot where easel and canvas once stood and the artist recreated the things that lay before him? Such places, really, should vibrate with painterly resonance. The first thing next day I set out to find some of them.

I did not really expect to see gaggles of naked women hanging about under the Pont des Trois Sautets at nine-thirty in the morning. It was in places like this – cool, shady and secluded refuges beside the River Arc – that Cézanne liked to place his groups of statuesque nude bathers. But they had existed only in his imagination. As a young boy Cézanne had bathed on the banks of the Arc, and as an old man an inner eye in search of harmonious forms had literally fleshed-out the well-known scene in front of him. Without any kind of dramatic content other than the bodies themselves, Cézanne had made such places appear as timeless as classical myth. What had existed then, and what remained now, though, was the bridge itself.

Holding a copy of the *Trois Sautets Bridge* (the original watercolour now hangs in distant Cincinnati), I scrambled down a steep slope to see the bridge from the same angle Cézanne had painted it. From both banks of the river it rose in a humpback. Its straight upper edges met like the peak of a roof while its underside described a smooth, circular arc that framed the water flowing beneath. I could see why Cézanne had chosen to paint it. It was in itself a harmonious, well-proportioned and voluptuous form – it hardly needed the addition of naked female bodies. And that was a good thing, really, because these days it was unlikely to get them. No longer in the balmy, bucolic Aix countryside, the Trois Sautets bridge had moved well beyond pastoral myth.

Close by, an elevated section of the Nice *autoroute* now ran past the bridge, cars and transport trucks howling along in an unending whoosh of noise. Just fifty yards away, beside a busy roadside vegetable stall where Jany and I often shopped, a tall sign proclaimed the day's special: five avocados for a euro and a half. What really bothered me though, was the water itself. For Cézanne's sake I hoped there had been a bit more of it in the Arc a century and a half ago – at the moment it would have risen half-way up his calves. For diving, grubbing for water plants, watching eels and other Huck-Finn-like activities it wasn't up to much at all. And when I climbed to the top of the bridge to look downstream I finally did see a naked body – paintless and rusty, the carcass of an old Peugeot lay rotting not far away in the water.

It was depressing. All around Aix the country sites that Cézanne had once walked out to in his paint-spattered coat were now built over or absorbed into the city. The only safe bet left, I realised as I squeezed avocados until I found five ripe ones, was Château Noir.

It lay not far from us out on the Route du Tholonet. Protected from development, the winding road had changed little since the painter's day. The chateau, an odd, gothic folly built by a Marseilles industrialist, was especially rich in Cézannia. Here the artist had rented a small studio in the château's courtyard, and for the last fifteen years of his life painted scenes of the building, its pine forests and its distinctive rock formations. The only problem was that Château Noir was privately owned.

As soon as I got home I did a little discreet phoning around. It didn't look good. Château Noir's owner was by all accounts obsessive about privacy. I couldn't say I blamed him – he maintained the place as an artist's colony for a small number of working painters, and had been fending off intruders all his life. In the mid-1990s, when a major Cézanne exhibition drew a million-and-a-half enthusiasts to museums in Paris, London and Philadelphia, he'd had an especially bad time. Interest in Château Noir had grown feverish – he'd been invaded by the casually curious, hounded by the press, had helicopters hover over his home. He had suffered greatly, it seemed, and not been quite the same person since. Perhaps it was just as wise, I was warned, not to attempt any *paparazzi*-style tricks, or I might end up looking down the barrel of a shotgun. The only visitors tolerated on the grounds of Château Noir, I learned, were guided student-groups from the Marchutz School – their teachers had once been resident artists there.

I did some more phoning. The Marchutz School was a small art school that had been around Aix for at least twenty-five years. It was run by American painters, largely for American university students, and offered summer courses as well as regular school-year programmes. It was reputed to have unconventional teaching methods. It also made field trips to certain well-known painter's motifs. I called the director, pleaded an exceptional and despairing case, and by noon had myself signed up for the next Cézanne field trip. It was scheduled to visit Château Noir the following Monday. Not all roads around Aix led into the retiring painter's world but here, I hoped, was one that finally would.

⤚

Just why females should favour Provençal summer painting courses over males was a mystery to me. There were twelve young women in the mini-bus that wound its way towards le Tholonet along the Route de Cézanne. Apart from the driver I was the only man. Certainly the driver wasn't complaining. These were Americans as Mediterraneans tended to imagine them – tall, long of leg and perfect of smile, they were the corn-fed blondes of American myth. But they were all adepts of that other myth, local and Mediterranean, of the small, frail man in the bowler hat.

The bus came to a halt below a thick wood of pines, and following our Marchutz School guide, an art-historian versed in all things Cézannian, we climbed up a track through the trees. There was a constant, impossible-to-locate drone of cicadas all about us, and over the shady hillside wafted an array of smells – cool pine, sweet rosemary, the sharper odour of thyme, the damp, fresh smell of the earth itself. Every now and then the trees would thin out and through the clear, luminous atmosphere that is peculiar to Provence – it is both sharp and soft, substantial and immaterial at the same time – the whole countryside below us glowed.

Château Noir was an odd place, an angular, slightly forbidding building, un-Provençal in its brick-built construction and high, arched gothic windows. There were odd features, like a row of unfinished colonnades – supports for a never-completed *orangerie* – that gave the place an air of romantic ruin. But there was also a comfortable, bohemian feeling of artistry-in-residence. There were pots of flowers balanced on walls, cats sleeping on stairways, pieces of sculpture and pottery sitting in unexpected places.

In the small courtyard where Cézanne had rented a room we gathered around a tree growing from an octagonal stone base. It was so old that one of its boughs was held up by a metal prop. I had seen the tree in reproduction – it was a pistachio that Cézanne had painted more than a century before. Apart from the iron crutch nothing about the tree, nor its courtyard background, had changed in the slightest detail.

And that was what bothered me. For the first time since I had begun following Cézanne's trail I was looking at precisely what he had looked at. Yet I felt no resonance at all, no alignment, no sense of connection. I was merely looking at a handsome old tree.

It was the same throughout Château Noir. At last I was seeing them life-sized, but the pistachio tree, the rocks, the pine woods, the chateau itself all looked far less grand than when Cézanne portrayed them on canvas. And when that afternoon we were taken to visit the painter's studio in a hillside suburb of Aix I knew something was definitely amiss.

There is no place anywhere quite as evocative of Cézanne's daily life and work as the studio he'd built at the turn of the century. High-ceilinged, its north wall faced with large panes of glass, it contained virtually all the objects the artist had left there at his death. I wandered about looking at Cézanne's stained smock hanging on a hook, his worn cape, his folding easel and backpack, his parasol and hats. It was as if he'd just stepped out of the room for a moment.

But if the painter's presence was so strong, why was I so unmoved in front of some of the most celebrated objects in art history? Here were the distinctive vases and statuettes, ginger-jars and woven baskets whose images populated museums around the world. Here was the tall porcelain pot in *Woman with a Coffee Pot*. There was the white dish in *Fruitbowl, Glass and Apples*. I even recognised the curlique-aproned table on which the still-life onions in my kitchen had been arranged. In the pictures these things had a kind of inner life and force. Now they looked small and insignificant.

I was stumped. I had tried it all. Cézanne's ghost was no

longer resident on the streets of Aix. Nor was his presence to be found hovering over the bridges, the pines and pistachio trees he had painted. It did not even emanate from these treasured objects sitting in his studio. Far from following in Cézanne's footsteps, I had lost the trail completely.

⌣

I slipped into the back of the class next morning and thought I had come to the wrong place. This was the Marchutz School studio, a light-filled building on a grassy slope above the Tholonet road. But there were no A-framed easels, no bright oils, no strong stinks of turpentine here. This was more like a creative writing course. Seated in a semi-circle, the students were reading and discussing an essay on the art of the short story by that remarkable writer of the American south, Flannery O'Connor.

It did not take me more than a moment or two to realise that I had stumbled into waters far deeper than anything the Arc had to offer. The essay was titled 'The Nature and Aim of Fiction', and the question under discussion was the one O'Connor started her discourse off with – what is truth in art? I took a stapled photocopy of the piece and slid into a seat. Having even less of an opinion about such things after the previous day's debacle than I did before, I kept my mouth shut.

But the question had everyone going. One young woman made me sit up and listen. If there is any truth in art, she

231

was saying, it is the most subjective of truths. Look at Mont Sainte-Victoire. With his eighty-seven paintings of the mountain dispersed around the world, Cézanne had single-handedly made it famous. Today the entire globe's perception of Sainte-Victoire was really just one man's impression of it. Where was the truth in that?

'Fair enough,' said the discussion-leader. Alan Roberts, the school's director, looked relaxed. He wore a beard, a short-sleeved shirt and khaki shorts. Even his voice was relaxed – after almost thirty years in Provence he still had a slight Carolina drawl. Rather than leading his students towards answers, he seemed content to let them ask their own questions and thrash matters out themselves. He intervened only when things went badly adrift. The point he was trying to draw out of O'Connor now was that for all its subjectivity, there was indeed some sort of truth inherent in art.

'It's a valid point,' Roberts went on. 'And it makes you ask yourself if Cézanne got the mountain right. O'Connor says "the person who aims after art in his work aims after the truth." Does she say anything about the basis of that truth?'

Nobody in the group had much difficulty in identifying O'Connor's opinion on the matter. While the others stopped their discussion for a moment one young woman read the passage from the essay aloud.

'"I want,' she intoned, 'to talk about one quality of fiction which I think is its least common denominator – the fact that it is concrete – and a few of the qualities that follow from this. We will be concerned in this with the reader in his fundamental human sense, because the nature of fiction is in large measure determined by the nature of our perceptive apparatus. The beginning of human knowledge is through the senses, and the fiction writer begins where human perception begins. He appeals through the senses, and you cannot appeal to the senses through abstractions. It is a good deal easier for most people to state an abstract idea than to describe and thus recreate some object that they actually see.'"[7]

The qualities that followed from this pre-eminent role of the physical senses were indeed many in Flannery O'Connor's view; as the morning progressed we made our way, with stops and starts and hesitations, with much debate and disagreement, through some of them. It was not easy going. O'Connor was not discussing formulas of rote, mechanical writing – through the lens of her mind we were looking at the basic underpinnings of the world's attempts to depict itself.

Fiction was not something upon which you imposed technique, said O'Connor; real technique was something organic; it grew out of the material itself, and was different for each story. Fiction was not abstraction, unfleshed ideas or emotions, either – it was full of matter and the concrete details of life. Nor were those details chosen either randomly or in their totality. Each was chosen for a reason, and arranged in a specific sequence to a reasoned end. Thus art, O'Connor said, was selective – its truth lay in the presentation of those essentials that created movement and life. Fiction was a dramatic unity, something that was valuable in itself, that worked in itself. Because it was an experience rather than an abstraction, a good story carried its own meaning – indeed, was its own meaning. But for the creator meaning was never a simple or superficial thing, and could not be discerned immediately. What was required was a lot of hard looking.

The longer one looked at an object, O'Connor asserted, the more of the world one saw in it. Not everything lay on the surface – the best writers subjected themselves to the limits imposed by reality, but reality was not always co-existent with the visible world. To discover it an artist had to use his reason, and to find an answering reason in everything he saw. Each object, each situation had its own essence and peculiarity, and to use reason meant finding the spirit which made each thing itself and not something else. It called for humility, a self-effacement which required the artist's recognition that his work sprang from a realm much larger than anything his conscious mind could express. In the end the creation of fiction was not a matter of technical competence, but of the larger vision that must precede it.

It was deep, dense stuff, and I could only sit there trying to keep my head above water. Even the class chatterboxes were silenced. But in every paragraph of the essay's twenty-three pages on truth in art there was the ring of truth itself. It did not matter that O'Connor was talking specifically about writing short stories. This was a description of a certain way of taking on the whole mystery of life; such an outlook carried lessons for painting as well. Both depended on those indispensable tools of perception, the senses. What counts most in any creative exercise, O'Connor was saying, is how we look at the world in the first place.

It was a long session and when it finished, well past schedule, the ladies scattered for lunch. I chatted with Alan Roberts as he tidied up books and papers.

The Cézanne field trip, I told him, had been a failure for me. I tried to explain why. Roberts expressed no surprise, but smiled. The reaction among his newly-arrived art students, he observed, was sometimes much the same.

He gestured at the O'Connor essay in my hand. 'You saw how this morning's reading affected the group. We're presenting them with lots of ideas about painting they have never had to deal with before. We are asking them to take a long step back and learn how to see.

'If you couldn't find Cézanne in all those places and objects he painted, perhaps it was because he was never there in the first place', Roberts said. 'Maybe his spirit isn't contained in the things he looked at. Maybe it lies instead in the *way* he looked at them.'

I gazed through the open door at the deep shade beneath the trees outside, at the sunlight bouncing off the bank below the studio, at the road beneath that wound its way out to the mountain. Obviously different painters looked at things in different ways. But I had never thought of looking as a distinct physical process, of observation as a creative act in itself.

But it wasn't simply looking that one had to begin with, Roberts told me. It was even more basic than that – it was learning to look.

'When our students arrive they're all ready for the spontaneous parts of painting,' he said. 'It's the long hard sessions of work they are less prepared for. We read vast amounts – letters, books, reviews, writers like Flannery O'Connor as well the great critics on great art through the ages. And we look at huge numbers of paintings. We study, analyse, and compare a range of art that's been produced over 25,000 years – everything from Lascaux cave-paintings to classical Chinese landscapes to Cézanne still-lifes. And we do a lot of talking about what we've read and looked at – it brings out all sorts of unnoticed relationships in art.

'In the end,' he continued, 'it's all something of a paradox. We get students to read like crazy, to look at a thousand pictures and to discuss the whole thing endlessly. Then we ask them forget it all. We ask them to let go of everything and head into the field, to use their senses and paint though the direct observation of nature. You would be surprised what comes out of it sometimes. The students certainly are.'

And where, I asked, already dreading the answer, would be a good place to learn about the way Paul Cézanne used his own senses? I had little desire to go back, I told him, to those verbose and self-important academics I had already tried reading.

'Try the painters and poets instead,' he said, pulling three thin volumes from a long shelf of art books on the studio wall. 'Roger Fry started as an average painter, but became an extraordinary critic. Joachim Gasquet was a Provençal poet, one of the few Aixois to know Cézanne well and recognise him for what he was. Rainer Maria Rilke never knew Cézanne at all, but had a poetic sensitivity to his art that's rarely been equalled. They all had ideas about the way Cézanne looked at the world.'

I took the proffered works with only a little more confidence than I had taken *In Cézanne's Footsteps*, and wished Alan Roberts *bon appétit*.

~

A few days later I went to return the books and found the Marchutz School deserted. Eventually I traced Alan Roberts and his young painters to a sun-dappled stand of plane trees outside Tholonet. Easels open and brushes in hand, they were spread out through the wood and hard at work. I wouldn't have known where to begin. All about us the country was enticing and alive – shadows danced on the boughs of the trees, tall, feathery grass made gentle, rolling waves in nearby fields, and beyond them, once again just an arm's-reach away, reared the great living mountain.

In slow, unhurried manner, Roberts was making the

rounds between one painter and the next. I joined him. He did more looking at canvases than talking about them, made inferences rather than critical comments, and let his students search for their own solutions to their own problems. It might be easier and faster to explain, he said as we strolled, but the lesson at hand would not be as well learned.

We stopped beside an athletically-built young blonde named Brianna and contemplated the landscape of field and hills she was working on. Roberts asked how things were going.

Brianna said she was frustrated. She showed us a painting of the same scene she had done the day before. The canvas was full and busy, but the different elements in it were unbalanced and confused. At least she had finished it, she said. Today she was stuck – in her mind she'd known exactly the painting she wanted to make, but now she couldn't transfer it to canvas. She was going backwards, she complained.

We looked at the painting. As she'd said, it was unfinished. But what was there was marked by graceful movements. There were balances and complementary colours that hadn't been there before. In its bare bones was a basic fitting together of things.

Roberts nodded. 'The only time I get nervous is when a student is *not* frustrated. When you are, it means you're making the effort to see.'

At home in the Midwest Brianna was an all-state hurdles champion. Roberts asked her if in her mind she pictured a perfect race before each event she ran. She nodded. And did it ever work out just like that? She shook her head.

'Cézanne was once asked what as a painter he would like most,' Roberts said. 'He answered, "*une belle formule*" – a beautiful formula. He knew there was no such thing, that each time is a new time and we can never tell beforehand how we'll work onto canvas what we see in front of us.'

Roberts started asking Brianna about the details of her painting, but I had lost my concentration. Instead I was thinking of what I'd been reading about – Cézanne's own progress as a painter, his painful working towards using his senses for his own way of seeing.

Like many young artists Cézanne had dreamed of taking the world by storm. And he had indulged what many young artists indulge – an emotional and agitated imagination. He sought grandiose effects. Without any natural inclination for Baroque tradition or technique he began imitating the Baroque masters, digging deep into his own romantic fantasies. Luckily for the world, the results were so discouraging that Cézanne was forced to look elsewhere. And what he began to discover and use instead was an inherent gift, something Roger Fry in his study, *Cézanne*, called the 'extraordinary sensibility of his reaction to actual vision of no matter what phenomenon.'[8] Cézanne, in other words, responded to anything and everything he saw in a way most of us don't.

Even in the most visionary and tormented of his early paintings, Cézanne showed a remarkable natural sense for the subtleties of colour, for their infinite gradations and the play between them. But when he began painting with Camille Pisarro in the landscapes of northern France Cézanne discovered Impressionism's open-air techniques. Instead of painting turbulent visions from his inner life or going to museums to make copies of old Italian masters, he opened his eyes to what surrounded him. Like the other Impressionists, Cézanne's concern became the capture of the fleeting and temporary effects of light on the real world.

Had he gone no further, Cézanne would have made an accomplished painter. But if he captured the fleeting and the temporary, it did not entirely capture him. For Cézanne was not using his senses passively or unconsciously – he also had a reasoning intellect that was asking deeper questions. In a short time Cézanne had moved on – or more precisely, in.

He continued to paint the variety that lay at the uppermost surface of nature. But at the same time Cézanne began looking at a deeper reality, at the fundamental visual principles that lay beneath appearances. And in the simple things of life – in coffee-pots and fruit-bowls, in onions and mountains – he discovered a permanent, underlying order of forms and structures that were almost architectural in their arrangement.

None of the invisible webbing he observed holding the world together was obvious or evident. Cézanne saw it as his task in painting to depict that hidden reality, to draw the harmony and balance he saw all about him out onto canvas. Involving not just an outer recording with his eye but an inner transformation with his mind, it was a job he called 'realising'. It was this effort, says Fry, 'which gave to all his utterances in form their tremendous, almost prophetic, significance.'[9]

෴

We walked on. Not every one of Alan Roberts' American students was tall, blonde and athletic – the next painter we met among the plane trees was petite and dark-haired. Jacqueline was a commercial artist working for a designer-clothing manufacturer in San Francisco. She'd spent years at a draughtboard practising the same specific technique – the isolating and replicating of individual objects. Now, standing in an outdoor world without boundaries, she told Roberts that she wanted 'to paint the whole painting.' She was trying, she said, to put objects in relation to each other, to make their existence dependent on their surroundings.

We looked at her painting. Her motif was a plane tree growing in deep green shade beside a thick tangle of bushes. Trying to paint the whole painting and connect all parts of her canvas, she had covered most of it in the same uniform shade of green.

'Stand still, Jacqueline,' said Roberts, 'and without moving your head concentrate on the mottled bark of your plane tree. Now, from a peripheral angle let your eye take in the green areas to the right, to the left, and in the background. What do you see?'

What Jacqueline saw was not quite what she had painted. To the left, where a shaft of sunshine was filtering through leaves, she saw tones of yellow. To the right, where the bushes were casting heavy shadow, she saw blue tints. Behind, where earth was showing through the grass, she saw hints of red. All these colours were still green, and all flowed smoothly into each other, but they were the different greens of a natural palette incorporating all the primary colours.

I am no painter and my own colour sense, I suspect, is basic. Neither am I an art-theorist, and the act of turning three-dimensional forms in nature into two-dimensional forms on canvas appears to me a very complex one to explain, much less perform. But I knew that the task that now confronted Jacqueline – using the subtlety of colour to give substance and reality to the painted image – was one that lay at the heart of Paul Cézanne's art.

Cézanne painted in the belief that volumes and forms were not best expressed on a flat surface by delineating shape or outline. Instead, he represented them through an infinitely painstaking use of colour changes. Each shift of planes – and, visually speaking, all objects are made of planes intersecting at various angles – could be designated by a change in colour, an effect that is produced by the difference in the angle of light reflected from its surface.

Thus even a perfect sphere, in Cézanne's way of looking, was only a receding series of planes foreshortened to the absolute maximum, the last visible one of which formed its contour. A sphere could be defined by colour alone. Put one way, each series of colour gradations determined the round-ness of an object. Put another, as Roger Fry did, Cézanne conceived of colour 'not as an adjunct to form, as some-thing imposed on form, but as itself the direct exponent of form'.[10]

It was a concept that took Cézanne a long way. In fact the painter perceived all objects in space as curved in shape – for him their culminating point was the point closest to his eye. Even flat and seemingly uniformly-coloured objects like walls or tabletops could be regarded as a series of planes, and subject to the same exacting scrutiny for colour variation. The result was such a finely nuanced treatment of surfaces that in some Cézanne paintings the wall behind the sitter in a portrait is just as captivating, has just as much character, as the face of the person itself.

What does it matter how Cézanne saw balls or walls? In the first place, his fascination with colour and form decided his choice of subjects. Cézanne could spend hours in infi-nitely detailed analysis without ever lifting a brush. In letters to his wife sent from Paris during a commemorative Cézanne exhibition in 1907, Rainer Maria Rilke recorded a painter-friend's observation on Cézanne's limitless patience in front of a motif: 'He sat there in front of it like a dog, just looking, without any nervousness, without any ulterior motive.' And when he did begin to paint, he painted only what he could 'realise'. 'Here,' the friend had said, pointing to certain place on one of Cézanne's apples, 'This is something he knew and now he's saying it; right next to it is an empty space, because that was something he did not know yet. He only made what he knew, nothing else.'[11]

Such profound and lengthy meditations on substance required that the substance involved did not move. Street-scenes do; fruits and vegetables don't. Removed from all narrative ideas, devoid of emotion, such objects allowed Cézanne to give himself up to pure form.

Cézanne's concepts had an effect not only on what he painted, but also on how he painted. Dispensing with heavy outlines and solid planes of massed colour, he evolved a style using small, parallel brushstrokes to lay on his colour gradations. And therein lay part of the secret that gave such extraordinary solidity and life to the simple objects he portrayed.

It was a curious process. In his still-lifes of apples, onions, skulls and other spheres, Cézanne actually began by drawing the contour with his brush. This, naturally, conflicted with the parallel brushstrokes he had surrounded such objects with. So he went back repeatedly over the contour with his parallel hatchings, building up thick layers of paint around it, continually covering his contour and then exposing it again.

Roger Fry recognised the extraordinary results of this procedure. 'At first sight the volumes and contours declare themselves boldly to the eye,' he wrote. 'They are of a surprising simplicity and clearly apprehended. But the more one looks the more they elude any precise definition. The apparent continuity of the contour is illusory, for it changes in quality throughout each particle of its length … We thus get at once the notion of extreme simplicity in the general result and infinite variety in every part. It is the infinitely changing quality of the very stuff of the painting which communicates so vivid a sense of life. In spite of the austerity of the forms, all is vibration and movement.'[12]

What applied to apples and onions applied similarly to entire mountains. In his contemplation of Sainte-Victoire Cézanne wrought a kind of magic. Long ago Celts and Romans had venerated Sainte-Victoire for its supernatural powers. Today, even if we knew something of the techniques used, the painted image seemed no less astonishing. Could an object like a mountain hold rock-steady and vibrate at the same time? When Paul Cézanne painted it it could.

⌒

The last young artist we encountered that afternoon was my favourite of all of Alan Roberts' students. She wasn't the best painter of the lot, but she had the best painter's perception. She was developing that Cézannian talent for seeing connections and correspondence wherever she looked.

Susanna was from Santa Fe. She had painted before in the harsh, dry landscapes of the New Mexico desert, but she had never painted colours like the colours she was finding in

Provence. She had fallen in love with greens – she said she hadn't known that in one place so many rich and varied tones of one colour could exist. Like Jacqueline, she was using them to try to paint the whole picture. But unlike Jacqueline, she had already more than covered her canvas. She had spilled far over its edges.

'I'm not just looking at the motifs differently', she said as we watched her mixing paints on her palette. 'I'm looking at *everything* differently. Walking to the art school in the morning I only have to see a tree and a house on a hill, and I start planning how I would arrange them together in paint. I've been turning in circles ever since I arrived. Sometimes I get so involved it's like I'm in the middle of a painting myself. It makes me feel wonderful.'

Being in the middle of a painting was Susanna's way of being fully engaged, of being wholly part of her surroundings. And for me that sense of connection was what Paul Cézanne was finally all about. What comes across most strongly in his painting is not colour in itself, nor shape, nor the objects painted, but the relation of each colour and shape and object to the entire painting. What creates the balanced harmony of the whole is the interdependence of each part. It's what Rilke thought when, after having long gazed at an subtly-coloured portrait of Cézanne's wife sitting in a red armchair, he wrote simply, 'It's as if every place [on the canvas] were aware of all the other places.'

Cézanne called his method of linking the world's

seemingly disparate elements 'joining hands'. As recorded by his friend, the poet Joachim Gasquet, no one described it better than Cézanne himself:

'There mustn't be a single slack link, a single gap through which the emotion, the light, the truth can escape. I advance all of my canvas at one time, if you see what I mean. And in the same movement, with the same conviction, I approach all the scattered pieces. Everything we look at disperses and vanishes, doesn't it? Nature is always the same and yet its appearance is always changing. It is our business as artists to convey the thrill of nature's permanence along with the elements and appearance of all its changes. Painting must give us the flavour of nature's eternity. Everything, you understand. So I join together nature's straying hands. From all sides, here, there, and everywhere. I select colours, tones and shades; I set them down, I bring them together. They make lines. They become objects – rocks, trees – without my thinking about them. They take on volume, value. If, as I perceive them, these volumes and values correspond to the planes and patches of colour that lie before me, that appear to my eyes, well then, my canvas "joins hands". It holds firm. It aims neither too high nor too low. It's true, dense, full. But if there is the slightest distraction, the slightest hitch, above all if I interpret too much one day, if I am carried away today by a theory that contradicts yesterday's, if I think while I am painting, if I meddle, then whoosh!, everything goes to pieces.'[13]

When the painting class broke up that afternoon I strolled a little way through the trees and rolling red fields until Mont Sainte-Victoire came into full view.

I took in its great bulk, then thought of that elderly man, small and none too sturdy-looking, who had so often stood here studying it. Flannery O'Connor had been right – the physical senses were not just the beginning of knowledge. They were a strength to be reckoned with, an instrument of concrete transformation. Paul Cézanne had not only joined straying hands. Recreating Sainte-Victoire in the minds of people on the far side of the world, he had literally moved mountains. Surely here was the powerful sensibility, the redeeming vision of the old Mediterranean that Nietzsche himself had spoken of. From start to finish the Mediterranean view of the world had a good deal to do with vision itself, with the whole panoply of human senses.

∽

A few evenings later Jany and I were once again having dinner in a restaurant. I have a certain weakness for Tarte Tatin, and Chez Charlotte in the centre of Aix can always be counted on for a good one. A lot of Aixois have the same weakness, so the place was crowded and it was late when we left, a little past midnight perhaps.

'Come,' said Jany, taking me by the arm and leading me up the rue Bédarrides, not our usual route home. 'I have something I want you to see.'

At the Place de la Mairie we turned right into rue Paul Bert and right again into rue Matheron. We had left the noisy, strolling crowds behind. Down on the Cours Mirabeau the sidewalks would be busy for an hour or two more. But here the metal blinds were pulled down over the shopfronts and the street was dark and empty.

'You've been rattling on about Cézanne and the senses all evening,' said Jany.

Had I?

'Not at all,' I protested. 'I merely wanted to say that when people get down to using them practically, the senses are a down-to-earth subject like any other. They're not so terribly mysterious.'

'Well, here's a mystery, then. I just want to show you that you are not the only Cézannian in town.'

Jany now marched me up to the window of a shop not more than ten feet wide. *Ecrivain Public*, Public Scribe, the sign read in French – 'letters, CVs, translations in all languages from English to pre-Islamic Yemeni.' There was nothing else in the window. This was not a typical Aix shopfront. But it seemed hardly remarkable enough to justify a late-night detour home.

'Well?' I said.

'Look at the number,' said Jany. '14, rue Matheron. Site number twenty-nine on your Cézanne site-map. This was the Cézanne family house from 1850 to 1870. Paul Cézanne spent his youth between this house and the family estate on the edge of town. He was registered for the census of 1860 here. His sister Rose was born here. Now turn around.'

I turned around.

'On the other side of the street,' Jany continued in the same tour-guide voice, '15, rue Matheron. Site number one in my own life. See that upstairs room, the middle window? That's the room I was born in. Lived there, too, until I was twenty-one. Roller-skated in this street. Walked this way to school every morning. Kissed my first boy on this very corner. I grew up in the shadow of Paul Cézanne's house. So enough about painting, all right? And a little bit more about us.'

So saying, she took my arm again and we walked down the sidewalk, homewards past the square known as the Place des Trois Ormeaux. Triangular in shape and marked at each apex by a tall elm tree, it is a modest little square, generally overlooked in the grander, more elegant scheme of things around it.

In Aix image is indeed everything. But what you see depends on how you look at it. Normally amid the noise and distractions of the day I didn't notice this square at all when I passed by. Now in the still of the night I saw how lovely it really was. I came to a halt and, for the first time, admired its simple lines and graceful balance.

What had made me pause? Of course I did not say a word about it to Jany. But in the end I had to admit that perhaps the physical senses did have their mysterious side after all.

For it seemed to me that I had noticed something from the corner of my eye. Hidden in the dark trees, in a shadow that may or may not have vaguely resembled a long coat and bowler hat, was a presence that asked me to stop and look a little harder.

Seven

It is inescapable and nothing to be ashamed of. Anyone who has ever even thought about living in Provence has a house fantasy.

My own fantasy was not so different from most others. It involved an old stone building, a couple of spreading shade trees, and a dark, flame-like cypress tree growing somewhere near the entrance. I had never grown a tomato in my life, but somewhere in the scene, perhaps around at the back of the house, I pictured a small patch of manured earth where I would grow tomato plants as good as the ones my father-in-law René grew. I could see myself in the cool of the late afternoon, pulling a tomato off its bamboo-staked vine, smelling the acid tomato-smell of the broken stem and biting into still sun-warm flesh. But above all, at the very heart of this waking dream, were calm and a view. My house sat high in a peaceful countryside, where the land fell sharply away to a perspective of far blue hills.

Jany, of course, had her own Provençal house fantasy. It was not at all like mine. She accepted, in principle, the same house of old stone. Ditto the spreading shade trees in the garden. The tomato plants, too, could stay, as long as I arranged for a babysitter with a watering can so we could get away for a few weeks in the summer. I would have to get rid of the cypress trees, she informed me – they gave her hay fever. But Jany's real interests did not lie in old stone or plant-life at all. She was too Mediterranean to want peace and rural calm. Her hills were peopled hills. Just beyond the garden gate of her fantasy lay a village and village life. She wanted sociable neighbours, children playing in the streets, a lively café, and a village baker who supplied warm, friendly talk along with the croissants. Jany wanted vivacity.

Given her determined character and the gap separating our two dream-houses I had bowed long ago to the inevitable: near Vaison-la-Romaine in northern Provence we bought a small holiday-home in the middle of a village. There were no shade trees or tomato plants; there was no garden at all. There was, however, a great deal of vivacity.

One example will do. When they hold their annual *fête de village* most small places in Provence are content to organize a *boules* competition and a community dinner, then call it a day. Our tiny village, however, laid on an all-singing, all-dancing extravaganza each summer. It continued virtually non-stop for three long, wine-bibbing days and nights. A high stage was set up on scaffolding on the square, there was a *pistou* dinner and other gargantuan feasts, and the merry-making went on until the very small hours. One year we had spot-lit go-go dancers in Brazilian thongs. It was an apparition that alarmed the elderly ladies of the village, but wholly delighted the male population of farmers and winegrowers. In the daytime the mayor toured the town-hall's bust of Marianne – official symbol of republican France, once modelled on Brigitte Bardot but today resembling pouting film-star Laeticia Casta – through the streets on the back of a donkey. For miles around other villages flocked to our village for its fête.

It was that kind of place, energetic, festive and forthright. Even the bell in the clocktower above our house was forthright. When it tolled its deep bells – five minutes before the hour and once again on the hour (that made twenty-four bells at midnight) – the glass panes in our windows vibrated.

The bell aside, I enjoyed the village as much as Jany did. But I had never entirely let go of my original vision of things. For years I had dreamed of a quiet house in the country not far from Aix where we could live year-round. Sometimes, when I felt time passing too quickly, a kind of house-hunting fever would creep over me. Then, between assignments to distant destinations for the paper, I would make shorter, more harrowing trips – I would drag Jany off to visit houses with our estate agent, Monsieur Lavoix.

He was not the most efficient property man even in the best of circumstances. I am not sure he should have been in real estate at all – he did not have the requisite shark-like nature. But I liked Monsieur Lavoix anyway. He was tall and thin and ascetic-looking, and wore his silver-grey hair long and swept back like a poet's. He was fond of reading and piano concertos. If he had to be an agent of some kind, his bent would have better qualified him as a literary or musical agent.

But in his heart Monsieur Lavoix was none of these things. He was a philosopher. He had huge admiration for Voltaire, and loved to quote the great man's witticisms and ripostes. He was also very good on Sartre, and displayed a weak spot for the musings of La Rochfoucauld. The only trouble was that all this got in the way of buying houses. How can you efficiently inspect creeping humidity stains on the wall when the man in charge is nattering on about man's uncertain role in the cosmos? How can you raise suspicions of terminal dry-rot when he is earnestly seeking your opinion on the possibilities of an afterlife? How can you peer up malodorous drainpipes as he speculates on being and nothingness? After a few visits like this the house-hunting urge would subside, and Jany and I would revert to being more or less contented town-dwellers. It was, to be honest, a bit of a relief – if ever we found anything one of us liked the other would surely oppose it.

In recent years, though, our prospects of finding anything at all around Aix, either inside a village or out, had dramatically declined. Monsieur Lavoix blamed it all on advances in transport technology combined with humanity's inherently unfaithful nature. Did we realise, he had asked us on our last visit, that with the *Train à Grande Vitesse* it was now entirely convenient for a man to maintain more than one household – to have a job and a mistress in the capital on weekdays and shoot down to Provence to become a dedicated husband and father on weekends? Imagine leading two existences instead of one! It knocked simple being and nothingness into a cocked hat. Obviously, he admitted, such possibilities raised certain moral contradictions that needed resolution. The *Philosophes* of the Enlightenment had never had to deal with sex and high-speed train-travel, so Monsieur Lavoix remained unaided.

Whatever the ethics of it, Provence's increased accessibility was a windfall for the local real-estate market – it was going through the roof. Parisians, Bruxellois, Amsterdammers, everyone was buying second homes in the Provençal countryside. As Jany and I continued to dicker over details, Aix's 200 estate agencies had settled down to a property bun-fight. By that point the supply of buns was fast dwindling and their price rising by the day. The time had finally come where even if we took on a non-philosophical estate-agent, a hard-nosed, market-savvy operator of the kind who called a house *un produit*, a product, the chances of finding anything we could afford were slim.

But that didn't matter now – when the familiar urge came upon me once again a few days after our stroll past the Place des Trois Ormeaux, I jumped at the chance. For with the excuse of house-hunting I saw the chance for another kind of hunt. Over the summer I had made some advances in my search for the fundamentals of Mediterranean existence – in urging me to use my own senses the painters of Aix had opened my eyes to an entire life of the senses. But painters weren't the only Mediterraneans to use their physical senses to serious purpose. No distance away in Haute Provence there were men whose search for older, simpler ways led them not to paint and canvas, but far past the fabric of the material world itself. There were monks in the rugged country up there, entire communities of holy men who lived a meagre life in hill-top monasteries. I wanted to find them.

'I have an idea,' I said to Jany as she sat reading the paper after breakfast. I preferred not to let her know that she might soon be spending time in remote places with men in itchy robes. 'What if we pooled our two house fantasies? We could look for an old stone house with a shady garden on the edge of a small hamlet that sits on top of a hill with a view.'

Jany looked up from the pages of *Libération* and blinked her eyes in consternation. 'Say that again,' she said.

'Well, it would be a kind of compromise. You'd get social life in a small hamlet, I'd get peace and a view from its edge, and we'd both get the house that we want. No go-go girls, no cypress trees. And to make our chances realistic, we must look further from Aix than we usually have. Anything up to, say, forty-five minutes away. You could still drive to the *collège*.

'Look.' I had a map all ready and spread it out on the

257

floor. When you took Jany on you had to be prepared. 'There's almost nothing left in the Luberon, on the coast, in the Rhône Valley – it's all been bought out north, south and west of Aix. But what about to the north-east, in the Alpes-de-Haute-Provence? That's rougher land up there, a tougher climate. There won't be so many house-hunters. And there's an *autoroute*.' I pointed to the string of towns that lined the Durance Valley. 'A 45-minute drive up the A-51 would take us as far as Forcalquier. Somewhere around there there's got to be an old hamlet on top of a hill.'

It was touch and go for a while; lately Jany had developed a tendency to resist even some of my best ideas. But I persisted, and before she got back to her paper she finally agreed to go exploring with me in Haute Provence.

꩜

At Les Ramparts, an estate agent's office beneath the high town walls of Forcalquier, the woman behind the desk did not merely blink her eyes. When we described what we were looking for – I said it all seemed simple enough – she rolled them around inside their sockets.

'That's *all* you want?' she asked. 'Monsieur, this summer I've been selling houses like warm *brioches*. To foreigners, especially – they cannot find what they are looking for anywhere else in Provence. They all want exactly what you want. And they are buying whatever they can get hold of.'

In truth I had expected as much. I went into a huddled

conference with Jany. We were not going to look at houses in any old place, I said. What we needed was a reconnaissance trip. If we could come back to the agencies with the names of half a dozen places we liked, I suggested, we could then ask what they had for sale there. It would save lots of useless and time-consuming visits. Jany sighed the sigh of one who has once again given herself up to an unpredictable fate, and nodded assent.

So began a tour up hill and down dale in search of the place that was supposed to make both of us happy for the rest of our lives. Of course we never ended up buying a house at all. We never even looked at one. But we did find the monastic community I was looking for, even if the route was a long and roundabout one.

It started simply enough. We sat in a Forcalquier café for a long while, poring over the map and marking likely-looking destinations in pencil. Then we were off, I driving and Jany navigating with the map on her knees. I am not sure if it was the closeness of the atmosphere – violent heat-storms often build in Provence towards the middle of August – or Jany's difficulty in keeping the multiple folds of her Michelin map under control. But relations grew a little strained. I wanted the window open for the breeze, she wanted it closed for her map. I wanted the radio on for the weather forecast, she wanted it off so she could concentrate on the printed lines of red and yellow that squiggled their way in front of her.

We couldn't even agree on a daily route. Jany, naturally,

wanted to head for the bigger, busier villages. I wanted to explore the remoter, quieter places. So we quibbled over this itinerary and that, until we finally agreed on a formula: Jany could have two days to see the villages she wanted, then I would have two days for mine.

Mane, Sauvan, Dauphin, St Maime … some of the places Jany directed me to were pretty. But on the whole they were too built-up for the kind of inhabitants I was looking for. On the second day Jany pointed us toward Simiane la Rotonde, Reillanne and Banon, places well outside our 45-minute radius but big enough for lively village life. I spotted her devious strategy right away. She did not really want to live in Banon at all. It was merely a tactical pawn – she was showing me villages so busy that when we finally came to our com-promise purchase I would, out of sheer relief, accept some-thing far less peaceful than originally planned.

Well, two could play at that game, I thought as we streaked up the *autoroute* on the third morning. Spread out across our map I had discovered dozens of small black printed crosses, symbols indicating churches, abbeys, priories and other ancient religious sites. I had circled some of the more remote ones, and was now aiming for what had to be among the most isolated ecclesiastic hideaways in all Provence. Never mind that in the last forty-eight hours the atmosphere had grown stifling and dark thunder-clouds lay piled high in the sky over Haute Provence. Behind Forcalquier I drove straight up into the thick forests that cover the flanks of the

Montagne de Lure. If Notre-Dame-de-Lure had been good enough for Saint Donatus it was good enough for me.

I had done my research the night before. Around the year AD 500 the reclusive Donatus, seeking a place of earthly peace and contemplation, had wandered into Provence along that old Roman road, the Domitian Way. Somewhere around Forcalquier he had wandered off it, and only come to rest high on the wild slopes of Lure. There in deep forests he built a church. It appeared to be the ideal place to start Jany off. Even the most dedicated of life-long hermits – grotto-dwellers, pole-squatters, wanderers in the desert and the like – would find it a touch lonely.

Jany said not a word as we rounded one steep bend after another, but I could see her inwardly recoiling at the unrelieved sight of all those trees. Only Canadians, she once told me, have the emotional equipment needed to deal with so many of them at one time.

'What a place!' I boomed with enthusiasm as we parked the car in the middle of nowhere and began walking down a grassy path to the church. Perhaps I was laying in on a little heavily. But negotiations with wily Mediterraneans are never easy. One can only meet Provençal cunning with more cunning.

'What a place!' I said for a second time when we emerged in the clearing at the end of the path. But this time I meant it. The church was a crude and primitive thing, its roof made of thick, irregular slabs of stone, its shape asymmetrical, as if one aisle had long ago collapsed. Yet it had a simple and appealing beauty, its rough-hewn texture only enhanced by the grove of gnarled and moss-covered oak trees that stood in front of it. They were very old, and gave the glade an almost Druidic feel. There was just time to make a circuit about the church, walking through thick, soft layers of leaf-mould, before raindrops began to patter down. In a minute the skies had opened and heavy rain began to fall.

The church door was locked. We loped for the small hikers' shelter that stood on the edge of the clearing, and beside a fireplace that smelled of cold ashes watched the rain fall. After fifteen minutes or so the downpour ceased as quickly as it had begun, and a hot summer sun unexpectedly emerged through a hole in the clouds.

Oddly, it seemed to animate the clearing – what had been old and dusty and tired now seemed new and full of life. Suddenly there was steam curling up in wavy sheets from the stones of the church roof. The bark on the great trees glistened and twinkled a shiny black. Long rags of white mist drifted slowly to unknown destinations through the woods. The air was soaked with the smells of earth and living things. It was as if everything long held in a state of suspended animation had suddenly been released.

I could see why Saint Donatus might have chosen to linger here. You'd have to put Jany's wrists in manacles to keep her here for more than half-an-hour, but for the moment even she was entranced. We hung on for a few minutes more, then headed back to the car.

My next circled destination, the priory of Carluc, lay a few miles from the village of Céreste. Carluc, which turned out to be far older even than Notre-Dame-de-Lure, was a once-pagan site built over a sacred spring. The setting was pastoral – rolling meadows and woods, herds of sheep, a stream running through the shallow ravine in which the priory lay hidden. It was the kind of secluded, out-of-the-way place that Jany abhorred.

Thunder continued to growl softly on the cloud-heavy horizon as we parked and walked towards the church that now stands beside the spring. It, too, had a saintly builder. Even in his 10th-century lifetime Saint Mayeul was venerated, becoming abbot of one the greatest institutions of his day, the Burgundian monastery of Cluny. But he never forgot his Provençal beginnings in Valensole, not far across the Durance River from Carluc. His extensive programme of construction and renovation in the region was eventually to make Provence one of the richest repositories of Romanesque architecture in all Europe. So popular was he because of his building mania – along with churches came pilgrims, peace, and prosperity – that when Mayeul was captured by raiding North African Moors a major military campaign was staged to bring about his rescue.

There were half a dozen other visitors to Carluc, and we joined them just as they were being shepherded off on a tour by a lively young woman with bobbed hair named Florence. There are so many Romanesque churches scattered about

Provence, Florence was telling her charges, that neither church nor state had the funding to maintain them all. Only *Les Amis de Carluc*, the volunteer organisation she belonged to, kept this beautiful old place going. There was no official presence here – no fences, ticket offices, parking lots or any other signs of administration around the thousand-year-old priory. Carluc, I complimented Florence, was that rare thing these days, a genuinely romantic ruin. She agreed, but said that romantic ruins have limited lives – if the farmhouses in the area looked particularly sturdy it was because many of them had been built with looted blocks of tailored Carluc stone. Once a major halt on the long pilgrim trail to Santiago de Compostela in Spain, the priory had continued to shrink over the centuries.

What locals had not been able to cart away were the chambers, stairways and galleries carved into the solid limestone walls of the ravine. Behind the church, where a large part of the nave had collapsed, ran a sunken hall carved into living rock. On each side of pillars and jambs that once supported a roof lay a series of sculpted tombs, now empty. Medieval monks must have been tiny – none of the receptacles carved into the stone measured more than five feet long.

We didn't linger. As we walked through antechambers and limestone-carved doorways we heard thunder growing louder, saw flashes of lightning illuminate the dark afternoon sky. Florence was growing more nervous by the second. She had seen lightning strike Carluc before, and had come close to being struck herself. She wanted to finish as quickly as possible. So did Jany – she hadn't forgotten the wind-storm in the Camargue.

But there was one place where even she took her time. Directly over the spring was a broad, raised shelf hewn in the rock. Florence called it her time machine. With it, she said, you could flip back and forth from one great spiritual age to another. At one end of the shelf a shallow semi-circle had been cut into the wall along with three square holes for supporting wooden beams – the remains of an early Christian altar, said Florence. At the other end of the stone shelf a circular channel was carved into the floor and joined to a depression leading over its lip – a place for pagan sacrifice, Florence indicated, with drainage runnels for blood.

We stood for a minute, gazing from one altar to another. The thunder was close now, and the heavy, ion-charged atmosphere literally electric. Jany was tugging at my arm, Florence was urging us to move along, and most of the other visitors had already scattered. I found it hard to take my eyes away. Both these things were just a few rough scrapes in the rock, but between them lay a world of difference. Finally a brilliant, violet branch of lightning streaked to the ground on the far side of the ravine, followed almost immediately by a deafening clap of thunder. Florence jumped, emitted a strange little yip, and we all ran helter-skelter for our cars.

It rained intermittently through the night, but disturbed weather was not enough to put me off my stride. Phase three of my plan was, as I saw it, the clincher. By now Jany was suitably softened up, terrified she was going to spend the rest of her days in some lonely and desolate place. When she saw Ganagobie, a Benedictine abbey perched 1,200 feet above the Durance River on a sheer-sided plateau in Haute Provence, it wouldn't seem so bad at all. After the last couple of days it would look like a thriving metropolis, and make buying a house in a similarly quiet place a cakewalk.

Heavenward we climbed, leaving fruit-orchards and olive groves in the valley below. The road was steep and narrow. There were dozens of hair-pin bends and spots where the roadside fell away to nothing. At the top we finally parked and walked on a stone-cobbled path through the forest. We rounded a corner and the walls of the abbey of Notre-Dame-de-Ganagobie came into sight. We might have expected it to resemble the primitive chapel at Lure or the half-ruined priory of Carluc. But it didn't look like either of them. It had a stone-sculpted façade that took my breath away. It was flanked by well maintained buildings. It was surrounded by neatly kept vegetable plots and rows of fragrant lavender. It was inhabited.

I gazed on. Like all Provençal Romanesque buildings, Ganagobie's church gave an impression of squat, almost fortress-like solidity. Apart from the single, large glass oculus sitting high over the entrance there were few openings. It was the tall arched entrance-porch itself, as ornate and decorative as the rest of the façade was plain, that was the star attraction here.

A triple series of recessed stone arches ran high above the church's stout wooden doors. Twelve apostles sheltered beneath a row of arcades carved into the doors' stone lintel. Seven hundred years ago their sculptor had tilted their bearded heads at different angles, trying to give each face its own personality. The apostles lacked the gravity a later and more sophisticated renaissance sculptor might have given them – they looked quizzically out at the world like Snow White's dwarves. But they gave the doorway a life of its own.

So, too, did the figure of Christ in Majesty, carved into the large central space between the door and its arches. I am not one of the faithful, and haven't been since spending long, tortuous Sundays on my knees in Anglican school church services. But you didn't have to be a devoted Christian to appreciate the serene figure, enveloped in a transparent and bubble-like orb, floating weightlessly up there in the heavens. He was not alone. Surrounded by an ox, a winged man, an eagle and a lion – the symbols of the four evangelists – Ganagobie's stone-carved Christ ruled over this lonely place in splendid repose.

Apart from the celestial company there did not appear to be a soul about. Behind the abbey we wandered down a long, tree-bordered alley that ended in a tall white cross. Beyond the cross was nothing at all – it marked the edge of the plateau and a sheer fall a thousand feet to the Durance River far below. We stood for a minute or two, looking down at miniature fields, toy cars on tiny roads, children's building-block villages huddled below. They were too far down, too distant to be disturbing or even to seem entirely real. This is it, I thought. Old stone, shady trees, peace and quiet, a gorgeous view – if I were a real-estate high-roller, this is what I would have gone for. Location, location, location ... Christ in Majesty had ended up with a prime site. The movers and shakers always do.

A bell began tolling from somewhere in the abbey. Even it was softer and more discreet than our brash village bell. We walked back to the church and were admiring the entrance-way once again when Jany stopped me. Behind the door she heard singing. It was faint but clear, a continuous rising and falling of unaccompanied voices.

'Gregorian chant,' she whispered as she laid her ear to the door's keyhole. 'They're singing psalms.' Then she began sniffing, her brows knit in concentration. In a second she had her nose where her ear had been, and was pulling in great lungfuls of air. 'Smoke,' she whispered more forcefully. 'They're burning incense.'

I nudged Jany aside. I couldn't see anything through the keyhole. But she was right. Clear, haunting musical voices were penetrating the door. Over the musty church-smell of stone and old prayer books that I could smell through the keyhole floated an odour of burning gums and essences. Jany gently pushed me away and replaced her own head. She was as captivated by it all as I was. For a few moments more we stood there, waists bent, taking turns at the little aperture.

But the heavens seemed determined not to leave us alone. For the third time in two days, as if on cue, it began to rain. It fell hesitantly at first, then harder and with more insistence, heavy drops of water bouncing up from the flagstones. We abandoned the great arched doorway, the keyhole, the bells and the smells, and raced for the car. By the time we got there we were soaked to the skin.

〜

'I'm not going. And that's final.'

Despite all my efforts, Jany turned out to be less than thrilled with my idea of a retreat at the monastery of Ganagobie. I had done my best, used all my wile to make the place appear civilised, sociable, lively – all the things she looked for in any residence. And in fact it wasn't the isolation of the place that finally led her to telling me that if I wanted to stay there I would have to stay there on my own. Jany was a convinced proponent of women's rights. And the monastery's policy on women, she said, made her just a little bit angry with monkish living arrangements.

'But women are welcome at Ganagobie,' I told her as we sat over dinner at home. 'This isn't the Middle Ages any more, you know.'

'Well, then, why aren't they allowed in the cloisters?' She gestured rhetorically with outspread arms, calling up the spectre of broad stone arcades in our little kitchen. 'Why can't women eat with the monks in the refectory? Why are they relegated to their own separate dining room outside the monastery walls? Medieval women were second-class women, and up there they still seem to be.'

I tried to picture Jany observing the strict Benedictine rule of silence at all meals. How could she eat, I was tempted to ask, if the only known way of silencing her was by tying her hands? It would be impractical – I would have to spoon-feed her – and look pretty silly besides. But I was growing wise, and held my tongue. And so in the end I phoned back to the *Père Hôtelier*, the monk in charge of monastery accommodation, and arranged just a single place at Ganagobie.

Jany wouldn't come to Ganagobie, but I did manage to persuade her to visit Silvacane with me. A Cistercian, rather than Benedictine abbey, it lay just twenty minutes from Aix. The real difference, though, was that Silvacane, once among the greatest monasteries of Provence, was no longer inhabited. I thought that a short tour of inspection, a sort of dry-run in a monkless monastery, would be a good idea. For, frankly, I was getting just a titch nervous. Perhaps I'd been too easily seduced by big views and a bit of quiet. I'd read *The Name of the Rose* – medieval monasteries can hold unexpected surprises. I was not quite sure what I had got myself into.

But as we drove up to it Silvacane did not appear threatening at all. On the contrary. With the Luberon hills blocking its northern horizon, the church lay on the outskirts of La Roque d'Anthéron, a village that in summer hosts a well-known festival of classical music. Silvacane itself is used for some of the more prestigious recitals. Here on the edge of Peter Mayle country the surroundings looked rather cushy and well-manicured. Even the neat rows of truffle-oaks in front of the abbey suggested that behind a simple exterior opulent treasures lay.

Things had not always looked this way. In the great age of medieval church-building begun by Saint Mayeul local architects had turned for inspiration to the old Roman remains – temples, arenas, amphitheatres, whole towns, even – that lay scattered about the region. Provence, in fact, had more examples to encourage the development of the Romanesque than anywhere outside Italy. To their window-less, fortress-like churches Provençal builders added the features of a rediscovered classical age. They transformed the atrium, the central feature of the Roman villa, into church cloisters. They appropriated geometrical and floral themes from pagan temple-columns for their own Christian church-columns. Even their glorious church porches were adaptations, entranceways harking back to the bellicose triumphal arches of Roman antiquity.

But the monks of Provence demanded one thing of their architecture that Roman civilisation never did – isolation. In their search for solitary and uninterrupted communion with the divine, the monastic orders sought the most remote corners of the country. And during the medieval age there had in fact been little to tempt erring monks at Silvacane.

As its Latin name *Silva Cana*, the forest of reeds, suggests, the monastery had once lain out in wild and inaccessible marshland.

It might be more enticing now, but not even the draining of the swamps and encroachment by famous concert pianists could hide the original austerity of the abbey. Once we had passed the ticket office, Silvacane proved as simple and unadorned inside as out, a jewel of precision-cut masonry that had changed little since it was first inhabited in the 1100s.

Where was the ornamentation, the carved decoration, the statuary usually devoted to religious glorification? We wandered from one vast, vaulted room to another. We gazed about a great, empty rib-vaulted church where spears of sunlight came shafting down through the narrowest of windows. We walked around the thick, solid walls of the cloisters. We stood in a long, high-ceilinged stone dormitory where monks once slept unheated and fully clothed on straw ticking. There was nothing to entertain the eye, nothing to provide variety or lead the attention onwards. Everything was stark and clean and untrammelled – I had never seen anything quite as visually frugal.

Like most people, I associated southern Europe with riots of Baroque fantasy, the sort of indulgence that had briefly inspired the young Cézanne. There wasn't much of anything for the physical senses to work on here. Why was this place so different? In the Monk's Room, a six-columned chamber once devoted to the copying of manuscripts, we sat on a window sill and looked for an explanation in an abbey brochure.

At the heart of the austere Cistercian abbeys of Provence, it seemed, had lain revolt, a 12th-century rebellion against moral slippage and soft living – even back then the Midi had been susceptible to that sort of thing. Remonstration was in order. The only solution to the church's growing taste for luxury, abbots were told, was a return to the old austerity. Five hundred years earlier St Benedict had written his famous Rule setting out the ideal conduct of monks. It was time to get back to it. Only by living in isolation, poverty and simplicity, Benedict had said, could they find God. His advice extended to every aspect of monastic life – even its architecture. Buildings should reflect spiritual purity; there should be no comforts, no visual temptations, no decoration to distract monks from a strict regime of prayer, study and work. Hence these bare and unadorned walls.

To me it all sounded like one of the more vicious boarding schools of my youth. The extraordinary thing, I thought as we wandered on, was that such spiritual rigour had produced such seductive architecture. 'Like the layout, the architecture is simple and stark. It was not designed to please and its simplicity makes no concessions,' the brochure sternly enthused. 'Its beauty results from the vigour of the proportions alone, from the harmony of its forms, from the perfection of its stonework and the way the light falls through rare openings.'

And it was true. The monastery was lovely, in a spartan

sort of way. If only life there had not been so dire. Silvacane did nothing at all to reassure me and I was more worried than ever. What if all through these centuries the monks in Haute Provence had maintained their medieval rigour? I didn't think that sleeping semi-refrigerated and fully clothed on an itchy straw bed would really suit me. With or without Jany, I suddenly wondered as we emerged outdoors into the warm sun, how was I going to make it through the next week?

⌒

It was late afternoon when I arrived at Ganagobie, and once again there was not a soul about. Around the corner from the church I found a heavy door set into high stone walls, and tugged tentatively at a metal bell-pull. Far inside I heard a faint tinkling.

The man who opened the door was my worst imaginings brought to life. He was elderly, in his late seventies perhaps, but straight-backed and strongly built. He was wearing a thick and voluminous black robe that had ample sleeves, a hem that nearly touched the ground and a pointed hood that hung downwards from his nape. Whisps of white hair clung to the sides of the monk's bald dome. His brows were massive and craggy, his nose hawk-like, his deeply recessed, slightly bloodshot eyes sharp and penetrating. He was an altogether formidable-looking character, and he spooked me.

But all anxiety dropped away the minute he spoke. The sub-prior was a gentle and kindly man and I grew to admire him. I can't say that we spoke a good deal during my stay, for at Ganagobie words are rare and dispensed with economy. But I liked the sub-prior immediately. He welcomed me to the monastery, then padded away on sandled feet to fetch the *Père Hôtelier*.

Ganagobie's *Père Hôtelier* was fifteen years younger, and possessed a brisk energy that made his robe swish when he walked. He led me up stone steps to an upper floor and a long corridor. 'The Baptism of Christ' ... 'The Presentation of Jesus' ... each door was labelled with a name. Just two others were occupied at the moment. My own room, when we halted in front of it, was 'The Transfiguration'. Behind the door I pictured a dark, damp hole with a tiny window and a flickering candle.

But the place I was shown into was no medieval monk's cell. It was comfortable, light-filled and airy. There was no straw ticking, but a perfectly normal bed on a floor of cheerful red terracotta tiles. This was cosier than the average French small-town hotel room. Only a Christ-figure cast in copper, ribs pinched and head lolling as it hung on the wall over the bed, reminded me of where I was. In a once most-Christian country such things are now hardly ever seen.

I confessed to the *Père Hôtelier* that I was a little nervous – I hadn't the faintest idea of procedure. He waved his hand, and with that puffing of the cheeks and purse-lipped expelling of air that in France signifies the total insignificance of the matter at hand, dismissed procedure entirely.

'*Laissez-vous aller*,' he said – let yourself go. There were no special schedules, requirements or activities here. Apart from the daily prayers and meals, one's time was one's one own. A few simple guidelines, the *Père Hôtelier* said on taking his leave, were laid out on a list on the desk.

I stood by the window for a minute or two after the monk had gone. It gave onto the monastery's inner courtyard, a large quadrangle that was part flower garden and part vegetable plot. There were gnarled almond trees, very old and much cut back; a heavily-laden fig tree growing out of a stone wall; rosebushes whose petals were now faded and dropping to the ground; ripening grapevines; a patch of plump and bright yellow melons. I could not imagine a more peaceful prospect – I was not surprised to see even the flame-shaped cypress trees and staked tomato-plants of my dreams. Beyond the quadrangle, shimmering across the river in the summer sun, was a panorama of the broad Valensole plateau with the high Alps rising behind. The view was divine.

I turned my attention to a typed page of house rules. First were the daily prayer offices and their different times: Vigils at 5 a.m.; Laudes at 7; Tierce at 9; Sext at noon; Nones at 1:30; Vespers at 5:30; Compline at 8. Then I was reminded that the *Père Hôtelier* was there for all my needs, spiritual, confessional, and material. Otherwise, communication with the monks was not encouraged. 'Silence,' I was admonished, 'facilitates the search for God. It aids in prayer, work and rest.' Underlined in heavy ink was the monastic convention that

Meals are taken in Silence. Apart from a short recreation-period following the noon meal, even talking to other retreat-takers was discouraged.

I could see that the art of *laisser-aller* at Ganagobie was perhaps not quite as uninhibited as the *Père Hôtelier's* puffed cheeks had implied. These precepts, however, were nothing compared to the injunctions of the Rule of Saint Benedict, a small volume that also sat on the desk.

Benedict had covered pretty well all the bases. Apart from Prayer and the Keeping of Silence by monks, the subjects treated included Humility (essential), Daily Work (required), Hospitality to Guests (mandatory), Monks in the Dormitory (one per bed and a lamp always lit), Clothing (two sets, the cheapest), How Much to Eat (two cooked dishes a day, no meat except for the sick), How Much to Drink (up to half a bottle of wine a day), Coming to Table Late (most inadvisable), and the ominous-sounding Monks Who Will Not Mend Their Ways. By the time I had finished glancing over the Rule I was feeling spooked again, and hesitant to set foot outside my room. But it was time to go to Vespers.

Clutching a Liturgy of Hours, I met my fellow retreaters on the way down the stairs. There were two other men and four women. Saying nothing but merely nodding greetings, I followed them outside, along the stone path between the monastery and its exterior garden, and around the corner to the church. The doors were open now and we filed from bright sunshine into the gloom inside.

In the 12th century the church interior would have been bright and colourful, its walls covered with frescoes, its slender windows fitted with stained glass, its floor covered with mosaics. And even today whimsical griffins, caparisoned elephants and two-headed birds danced across the mosaic floor of the chancel. But after Ganagobie's partial destruction during the French Revolution not even the best artisans had attempted to restore it fully. As my eyes adjusted to candlelight I discovered a church interior that was now every bit as sober as Silvacane's.

The focus of attention, the altar, was a simple, slab-like table of stone. Everything else, from the arches of the high, narrow nave to the vault of a chapel facing east to Jerusalem, was equally austere. The church walls were naked grey blocks of stone. A large wooden crucifix hung suspended from a chain by the altar. A carved Madonna and Child sat mounted on the wall in the transept. And that was about it for decoration. Ganagobie was beautiful, but it was severely beautiful. What was going to hold my attention, I wondered a bit desperately, through endless hours of prayers in the days to come?

The answer arrived through a door to the adjoining cloisters, fourteen black-robed monks walking slowly and ceremonially into church in double file. We rose. One of them seized a long, heavy rope that hung from the ceiling and waited, glancing at his watch. At 5:30 precisely he began heaving energetically – from inside the church the bell ringing above the roof sounded faint and muffled.

There were a few younger monks, but most of the men who emerged through the door looked ancient. They didn't need tonsures – they had precious little hair about their heads anyway. Deliberate and unhurried, moving with the dignity of their office and the accustomed habit of their years, they took their places in the simple wooden choir-stalls before the high altar.

Only one of the company stood out. One young man had hair growing over his ears and collar, and was dressed in green corduroys and a blue nylon anorak. He looked completely out of place. He was, I supposed, a postulant, an apprentice-monk undergoing a trial period before committing himself in earnest. And a good thing, too. Nobody, but nobody, I thought, thinking of the self-denial of these men, should take up monastic life without a little reflection. Of course the door is never locked, but in some ways monasticism is like the IRA, the Mafia, or the Foreign Legion – it's harder getting out than it is getting in.

The service began. It was conducted almost entirely in chant, with very few spoken words at all. Solo and collective voices alternated. One monk, a tall, thin, ascetic-looking man with a heavy gold cross hanging from his neck, would sing a line or two. The rest of the monks would join in, their pitch rising and falling. It was like following the progress of a band of travellers moving through desolate and uneven country. They might have been travelling over the landscape of Ganagobie itself. For a moment or two the voices would hold steady as they traversed a high, monotonous plateau; the next they would drop without warning into some deep, uninhabited gorge. Eventually they would climb out the other side, ready to cross the next desolate stretch of highland. It seemed lonely and solitary stuff. Each monk in the end was singing not for the other or for the benefit of our tiny congregation, but for an invisible and divine audience of One.

It took me a little while to find my place in the Liturgy, but when I did I cannot say I understood a great deal more. The French words, if not incomprehensible, had nothing of the reassuring Anglican heartiness of the hymns of my boyhood.

> *It is You, God, who tested us.*
> *You refined us as one refines a metal.*
> *You led us into a trap.*
> *You tightened a vice on our hearts.*
> *You gave us mere mortals to lead us.*
> *We went through water and through fire.*
> *You led us out towards abundance.*
> *I come to your house with troubles.*
> *I will keep my promises to you,*
> *The promises which opened my lips,*
> *The promises which my mouth made in my distress.*

What kind of lyrics were those? On and on it went. There was no resolution, no resounding climax, no crescendo of

Christians marching victoriously to triumph. There was just an interminable progression that rose and fell, fell and rose, leading to some distant, unknown place that never seemed to get any closer.

If the lyrics failed to warm, the physical act of praying certainly did. It was like callisthenics. Our tiny congregation in the pews followed the lead of the monks in the stalls. One moment we were standing, the next kneeling, then sitting, and a few seconds later bowing in supplication. It was a demanding rhythm. The bowing, especially, was tough. It was no mere lowering of the head and shoulders, but a full, sustained body-bend from the waist that kept the trunk parallel to the floor. I'd had gym teachers who demanded less. The elderly monks were in far better shape than I'd imagined.

The obvious benefit of this workout was that it kept everyone moving and awake. For after a few minutes chanting psalms seemed like sitting in a running car with the garage-door closed. The brain fogged over and the eyes went glassy. It seemed to go on forever, yet when I looked at my watch I was astonished to see that scarcely half an hour had passed.

The service ended with the sub-prior lighting a censer. Around and around he swung it on its chain in expanding orbits, the rush of air through its holed silver body causing it exude ever-thicker clouds of billowing white fragrance. Once it was going the craggy-browed cleric wafted the censer around the monks, then swung it some more around our little herd of retreaters. When holy smoke had well and truly suffused the church and its supplicants, the sub-prior made one last, low obeisance to the altar. The monks filed out, the candles were extinguished, and Vespers was over.

~

A minute or two before dinner the *Père Hôtelier* met his three male charges, as convened, at the bottom of the stairs and led us through the abbey doors. The women had disappeared into some nether-region on the outer monastery walls to eat on their own. We crossed the inner courtyard past rosebushes and cypress trees, then plunged into the stone-carved innards of the monastery. There were long, dim, flagged hallways, twists and turns to left and right, stone stairways leading up and down. Finally we were in the cloisters in the heart of the abbey.

It was a beautiful place. Beneath broad barrel-vaults bordered by columned arcades was some of the decoration so conspicuously absent elsewhere. Little faces of fanged beasts and bearded men peered down at us. The capitals on the arcade's columns were sculpted into intricate flowering petals. The columns receded down the sides of the cloisters in an alternate series of doubled and quadrupled groups, an ornate geometry that was decoration in itself. In the middle of the cloisters and open to the sky lay a lawn of green grass, a deep well of water, and sweet-smelling bushes of rosemary and thyme.

I had a little while to take this all in, for as the other two retreat-takers continued on into the refectory, the *Père Hôtelier* took me aside. If I wouldn't mind waiting, he said, there was a small ceremony arranged for each new arrival at the monastery. In a minute the tall, thin monk with the heavy gold cross arrived. He had the look of a man used to bearing heavy responsibilities. This was Père Abbé René de Lacheisserie, the abbot of Ganagobie.

He shook my hand, bid me welcome, and was handed a silver pitcher by the monk in attendance behind him. While the second monk held a wide bowl beneath them, the abbot poured a high stream of cold water from the pitcher. I washed my hands, then dried them on the cloth he proffered. Fifteen hundred years after the writing of the Rule, Benedict's injunction, a ritual of water to welcome tired and dusty travellers, was still intact. I tried to recollect any other symbolic display of hospitality that old, but couldn't.

We continued on into the refectory. It was a vast stone hall, chilly even in summer, its clustered columns rising to arches thirty feet above our heads. I joined my companions at a table in the middle of the room, while the monks filed in and took seats at long tables ranged around its edges. Finally the abbot, the prior and sub-prior assumed their places at a head table. Why the abbot's central place-setting included a wooden gavel I don't know, for I never saw him use it. I wouldn't have been surprised to learn it was kept for the rare, ritual dressing-down of Monks Who Will Not Mend Their Ways.

There was a long dinner prayer and we then all crossed ourselves and sat down. Each monk unrolled a large white napkin and tucked a corner of it around his throat. Set against the black of their robes these diamonds of bright white somehow made the dim medieval hall seem even more medieval. Then we set to eating.

I glanced at my two fellow retreat-takers as they passed a basket of bread. Already I knew their backs well; I'd been sitting behind them in church. But this was the first time I'd had a chance to look at their faces. They seemed to form a pair of opposites.

Ariel – I could read his name from the small slip of paper inserted in his napkin ring – was middle-aged and distin-guished-looking. He was dressed in expensive, perfectly ironed clothes. Sparely built, his features were fine and his manner fastidious. He broke his bread delicately. None of this finesse, though, managed to conceal an infinite sadness that seemed to well up from some great reservoir deep inside and immerse him. Occasionally I would catch an unguarded look on his face, a gaze so sightless and sorrowful that one could only imagine that Ariel continued to live vividly on in some overwhelming tragedy of the past.

I strained to read the name of the younger man across the table. Emmanuel was about thirty. He had a blunt potato-face and a ragged, self-inflicted haircut that only drew atten-tion to his prematurely balding head. He wore an unravelling hand-knit sweater, trousers bagged at the knees and scuffed

284

trainers. His clothing matched his tired, travel-worn manner. He had the look of someone who is constantly on the move. Ariel and Emmanuel – by chance both names were biblical, and I don't know why, but it wasn't long before I was thinking of them as some sort of heavenly pair. It was as if they were divine visitors, temporary residents from some lower order of flawed angels come to redeem themselves.

A fanciful idea? Undoubtedly. But when you find yourself isolated in a monastery on a remote mountain plateau, when you cannot seek a word of explanation for anything, when you are surrounded by aged, silent men in black robes with pointed hoods and white-diamond fronts – well, then, it is easy to imagine anything at all.

There was no further time for reflection, for it was hard to keep up with the monks. I was surprised at the speed with which these elderly men dispatched each dinner-course set before them. They were downright spritely – they hardly seemed the same individuals who just an hour before, heedless of the passage of earthly time, had proceeded through the slow, celestial observances of Vespers.

No sooner were bowls and platters of food brought out from the kitchen than they were divided, dished up and devoured. There was nothing sparse or meagre here. There were steaming tureens of thick and hearty soup, salads of fresh vegetables from the monastery gardens, a *gratin dauphinois* of creamy baked cheese and potatoes; a savoury *ratatouille*, cake and fresh fruit for desert. Each was excellent.

Each was rapidly eaten. There was not even the time to set spoon or fork down between mouthfuls.

It seemed a pity to polish it all off with such haste. But this, too, was part of Benedict's monastic regime. If the architecture of Silvacane was not intended to please, neither was the food of Ganagobie. There is nothing more shameful in any Christian, the saint had emphasised in his Rule, than an excessive fondness for food – it should not be savoured or lingered over but regarded by monks as mere sustenance.

Like the architecture of Silvacane, however, it was too good not to appreciate. The wine was also good, and we tucked into that too, serving ourselves from bottles set on the table. Mahatma Gandhi, I remembered, used to repeatedly test his ascetic's power of resistance by having young women sleep with him in his bed. Was this a Benedictine equivalent, laying on a delectable spread and then defying diners not to enjoy it, or at least not to enjoy it too much? Only in France, I reckoned, could such a test be devised.

Even more surprising than the speed of the meal was the edification that came with it. Apart from an occasional scraping of spoon on soup bowl, not a sound escaped the dining monks. But far down at the end of the refectory, at a desk fitted with a shaded reading lamp, a monk sat before an open tome. He read in *recto tono*, yet another monastic voice-style – instead of rising and falling like the chant of the offices, *recto tono* pursued a steady monotone. The words were spaced regularly and wholly devoid of any inflection or emotion – it sounded a bit like my computer's voice program.

It wasn't a style that suited the evening's reading, a dramatic history of 20th-century Christian martyrdom. Suddenly there were Belgian nuns being raped by Congolese rebels, Russian patriarchs being burned alive in monasteries by Red Army commissars, Spanish priests being shot by Republican anarchists against the very doors of their own churches. As the monks worked their enthusiastic way through one dish after another, we listened to horrific accounts of slaughter, torture and butchery, the whole intoned without the slightest flicker of feeling.

It was a strange meal. I was happy the wine was there in good supply, for it made things a little more cheerful. When dinner was over – the entire affair took little more than twenty minutes – we rose, said another prayer of thanksgiving, crossed ourselves and filed out.

Twilight was falling as the retreat-takers gathered outside the great doors for Compline, the last office of the day. It was dim now in the church as we entered ten minutes before the service, and I heard, before I saw, the monks praying in their stalls. As if prayers seven times a day were not enough, they had come in early for a little additional adoration.

'*Je vous salue, Marie.*' Hail Mary, full of grace, the abbot intoned.

Hail Mary, mother of God, came the response from the gathered monks.

The exchange was repeated with slight variations countless times, the invocation slowly turning from words with meaning into a sort of hypnotic mantra. Eventually a great silence descended upon the church, and for a long while the monks remained on their knees in mute contemplation. A complete and utter lack of sound is rare enough when you are on your own; when you are in close proximity to twenty other people total silence is really remarkable. When not a chair creaks, not a throat is cleared, not a breath of wind sighs outside, when both men and the world around them temporarily come to a complete halt, silence becomes its own message.

I had never heard such quiet, and when the Compline service began it seemed almost festive, a return to a world that was human and sociable. The chant, the prayers, the repeated standing and kneeling were as solitary and remote as Vespers had been. But the evening ended with a gathering that celebrated not eternity, but the living community of monks.

When the last chant was over, the last prayer uttered, the monks left their stalls and congregated around the wooden sculpture of the Madonna and Child. All lights were switched off, all candles except the votive offerings beneath the Madonna extinguished. Together, their faces lit in flickering light, the monks sang *Salve Maria*, a simple, moving Latin hymn dedicated to the Virgin. And this time the monks really sang together, each one no longer out on some lonely quest of the infinite, but happy to share the other's company. It was almost as if they were relaxing together after a hard day's work – it was what other men do over a beer in a bar before heading home.

When the *Salve Maria* was finished the abbot walked among the monks, dipping an aspergillum, a spoon-sized sprinkler, into a small silver pail as he went. With each flick of his wrist the monks were blessed with a light dousing of holy water. The retreat-takers, too, were showered. Then a monk seized the rope hanging from the ceiling and tolled the bell three times as his fellows filed silently out. The day at Ganagobie was over.

I had set my alarm for 4:30 and the next morning slept through it without hearing a thing. It was still dark and cold when I got up an hour and a half later, and looking out of the window I could see monks with their hoods over their heads and hands pushed deep into their sleeves for warmth. Flitting silently like shadows across the courtyard, they looked more unearthly than ever.

Pre-dawn is not my best time of day, and I was feeling fairly unearthly myself. I struggled into clothing and tried to wake up over a sinkful of cold water. I was worried. What fate lay in store for miserable retreat-takers who had missed Vigils? Would the Abbot strike his gavel on the table at the next meal and in the deadly quiet point his long, bony finger at me?

He would not. On the stairs on the way out I met other backsliders who were yawning as sleepily as I was. They didn't look worried. The Benedictines are a tolerant lot. The monks themselves never miss their 5 a.m. rendezvous with the everlasting, but happily excuse less diligent visitors from the outside world who do.

Laudes at 7 o'clock was a different story. If you didn't make it over the cold cobbles, past the dew-drenched rows of lavender and into church as the morning sun broke the horizon you didn't get breakfast. As soon as the chanting, kneeling and semi-prostrations were over we were lead straight through the cloisters door and into the refectory for breakfast. The monks had eaten long before. We drank our café au lait and buttered our baguettes alone but in the same monkish silence. The rule of silence works wonders for table manners – unable to talk, we filled the hushed void with grave attention to the passing of jam.

Tierce came and went at 9 o'clock; Sext at noon; Nones at 1:30. There seemed barely a moment when we had not just emerged from the dim, echoing church or were preparing to enter it again. There was little time for anything else – prayer was the pivot around which each small remaining portion of the day turned.

And what of prayer itself? As the voices continued to rise and fall at each service like some endless, unhurried tide, I spent most of my time trying to reason things through.

Here were a group of men, dedicated, disciplined, and

intelligent, who had voluntarily cut themselves off from the ambitions and satisfactions of the outside world. They spent their time instead in prayer and contemplation, giving their lives to communion with a divine, omnipotent being. There is nothing, Benedict wrote in his Rule, that a monk should prefer to prayer. Even manual and intellectual work, accomplished in silence, is an extension of prayer.

In theory, at least, I could understand that. It was a bit like Paul Cézanne's perception that, beneath life's ephemeral and constantly changing surface a truer, more permanent reality lay hidden. If only one looked a little harder, carried on past the shallow and fleeting things of ordinary existence, one might find an organised and harmonious universe. What Cézanne sought with his geometry of volumes and correlations of colour the monks sought through prayer.

My only problem was believing it all. Cézanne's universe made some sense to me. But an omnipotent, all-knowing, divine being who had looked out over the world and its affairs since the day he created it? My non-belief made prayer pointless, turned the chanting, the censer-swinging and scattering of holy water into so much hocus-pocus.

The lunch that followed Nones I could understand much better. Though just as hasty, it was even more impressive than the previous evening's dinner. There was an entrée of dried sausage, cherry tomatoes and black olives. There were platters of ham-hocks drenched in a mushroom sauce where whole cloves of garlic, cooked through and sweet, floated about. There was chard baked in a rich béchamel; cheese, bread and wine; ice cream and pastry sprinkled with pistachio nuts. So when lunch was over and the *Père Hôtelier* led us into the outer monastery garden for our half-hour talk-and-recreation period, I asked him if the food was always as good.

He admitted it was. Not so long ago, he recalled as he poured espresso for us, it had been even better. Had I noticed, he asked me, the big monk with the bushy black beard at the end of the choir-stalls? I had – he was a large, stout Friar-Tuck sort of monk. Well, before he'd taken monastic orders, the *Père Hôtelier* said, he had been a well-known *bon vivant* in his native Lyon, the nation's gastronomic capital – he had wined and dined, hobnobbed and cooked with Paul Bocuse, the Troisgros brothers and other celebrity chefs. Of course when he arrived at Ganagobie he had immediately taken over the kitchen. Within weeks his use of the finest ingredients available had not only spoiled the monks but exhausted the monastery's kitchen budget. With regret the abbot had moved him on to less extravagant duties. Still, the *Père Hôtelier* smiled and sighed in fond remembrance, it had been good while it lasted.

I tried to imagine high-class gastronomy eaten in total silence and record time, and was about to ask the *Père Hôtelier* to describe it. But my ragged-sweatered co-retreater Emmanuel, who was drinking coffee beside me, moved the conversation to higher planes.

The food on the pilgrim trail to Santiago de Compostela had been good, too, he said. After trudging day after day in a hot sun anything tasted good.

Had I ever made the pilgrimage, he asked? I admitted I hadn't. If I ever got the call I should certainly do so, Emmanual admonished. He had got the call, and immediately dropped everything to spend two months walking fifteen miles a day to the coast of north-west Spain. Emmanuel seemed as busy as a receptionist – he often received calls, he told me, and he found it advisable to act on them. As long as he prayed hard, listened diligently and took the advice offered, life went well; the minute he let up, evil began its work and things went wrong.

So began a series of post-lunch conversations that took me on zigzag spiritual paths across half of Europe. Emmanuel was a kind of full-time retreat groupie. He had spent years moving from one monastery to another. Apart from his own labour he had nothing to offer the monks in return for living and praying with them. He was penniless and he was homeless. Directionless, though, he was not. He never stayed in any one monastery long, but moved on whenever and wherever his spiritual counsel advised.

He was a living monastery-directory; he could tell you about the Benedictines and the Franciscans, the Cistercians and Dominicans, the Jesuits, Trappists, Carmelites and Carthusians. Some were gentle and friendly. Others were so fiercely dedicated, he avowed, that merely to think of them gave him goose-bumps. He had stayed with fundamental-ist monks in northern Provence who were just waiting for a chance to change the modern world – for them the holy Crusades were not simply memories of the past. There were other monasteries that denied the existence of the modern world altogether – he had herded goats in the Ardèche hills with monks who rejected electricity, running water and every other convenience. With its welcoming, humanist outlook, Ganagobie rated high on Emmanuel's monastic league-table. Whatever its ideology, though, Emmanuel knew his resting-place was not here. He was waiting for the Word. God knew, he said, when and where he would finally settle down.

Was Emmanuel a crackpot, a religious eccentric unable to cope with the demands of daily life? Perhaps he was. But in his restless, down-at-heel way he was a relatively happy crackpot, and oddly self-reliant. Nor was he without prec-edent. In the Middle Ages wandering mendicants, itinerant friars who lived solely by the giving of religious alms, were a regular part of the rural landscape.

And who, finally, was to say if Emmanuel was any worse off than his opposite, Ariel? In his erratic and temporising existence, every day was for Emmanuel a new day rich with possibility. Ariel, on the other hand, despite his success and wealth – he revealed at one break that he was a company director – seemed irretrievably stuck in some sad past. In a monastery one prays but one does not pry, and I never did find out what had set either man on his path in life. It didn't matter. What counted was the present moment and the safe refuge, unchanging from day to day, that lay high over the Durance River.

⌒

Time passed, the bells rang the hours, and very soon each day at Ganagobie began to resemble the last. Like prayers endlessly repeated with only the smallest variations, they gradually lost their significance as separate units. That, perhaps, is the purpose of monastic life – a slow melting away until all things fuse into a larger existence. Only the small details distinguished life's progress.

Without a word on their part, I began to discern character traits among the men in the black robes. Talk, any monk will be the first to tell you, is not the only tool to learn by. I got to know these men by their facial expressions instead, by their gestures, posture, and eating habits. There were some monks who remained as cool and removed as distant planets. There were others, like the small, bespectacled monk who served food and cleared the tables, whose engagement was total – his face was so bright and beaming as he went about his work you envied him his tasks.

I became more familiar, too, with the routine of meals, and the pace at which they were eaten. I also began enjoying the *recto tono* readings that accompanied them. After a day or two of 20th century Christian martyrs we moved on to a life of Vauban. Not only was Sébastien de Vauban a pious

295

Christian, and so a suitable subject for refectory readings; he was also Louis XIV's brilliant chief military architect and one of the greatest engineers in French history. He brought a bit of life and excitement to meals. There is nothing like rapidly demolishing a light-as-a-feather soufflé while at the same time learning the kind of embrasure-construction that permits you to pour withering cannon-fire down on your foes. I think the monks enjoyed it, too.

I even did a little constructive work myself – tiring of meditative strolls about the plateau each afternoon in the break after lunch, I joined Emmanuel in tending the sub-prior's rose garden in the monastery courtyard. Roses have now joined tomato vines and cypresses on the list of plants growing outside my fantasy house.

All these things gave me some satisfaction. Day after day, though, there was one activity I remained entirely incapable of getting my mind around. It was the main business, the sole concern, really, of the monks of Ganagobie – prayer.

It came to a head at Sunday Mass. It was a service at which for the first time the young postulant finally appeared among the other monks as one of them. Gone was the blue anorak and the hair over the ears – in their place were the long black robe of the Benedictines and a newly-shaved, prickly-looking scalp.

The young man's admittance to the order was almost a public event, for Sunday Mass is the one service of the week when Ganagobie is open to churchgoers ascending from the lay world below. After days of perfect peace the church grew crowded and noisy, the pews packed with strangers, the air full of uncustomary coughs and conversations.

Along with other churchgoers a Catholic school-group of a dozen or so teenagers arrived and installed themselves. From the moment that three of the schoolgirls, obviously close friends, took places directly in front of me I could see that, ecclesiastically speaking, they were trouble. No god-fearing monk under the age of eighty would want to be left alone in a room with any one of them. They were only fourteen or fifteen years old, but already well-developed young women. They might have been dimly unaware in every other department, but in the company of their male adolescent schoolmates they were entirely conscious of the gazes they attracted and the kind of power they pulled – if you'd put them in pig-tails and given them sunglasses and lollipops they could not have been more Lolita-like. They were sexy, they were brazen, and on this Sunday morning in church they were bored out of their minds.

They started playing up the moment the Abbot, dressed for Mass in a white alb and embroidered green stole, came through the church doors swinging his silver censer. The congregation rose to its feet as the abbot paced down the aisle towards the altar. He was followed by the *Père Hôtelier* holding a large, leather-bound bible above his head, then by a double file of chanting monks. Monastic decorum was at its peak, liturgical observance at its most dignified. But as the

Abbot passed by, the girls began giggling and twittering, and once they had the attention of the boys on the other side of the aisle there was no stopping them.

They blew large pink bubbles of chewing-gum, snapped the shoulder-straps of each other's brassieres, twirled their gold-chained crucifixes about on nail-varnished fingers. They were being as provocative as they possibly could – there is nothing for tweaking adolescent rebellion like the taboos of a stern and forbidding church. By the time the girls got to the point in the service where monks and congregation began deep prolonged bows, they were wiggling their bottoms high in the air. It all worked miraculously – the boys opposite were just about ready to start a church riot.

I was working up to a fit myself, for after even just a few days retreat-takers begin to feel part of a small and intimate community. Who were these booty-shaking hussies to invade the tranquillity of Ganagobie? They made go-go dancers in Brazilian thongs look discreet. Just as I was about to lean forward and tell the girls to quit goofing around, I was halted by looking up to see sub-prior arrive at the culminating act of the communion – the consecration of the host.

Surrounded by drifting clouds of fragrant smoke, the monk was standing behind the altar with head bowed. Raising it, he grasped a small, round wafer in both hands and raised it high in the air. It was not by chance the architects of Ganagobie had built the only good-sized church window in the eastern wall behind its altar. A great bolt of sunshine, angling down towards the sub-prior, surrounded him in a nimbus of white light and caught the raised host at the moment of transubstantiation – the mystical conversion of wine and wafer into the body of Christ.

For me at that moment the kind and gentle sub-prior might just as well have been an Aztec priest triumphantly holding a dripping human heart aloft at a temple sacrifice in the Andean jungle. The whole communion ceremony was all so entirely outlandish as a concept that on any rational level I had to reject it. But for the first time since arriving at Ganagobie I began accepting its rituals of worship in another way. And, oddly, it was thanks to the presence of the three Lolitas.

On the face of it, it wouldn't seem fair to compare the flirting of brash adolescents with the dry ceremonials of elderly clerics. One group was rejoicing in an awareness of its pure physicality. The other was celebrating a consumma-tion of flesh and blood that was entirely metaphysical. But at the heart of both rituals lay the same thing – the life of the senses.

The world has largely lost its ritual sensuality, the physi-cal symbolism that once accompanied the major events and transitions of life. We have left it behind for the more literal, in-your-face messages of a modern material society. But that older ritual of the senses was still here at Ganagobie, a spare, pared-down use of carefully chosen signs and symbols. Of no value in themselves, they represented something of greater significance beyond – they were, as the theological formula had it, the outward and material manifestations of an inward and spiritual state.

So in the end I did not lean over and tell the girls to cut it out. Instead I sat back and enjoyed the contrast of sacred and profane. And whose sensuality, finally, the girl's or the monk's, was being used to better purpose? Which propelled humanity forward? In the end both were essential to its ongoing existence.

But what I did do from that point on was stop trying to find a logical explanation for prayer. I put the question of belief and non-belief to one side, and began to enjoy the sensuality of symbols for their own sake: the reverberation of monastery bells spreading out over the Ganagobie plateau; the mysterious darkness of the narrow, high nave; the flickering of candles against bare stone walls; the billowing of near-invisible smoke which, rising out of the gloom, suddenly took on the solidity of stone itself in the sunlight over the altar. Strong and simple outer signs reflecting deeper inner beliefs, these things, too, I recognized as part of that older life of the Mediterranean.

And above all there was the slow, musical rise and fall of those interminable, imponderable voices at prayer. It was a strange thing, but once I stopped thinking about it the chanting ceased to seem dull and onerous. Instead of merely watching the tiny band of monastic travellers set out in song over an empty horizon, I let them carry me with them. The chant became a kind of open-ended meditation, outside of time, that took me wherever I wanted. The *Père Hôtelier* had known exactly what he was saying when on that first day I'd asked his advice. *Laissez-vous aller*.

⤳

Back in the world of men and earthly affairs, I found myself a day or two later at Chez Charlotte lingering over a Tarte Tatin. I found it difficult to describe to Jany the praying and prostrations; they seemed to have little existence outside Ganagobie. On the other hand, I had no difficulty at all describing the Benedictines' refectory meals. To be honest, with the taste of Ganagobie figs still on my lips – they grew from the monastery walls and were the sweetest I'd ever tasted – Charlotte's Tarte no longer seemed quite the same desert it had once been.

I was about to describe yet one more sublimely monkish meal when Jany broke in. I think she still resented the male prerogative in refectory dining.

'It seems to me you spent more time thinking about food up there than you did about God,' she mused. 'If you've chosen not to become a Provençal monk, perhaps you should become a Provençal cook.'

And with that she stopped me in my tracks. I had done a fair bit of reflecting on God and how, if only one believed, it might change the meaning of life. But Jany was right. There were also times when I'd thought of food and believed it *was* the meaning of life. Now the seed of an idea was planted, and I looked at her for a Ganagobie-minute, sixty seconds that lasted infinitely longer than most other minutes.

'Well, perhaps I should,' I meditated out loud at last.

Eight

When it comes to Provençal food there are only two authorities I really look up to. One is Jacques Médecin, deceased author of *La Bonne Cuisine du Comté de Nice*. The other is my mother-in-law Odette, still very much alive and cooking.

What I like about Jacques Médecin is his straightforward style. It's been half a century since Anglo food writers like Elizabeth David began saying it was actually OK to enjoy eating. But the lesson has been more than learned – today kitchen celebrities have no hesitation about piling on a language of foody self-indulgence until one begins to feel, at least lexically, just the slightest bit overfed.

Exponents of Mediterranean regional cuisine are especially prone. Purple aubergines seem to lead unerringly to purple prose – the temptation to match highly-coloured food with highly-coloured language is hard to resist. Shopping trips to outdoor Provençal markets can have some writers dangerously swooning with the heady scents of aromatic herbs and the apparently ineffable sight of stacked vegetables. But any situation will do.

'We passed the salt pans and suddenly the sea was there, deep blue, seemingly drunk with joy under the azure sky. We screamed and cheered at the glory of it.'[14] That is one well-known food celebrity reminiscing in her Mediterranean cookbook on a childhood drive to Alexandria and a Greek fish restaurant there. I have seen a few Greek drunks in seaside fish restaurants, but this was pushing it a bit. And to this day I have yet to hear anyone use the word 'azure' in real life.

Jacques Médecin would have none of this. Although he wrote about what many would consider the most elaborate and tasteful of all Provençal cuisines, his descriptions of the cooking of Nice are simple and clear. Aside from precise directions for the making of the dishes themselves, his text is spare, and composed for the most part of brief commentaries preceding each recipe. He was a no-nonsense food-lover who remained a staunch upholder of tradition, authenticity, and good, honest cooking.

Which is surprising, really, for in no other respect was Jacques Médecin even vaguely good or honest. If he was widely known as a cook he was far better known as a crook, one of the most corrupt politicians the city of Nice has ever known. And on the mob-ruled shores of the balmy French Riviera that is saying something. The grasping and all-powerful mayor of Nice for a quarter of a century, the only thing Médecin preferred to the delicate aroma of a slow-baked *estouffade* was the smell of money. Casinos, airports, urban infrastructure, the Nice opera house ... he had a finger in every pie. Graham Greene, a resident of Nice towards the end of his life, got so fed up he targeted Médecin and coastal corruption in his muckraking book, *J'accuse!* In true gangster-style Médecin eventually fled to South America just one meal ahead of the law. He was extradited from Uruguay, and spent his last years in prison after conviction on multiple charges of fraud, embezzlement and the misuse of public funds.

But you couldn't take it away from him – the mayor knew the correct use of an aubergine. There were no kickbacks in his kitchen; he gave full value when it came to cooking up sea-urchin omelettes, stuffed courgette flowers or any other Provençal delicacy. Take, for example, Médecin's recipe for that universally known summertime dish, salade Niçoise.

You will find it listed on every restaurant menu from Menton to Montélimar and beyond. And slung into the salad itself, apart from the essential tomatoes, you will find any old objects the cook feels has been hanging around in his fridge too long. Ham, croutons, cheese, muscatel wine, smoked mackerel, diced beets, melon-balls – these and a hundred other haphazard items eventually find their way into so-called Niçoise salads. But even among self-respecting chefs aiming for the real thing you will find ingredients Médecin says no true Niçois would dream of using. Boiled potatoes are one particularly common culprit. Green beans are another.

You get the feeling that Médecin would like to fit these miscreant cooks with size twelve cement shoes and drop them into the waters of the Baie des Anges. 'The crimes that have been committed in the name of this pure and fresh salad … !' he indignantly cries in his own paragraph-long *J'accuse* at the top of his recipe for *La (Vraie) Salade Niçoise*.[15] It is one of his few emotional moments – you'd think he was execrating the rape of young virgins. With the exception of hard-boiled eggs, Nice's former Supremo points out, this is a salad that contains only uncooked ingredients. All the vegetables, including the artichokes that go into it, are raw. Médecin also frowns on countrymen who put tuna in their salad; tuna was all very fine for the wealthy, he says, but salade Niçoise was originally a poor man's meal, and the cheaper choice of anchovies is appropriate. Given Médecin's own vast wealth, such an uncompromising stand on authenticity is truly impressive.

Which brings me to ratatouille and the afternoon, not long after my return from Ganagobie, when I sat peeling courgettes and aubergines with Odette in her Aix kitchen. In *La Bonne Cuisine* Jacques Médecin gives an authentic and demanding recipe for this Provençal dish, a speciality which is almost as regularly dishonoured by those who make it as salade Niçoise. It is a preparation that many cooks seem to think requires nothing more than rapid assembly in a single pot. Wrong, says the coastal Caïd. Ratatouille is particularly long and difficult to prepare, and can easily turn out unsuccessfully. I agree. I have never eaten the mayor's ratatouille, but I have eaten Odette's version of the dish many times.

It was indeed long and difficult to prepare. And it always turned out exquisitely.

That is not the reason, though, that I respected Odette's Provençal cooking as much as Jean Médecin's. For all his refusal to wax poetic, Médecin was in some ways even more of a put-on than the food-writer who succumbs to a few over-blown adjectives. Odette, on the other hand, was entirely authentic without even knowing it. She had never written a Provençal cookbook. In her entire life she had never even *owned* a cookbook. If you asked her how she characterised her cooking she was at a loss for an answer. She certainly didn't call it Provençal – she didn't know any other kind, and had nothing to compare it to. It's just cooking, she said.

But it wasn't. It was the cooking of a Provençal rural childhood, stored away in her memory for eighty years without measurements, cooking times or corrective com-mentary. Every day in the kitchen she returned to it, her hand and eye attentively recreating dishes she had once made in precisely the same fashion for her farming father. It was all done to the immense satisfaction of René and anyone else lucky enough to be around at the time. But it was done, too, for those no longer sitting at the table. It was Odette's way of reviving the shared pleasures of the past. Here was a woman whose belief in her physical senses was strong enough to call up vanished generations, and if she couldn't teach me some-thing about Mediterranean ways then no one could.

Our ratatouille session began with a telephone call earlier that day. Would I mind, Odette asked, coming over to help with a little shopping? Odette had never learned to drive, and while René still chauffeured her to shops that were nearby, there were other, busier roads that at his age he preferred to avoid.

Armed with straw baskets, we drove out on the Route de Berre to a fruit-and-vegetable shop particularly esteemed by Odette for the freshness of its produce. Odette never shopped more than a day or two in advance of any particular meal. When I first arrived in Provence I was astonished at the meagreness of her larder. Was this the truth of much-vaunted French cuisine, I wondered – a few potatoes in a crate in the cellar and some tomatoes ripening on a window-sill? By the freezer-bulging standards of North America Odette's kitchen was woefully bare and under-equipped. There were a few knives, some thick-bottomed pots and pans, a heavy stone mortar and pestle. There were some implements that were slightly more advanced, but not much – her *moulin à légumes*, a hand-cranked food mill, looked as if had been invented and manufactured by Archimedes.

Once, when René and Odette flew to Washington to visit Jany's sister Mireille, Odette's most curious discovery was a kitchen-appliance shop. 'Imagine,' she marvelled on her return, 'an entire shop, nothing but aisle after aisle of gadgets!' Seen by American cooks as basic equipment, for Odette most such items were fanciful and unnecessary extravagances – she bought nothing there because she saw nothing that would improve on what she already did.

Yet from her kitchen Odette regularly and unostentatiously turned out magnificent Provençal meals. René, who liked the ceremony and sociability of restaurants, had only one complaint about them – the food there was rarely as good as it was at home. Daily shopping, Odette reasoned, was a small price to pay for such consistent satisfaction.

But when it came to buying fresh produce Odette herself was hard to satisfy – when you have lived on a family farm that grows the best Provence has to offer you tend to be choosy. With baskets in tow we made our way past stands of bright-skinned vegetables that to me appeared to be at the peak of perfection.

'Too big,' Odette said, surveying a pile of small, purple-tinged *artichauts violets*, a delicate local variety that made ordinary globe artichokes look coarse and unpalatable. 'Picked too early,' she murmured, gently palping a marrow that might have done with a day or two more sunshine.

We arrived in front of a pyramid of Cavaillon melons. When it came to buying these small, round, smooth-skinned fruits Odette was a champion. Their orange flesh, when it is perfect, is about as delectable as any food can get. But the melons of Cavaillon, at least according to a Provencal housewives' dictum, are just like men everywhere – you have to try a few before you end up with a good one.

Among aficionados there are various schools of procedure – the simple look of the things is for rank beginners alone. Some cognoscenti go by smell. Others believe the flexibility of the stem is the best indicator of excellence. Both schools have their merits. Odette herself, though, belonged to that small but distinguished class of melon-experts, the hefters. Infinitely practised, such judges rely on a subtle ability to closely estimate ratios of size and weight – simply put, a good melon, no matter what its dimensions, weighs more than you think it should. The best are like little cannonballs. Odette hefted first one melon, then another, finally testing half a dozen before she found one to her satisfaction.

But if Odette used the science of relative sizes and weights to her own advantage, she knew it was used against her as well. There was nothing worthier of Odette's disdain when shopping or cooking than a vegetable gorged on water. Odette had grown up in an age before agricultural irrigation became widespread in Provence. It was certainly not used on Le Marronnier, her father's farm. In her firm opinion the only good vegetable was a stressed vegetable, taken from a plant that grew in extremes of temperature, in non-fertilised soils and with a minimum of water – a Le Marronnier vegetable, in fact. I am not sure that Odette didn't consider vegetables a little bit like human beings – over-indulge them, fail to give them challenges, and they grow up flabby of character, incapable of showing any real personality. Sold by weight, big, watery vegetables were of course good for market-farmer's wallets. But they were no good for Odette's ratatouille.

'Take the smallest ones; they're firmer,' Odette said to me as we surveyed the shop's stock of courgettes. The aubergines were just as carefully chosen. 'Avoid the fat ones; you don't want too much pulp and seeds in the middle,' Odette advised, and we picked the longer and thinner of the shiny, purple-black eggplants. Tomatoes, onions, red peppers ... all were bought with the same attention to freshness and quality.

Once I had her back home I wanted to see how Odette sorted out her problems and got that rich flavour, concentrated yet subtle, that made her vegetable dishes so memorable. And somewhere also, half-consciously in the back of my mind, I was turning over Jany's comment about Provençal restaurant cooking. So I stayed on to help.

While Odette peeled and sliced aubergines on one side of the table in her cheerful yellow kitchen, I did the same with the courgettes on the other. 'Don't take all the green off,' she instructed as I removed lengths of skin with a knife. 'Leave alternating strips. If you don't there will be nothing to hold the slices together – they'll fall apart when they're cooking.'

But it was the removal of the maximum possible amount of moisture that was Odette's greatest concern. After slicing the courgettes she drizzled them with olive oil in a shallow baking pan and put them in a low-temperature oven. She

311

salted slices of aubergine to sweat the humidity out and dried them off with paper towel. Still not satisfied, she cut them into quarters and tossed them in a colander with more salt. She turned over the courgette slices in the oven, already much reduced in volume by the heat. Having skinned and deseeded the tomatoes, she squeezed them in her hands until the excess juice ran from between her fingers.

As she worked Odette talked, the much-repeated gestures reminding her of earlier occasions in other kitchens. She might have made ratatouille a thousand times, but each time it brought her back in some small way to that farmhouse in the Dôa Valley behind Apt.

The kitchen in Le Marronnier, she said, had been the simplest imaginable. But it was no different from any of the neighbours' kitchens – in the 1920s rural Provence had remained well behind the rest of France. There was no industry, no large-scale agriculture, and not much money. Life had been simple, and the first meals she'd made had been cooked in a farmhouse without electricity. Nor was there plumbing – water was collected from the stone fountain in the courtyard and, once used, emptied from a bucket below the sink. Until the 1930s there hadn't even been a wood-stove to cook on – soups and stews were cooked in an iron pot that hung in the fireplace, while *gratins* were browned in a metal baking-box that was banked above and below with hot coals from the fire.

It sounded like a lot of work, I said. Had she enjoyed cooking?

It wasn't really a question of enjoying or not enjoying, Odette replied. When she was nine her mother, still young, had a stroke that left one side of her body paralysed. Out of necessity it was Odette who not long after was cooking for the men in the family. It was her father who'd got her started. A fine cook himself, Louis was famous among his relatives for his unabashed love of good eating – when invited to dine at a brother's or cousin's house down the valley, he would march straight through to the kitchen and begin lifting pot-lids, sniffing roasts and testing sauces with a spoon. At first he'd shown his daughter easy things, how to make dishes like tomato or spinach omelettes that could be carried out to the fields during busy harvests and eaten any time, hot or cold. She progressed from there – by the time Odette was fourteen she'd assumed practically all the domestic responsibilities on the farm.

At this point Odette was sweating chopped onions in olive oil in a heavy pan, preparing the tomato sauce that would hold her red peppers, aubergines and courgettes together. In went some *herbes de Provence* – dried thyme and rosemary – and a generous amount of pressed garlic. Like most Provençal cooks, Odette loved the flavour of garlic – not the powerful, rough bite of the raw clove, but garlic which, slowly simmered, melted into other ingredients and met other, less aggressive herbs and spices half-way.

It was the same with basil, capers, anise, olives, sage, anchovies and other pronounced Provençal flavours – Odette

313

enjoyed their presence, but never let them crowd out the tastes they were supposed to be helping. The only time she really let go was when she made aioli, pounding clove after clove of raw garlic in her old stone mortar, adding olive oil drop by drop until she'd beaten up a mayonnaise fierce enough to rip your head off. But ratatouille was a dish that honoured Provence's most fondly-regarded vegetables, not its feistiest raw material. Now Odette paused to remove her courgettes from the oven, reduced after an hour by about two-thirds. In their place she put whole red peppers.

It must have been difficult getting provisions in, I said, thinking of the distance from the farm to the market town of Apt. How did they get they get their shopping done?

Odette only laughed.

'Le Marronnier in those days produced mostly wheat and wine,' she said. 'Along with olives those were the essentials of life in Provence. But country people never thought about buying much more than sugar and coffee in shops – we lived from our barnyards, grew things in gardens and orchards. There was plenty to be found up on the hillsides, too. We didn't have much money then, but we had plenty of time. We ate far better than most people eat today. Even during the war, when people in the cities were living on ration cards, we were never short of anything. Except coffee, maybe – we made it from chicory.'

Odette turned the oven off and the grill up high. 'It wasn't like today, of course – no one ever dreamt of eating

314

strawberries in November. You just had to wait until spring. Waiting made things taste better. Each season of the year had its own produce, and we looked forward to them all. Different weather still makes me think of different dishes.'

'Snow,' I said, thinking of the leanest season and looking to put her off balance. 'What dish does snow make you think of?'

'*Lapin rôti à la moutarde*,' Odette answered without missing a beat. 'My father used to hunt rabbits in the winter and bring home a dozen at a time. I was the one that skinned and cleaned them. But they were delicious. I'd cook the livers apart and when they were hot I'd crush them with a fork, mixing in mustard, vinegar, olive oil and pepper. After the rabbit had turned in front of the fire I'd pour the liver sauce over it. Yes, that was good in cold weather. And so were thick pumpkin soups. Oh, and wintertime was truffle-time, too – we used a dog to find them in the oak forests above the farm. We put them in salads and omelettes and sautéed them with potatoes.'

Winter snow did not seem to have fazed Odette at all. 'Spring rain,' I tried.

'Baby radishes, white asparagus with vinaigrette, cherry clafouti.'

'Summer heat-waves.'

'Melons cooled in the cellar. Bottles of rosé stood beneath the spigot of the courtyard fountain. *Pistou* soups with green beans and white beans and plenty of basil. *Mangetout* peas cooked with tiny onions and small chunks of *petit salé*. After Bastille Day, when the first tomatoes were off the vine, ratatouille served cold, and *tomates provençales* grilled with breadcrumbs, garlic and parsley.'

'Autumn storms.'

'*Poule en sauce*. They were farmyard chickens that were headed for the pot because they no longer laid any eggs. They were tough old birds, and had to be simmered a long time with white wine and onions and herbs. After hours of slow cooking the meat was soft and tender, and only then did we add wild mushrooms, the *lactaires* and *girolles* my brother Robert and I gathered in the pine forests after the rain was over. Nothing smelled as good as those bubbling pots of chicken.'

Were there tears of remembrance in the corners of Odette's eyes? Was that why she rose and bent busily over the oven door? Perhaps, instead, it was because a charred odour was telling her that the red peppers had a nice smoky flavour and blistered skins that could now be easily peeled off. Odette would rather cook her way through the past than make an emotional fuss about it.

Soon the top of her cooker got very busy, with four heavy pans slowly cooking away at the same time. The point of a genuine ratatouille, as opposed to the inferior, fifteen-minute throw-together variety, is that each vegetable contributes its own distinct and separate flavour to a single dish. They must be cooked long enough that they are tender, but not so long that they start losing taste and colour and texture. Because each vegetable reaches its optimum point at a different speed, aubergines, courgettes, peppers and tomatoes must be cooked separately for different lengths of time and only combined at the end. Ideally they should all be put together at the moment each of them reaches perfection – it means starting them off at different times so they all arrive together in unison.

At last I watched Odette combining the contents of all four pans at precisely the right moment. Some four hours after starting the job, Odette's ratatouille was finished. She thought nothing at all of the time involved – for the same supper that evening she went on to cook a garlicky gigot of lamb and a gratin of courgettes. As a reward for acting as *aide de cuisine* I made sure Jany and I were invited. As always, the results were incomparable.

There was nothing water-gorged about these vegetables any more. Odette's seven aubergines, six courgettes, four onions, three large red peppers and three and a half pounds of tomatoes now all fitted comfortably into a shallow baking dish. We sat on the garden-terrace outside the house savouring the dinner, a bottle of chilled rosé, and the glorious cool of evening falling from a clear sky. Fragrant and appetising, the ratatouille was like a concentration of the Provençal summer. After a mouthful or two I sat back and gazed upwards in rapture.

Here was a dish, I thought, that was as deep in flavour

as the sky above was profound in colour. In fact, the more I gazed upwards, the more the sky looked not just deep blue but, well – there was no other word for it – azure. In such circumstances it was easy to grow emotional. Another glass or two of rosé, and I might have started screaming and cheering at the glory of it all.

⌒

Not long afterwards I found myself spinning up the *autoroute* northwards past Avignon to our little village-house near Vaison-la-Romaine. Jany had stayed behind in Aix, for this was serious business and I was not planning on staying at the house much. Jany alone had not been influence enough to help me make the decision. But Jany and her mother's cooking were. I had decided I was going to spend a few days messing around in restaurants. I wanted to see how Mediterranean senses were used on the other side of those swinging kitchen doors.

The restaurants of Provence are, on the whole, not terribly distinguished. It has nothing to do with the strength of local culinary tradition or the local raw ingredients themselves. Odette had shown me why both those things are renowned. Provence might not have the dairy products and elaborate, cream-based sauces of the north, the duck and goose *confit* preparations of the south-west, the rich, pork-based charcuterie of Alsace and the east. The principal glories of Provence lie in its vegetable fields and fruit orchards and herb gardens,

318

and in a southern sun strong enough to wrest the maximum flavour from all of them.

And therein lay the problem. The Provençal summer sun is good not only for plant-life. It seems to do a powerful lot of good for humans as well. In other, less touristy parts of France restaurants have to work hard throughout the year to keep their customers. But the holiday crowds that pack Provence every summer are on the whole a carefree and unpicky lot when it comes to eating – what they want is sun and fun. They rarely return to the same establishment anyway.

So with no reputation to protect, restaurants can dress up a mediocre dinner in crushed garlic and basil leaves, ask a higher-than-average price, and get away with it. In a tourist-town like Aix-en-Provence there are scores of restaurants that regard food as a high-profit, high-risk, short-term business opportunity; they literally come and go with the seasons. Turn your back, and the place that yesterday was called Zola's Bread-basket is today Cézanne's Salad-spinner – the management and décor have changed, but the food, disappointingly, is the same.

Northern Provence is almost as popular with summer visitors as Aix, and no one who stops in Vaison-la-Romaine to see its Roman ruins is guaranteed that they, too, will not end up eating a dud salade Niçoise. But there was one big difference that made me happier following the food-trail from our village-house near Vaison than from Aix. Where Aix is urban and its *raison d'être* the production of high culture, northern

Provence is essentially rural. Its culture is agriculture. The foods the area produces are superb. Considered in the grand scheme of all things French, I regarded its *mission civilisatrice* as even more elevated than Aix's.

On arriving in the village, I did what I always do after swinging open shutters and turning on water and electricity. I stumped up three flights of steep and narrow steps to the top of the house. We had no garden, but we did have a rooftop terrace, one of the highest in a village that climbed a rocky outcrop. After an absence it was always a good spot to get reoriented, to replace Aix's Sainte-Victoire with a view of Mont Ventoux, the even larger, cone-shaped giant that looms on the horizon. Like Sainte-Victoire, the highest mountain between the Alps and the Pyrenees is a powerful presence.

As I climbed upwards this time, though, I didn't have mountains on my mind. Instead I was thinking of food. I might not be able to grow tomatoes up on the terrace, but from here I could at least look out and see what other people were growing. In virtually every direction there were different areas specialising in the production of one thing or another. To me they all seemed extraordinary.

I gazed out across village roof-tiles and chimney pots. To the south-east, a great sea of vineyards stretched away over the alluvial plane towards the Rhône River. Not far away, it harboured some of the best-known wines of the Midi – Gigondas, originally named Jucunditas, or 'happiness' by the Roman troops who retired and found their vines to be especially fruitful there; Châteauneuf-du-Pape, 3,000 hectares of stony, dry, clay-like soil producing a wine so divine it became the exclusive prerogative of the popes of Avignon; Beaumes-de-Venise, the sweet and fruity Muscat wine that is the closest thing I know to the nectar of Greek myth.

But you didn't have to be a retired Roman to enjoy the land the wine sprang from. Even without wine-tasting from one village to the next, I always found it a pleasure to simply drive through the vineyards. In spring bright rosebushes flowered at the end of the vine-rows. In autumn after the harvest the broad vine-leaves turned fiery red and set the whole country alight. And any time in between you could mark the slow and steady progress of the season by the clusters of hanging grapes that grew rounder and riper and heavier by the day.

I turned to the north-east, looking in the direction of the little village of Richerenches. When a local phylloxera blight wiped out wine production there at the turn of the last century, desperate peasants ripped out the vines all around the village. In their place they planted oaks, the trees around which, with a little luck, truffles like to grow. Today Richerenches has the largest truffle market in France.

Buying truffles is not like buying cabbages; this weekly winter market attracts professional buyers and restaurateurs from all over Provence. The amounts of money are large and competition is fierce. Deals are negotiated in low voices beside the barely-open trunks of cars. It is all rather cloak-

and-dagger, but in the end nobody hides their gratitude for the wealth bestowed by these little black tubers. Each year at a special church truffle-service a collection bowl is passed around; dealers dig deep into their pockets not for money, but for fresh and fragrant earth-encrusted truffles. Once the priest has blessed the collection it is put up for public auction. The money goes to the glory of God, the truffles go down gourmet gullets.

I swivelled due north to gaze towards Nyons, olive capital of Provence. The gnarled, silvery-grey olive trees that grow around the town appear much like olive trees in other parts of Provence. Nor is their fruit anything special to look at. Nyons olives are small and dull black and harvested late – their skins are puckered by winter frost. But so prized is their flesh that they were the first olives in France to be awarded their own certificate of *appellation d'origine contrôlée.*

There are connoisseurs who speak of olives with the same refined sensibility as wine-lovers. It is said that while the *verdale* olive of Haute Provence presents subtle undertones of artichoke and the *cailletier* olive of the Massif de l'Esterel is reminiscent of acacia and hawthorn, the *tenche* of Nyons suggest notes of green apples and cut hay. I hadn't got the nose for it, and suspected that just as there are wine-snobs who over-do this kind of thing, so there are olive-snobs. But one thing was certain – I had grown attached enough to the cold-pressed virgin oil of Provence that cooking with butter now seemed a slightly odd and foreign thing to do.

I turned once again, looking west now into the rugged country of the Baronnies. There in the thick forests covering the hillsides grew the area's most celebrated tree, the *tilleul*, or lime. The Baronnies boasts the only community in France where lime-blossoms are traded – on the first Wednesday of July each year the little medieval town of Buis-les-Baronnies overflows with herbalists, pharmacists and makers of that gentlest of French post-prandial comforts, the *tisane*. Lime-blossom infusions, of which Jany was a great admirer, are reputed for their soothing, calming effects – they are nature's tranquilliser, and often drunk before bed.

I could only speak for *tilleul*'s efficacy in concentrated form. I once helped the *employé municipal* – the man who sweeps the streets, buries the dead and clips the trees – pick the blossoms on the lime-tree in the street below our house. Was it the sticky gum on our hands or the saturated air up in the tree's leafy boughs? Either way, the stuff seemed to work like Provençal Prozac. Our harvesting went more and more slowly, until both of us were sleepy and quite content to be standing nearly motionless at the top of our ladders. We might have stayed up there all night, brainless and nodding, if someone hadn't noticed and called us down.

The only direction left to look now was south-west to the slopes of Mont Ventoux itself. But even there the land was carefully tended and worked. On its north side Ventoux's lower flanks are covered with the apricot trees known as *Orangés de Provence* – they make the best apricot syrups and jams in France. On its south side are orchards of firm, sweet *bigarreaux* cherries. Some people think the highest summit in Provence has the rugged, monumental look of a Kilimanjaro. In early springtime, with acres of frail pink and white fruit blossoms covering its base and snow still layering its summit, I think it has the delicate colours and zen-like repose of a Japanese print. At that time of year it is Mount Fuji for me.

Wherever I looked, the whole countryside was busy with plants growing, with men pruning and harrowing and hoeing and harvesting. All these places lay just minutes away, and I couldn't imagine any other spot on earth more entirely surrounded and bountifully provided for by food and drink. It was a reassuring thought, all that sustenance and succour lying so close at hand. But I didn't, in fact, have to go any distance at all to find my first source of comfort. Just below the house, not 300 yards away, stood the village wine co-operative.

It was the heart and soul of the little community. It was the reason the village had not become a ghost town like so many others, populated by tourists in summer and deserted in winter. It was the reason Jany and I had been able to buy an 800-year-old house with age-bowed beams – such things were all very well for romantically-minded foreigners, but prosperous farmers built themselves spanking new villas out of town. It was the reason the place was happy and energetic – without wine there would be no children in the village school, no grapegrowers in the village café, no grapegrowers' wives gossiping in the village bakery. Just as critical from my point of view, without wine there would be nothing to put in the five-litre jug with which, every now and then, I strolled into the co-op's cool, well-scrubbed interior.

Regular or super? I think it was the half dozen petrol-station-style pumps, each delivering a different blend of wine varietals, that I liked there most. Large-diameter hoses and heavy-duty nozzles reinforced the idea of unlimited supply, and with a very acceptable Côtes-du-Rhône selling for the equivalent of $2 a litre you couldn't go wrong. Never mind that French transport strikes occasionally exhausted fuel reserves at real petrol stations. We weren't likely to run out here any time soon – there were seven million litres of wine held in storage tanks at our co-op.

'That's too bad,' I would think as I watched the rich, dark-red liquid pouring from the nozzle and swirling upwards to the rim of the jug. 'Now there are only six million, nine hundred and ninety-nine thousand, nine hundred and ninety-five litres left.'

How could such a countryside not be reassuring?

〜

Through mutual friends I had scraped an introduction to Bruno and Salva, co-owners of a restaurant in Vaison-la-Romaine. Leonardo was a tiny place on a cul-de-sac in the centre of town. So small a restaurant was it that there was

no room for that summer-visitor's non-negotiable require-
ment, an outdoor terrace. Instead, Bruno had obtained sea-
sonal rights from the town hall to install his tables in the
street itself. With creative flair and effort he managed to
make the tarmac virtually disappear, dressing it in feathery, potted hedges and bright pimento plants growing in
large terracotta vases. In the evening a flowering jasmine
vine growing over the door dispersed its perfume halfway
down the street, pushing the little restaurant's frontiers even
further outward.

But it wasn't the size of the place that interested me. It
wasn't even the kind of food it served, for Leonardo was not
Provençal, but a trattoria-style Italian restaurant. By all
accounts, though, it was a cheerful, well-run, finely-tuned
establishment that consistently turned out good Mediterranean food at reasonable prices. And that interested me no end.

It was a few minutes to eight on a Tuesday morning
in late August when I walked into Leonardo, and already
the day was warm – by noon it would be scorching. Bruno
was outside setting up tables and parasols and watering his
plants, Salva inside preparing the day's desserts. They did not
have far to come to work – they lived above the restaurant
– but they had been up since six o'clock. While each had
dozens of different chores, their labour was clearly divided.
Bruno worked the front end of the restaurant, taking orders,
serving and clearing. Salva, with single-minded attention,
ran the kitchen behind.

Which was just as well, for a single mind was about all that Leonardo's kitchen had room for. It was minuscule, a bright place of stainless steel and white tiles where nothing lay more than two steps from anything else. There was no room for a conventional layout – prep-station, salad-station, grill, mise-en-place and the rest of it. It all happened at arm's length. Salva looked after the preparation and cooking alone. At mealtimes a *plongeur* – a 'diver', or dishwasher – took his place by a sink in the corner. Luckily he was skinny.

Like the restaurant itself, the Leonardo pair looked relaxed and hiply casual. Both men were in their late forties. Bruno wore short, dyed-blonde hair, two-day stubble, and his shirt-tails out. Salva's head was shaved, the frames of his glasses were heavy and black, and from a ring in the lobe of one ear hung a tiny silver bullet. 'We please ourselves,' the attire and attitude seemed to say. 'What we hope pleases you is the food on your plates.'

And they seemed entirely devoted to just that. Tuesday in Vaison is market-day, and after conferring with Salva, Bruno was about to set out into the streets to do some shopping. He invited me along.

'And don't forget aubergines, at least eight for the capo-nata,' Salva shouted once more as he whisked confectioner's sugar into a saucepan of heavy cream heating on his range. He was making panna cotta. On the little work-surface in front of him were packets of gelatine, almond essence, and the dozen ceramic ramekins he was going to fill.

'What's caponata?' I asked, as we walked through the dining room towards the door and the glare of light in the street outside.

'We serve it as a starter,' Bruno answered. It's a kind of vegetable stew made with aubergines and red peppers and onions. It's an Italian ratatouille, really.'

'*ET MERDE!*' Salva shouted even more loudly from inside the kitchen. He'd been listening carefully as he stirred. 'What do you mean, Italian ratatouille? Don't start telling him rubbish.' He emerged from around the corner and addressed me directly. 'Caponata's from Sicily. Yes, it's got some of the same vegetables as ratatouille. It can also be served hot or cold. But it's made with sugar and vinegar. It's got olives and capers in it. It's complex and balanced, sweet and sour and salty all at the same time. Ratatouille is simply a bastardised cousin of caponata, introduced from Piedmont into Provence by the Niçois. What do you expect? They're all half-Italian and half-French down there.'

He said it if as if he were dismissing some presumptuous race of hybrid poodle. Bruno was from Provence, but Salvatore was from Puglia, deep in the heel of southern Italy. He may have been cool and casual, but he had his regional pride, too – and he was not going to let his associate get away with culinary approximations. I liked that.

We walked outside and into the middle of a great noise and bustle that showed no sign of letting up whichever way we turned. With every inch of every street in town filled with stalls, Vaison has one of the largest, most attractive weekly markets in Provence. On the other side of the post office I glanced briefly downwards past a protective iron railing at the chariot-rutted flagstones and carved columns of antique Vaison. The town has been a market centre for a very long time. The excavated street below me was known as the rue des Boutiques; 2,000 years old, it had once been as busy with Roman hawkers and shoppers as the street I was now walking in.

The crowds were so thick that it made slow going. It was not Latin, nor even French, but German, Dutch and English voices that rose into the air as we worked our way past one food vendor after another. Most stalls sold local specialities – picodon goat-cheeses, olive tapenades, thyme-flavoured sausages, lavender honey. It was all gorgeously displayed, and all expensive.

'Don't get the idea that Provençal restaurateurs do all their shopping in outdoor markets. That's only for television cooks,' Bruno said as we slowly progressed. 'I'm just buying the bare minimum today, and that's only because we've been closed, as usual, for the last two days. When the last dish is washed and stacked on Saturday nights in summer we hop into the car and drive down to Cap d'Agde. We get there about three o'clock in the morning. There's a nudist beach there. We drive back late Monday night. This market just holds us over until we can do some real shopping.'

It didn't sound like the kind of lifestyle that television-cooking might accommodate. I doubted even Jamie Oliver, the Naked Chef, indulged in quite as bare a minimum on his own weekends. Bruno and Salva seemed less concerned with promoting the prestigious, self-important image of the French cooking establishment than with enjoying themselves.

We stopped at a tiny stall where a man in a flat cap sold nothing but herbs – Bruno bought his entire supply of basil, chives, mint and fresh bay leaves. Further on we filled a basket with artichokes – the good small ones, Bruno said, were hard to find, and Salva's *Carciofi alla Nonna* always sold well in warm weather. At a third, larger stall, we bought the makings for caponata. And as we carefully inspected aubergines and red peppers Bruno described the pleasures of small-town, small-restaurant ownership in the south of France.

Bruno and Salva had been cooking and living together a long time – twenty-three years. They had started their first restaurant not far away in the Vaucluse town of Orange and then, energetic and youthfully ambitious, headed north from the Midi to run a larger, more serious establishment. It, too, did well, and eventually they were setting more than a thousand covers a day, with teams of twenty employees working shifts. It was challenging and invigorating, Bruno said. And then it was exhausting and stressful. The same restaurant life went on for fifteen years. Finally the pair had had enough – they wanted less restaurant and more life.

'Leonardo is perfect,' said Bruno as we packed his purchases into baskets. 'We couldn't put out one more table or serve one more meal even if we wanted to. It is just the two of us. Now, if we want, we can go to the beach in summer and close for holidays in winter. And at last Salva has the time and leisure to cook the way he likes. We like our life.'

When we got back to the restaurant Salva had long finished making panna cotta and moved on to tiramisu. While he was waiting for his *génoise* sponge cake to cool he began removing the petals from a large pink rose. One by one, he carefully dipped them into egg whites, then lightly sprinkled them with caster sugar.

'I bake them for an hour at seventy degrees', he said. 'The petals come out crackly and full of rose-flavour. They're organically grown. They're a perfect garnishing for ice-cream.'

Salva made his cooking seem a relaxed and delicate art. It was only when I returned that evening that I realised it could be something else as well.

There might have been only three or four tables occupied at Leonardo when the sun began setting on Vaison-la-Romaine. It was still warm outside, but Bruno's tarmac terrace was a model of cool elegance – tables set, glasses gleaming, candles barely flickering in the still air. But inside the kitchen the atmosphere was already very different. With the range going full blast it was ferociously hot. And with numerous paper slips on his order-board now calling for immediate action, Salva's mood had changed.

Intense and edgy, he was stripped to the waist beneath

his chef's apron and moving at a pace I found difficult to imagine sustaining for more than a few minutes. Each movement was precise, without a split second being lost between any of them. At first I was at a loss to see any pattern at all, for Salva was accomplishing half a dozen different tasks at the same time.

'What are you cooki ... ?' I began.

Salva abruptly held up his hand like a policeman stopping traffic and shook his head, then went back to work. This was no time for questions.

One moment he was coating veal in breadcrumbs and Parmesan, the next he was frying it. At the same time he was slicing coppa, plunging fresh tagiatelli into boiling water, pulling trays of lasagne from his oven, flambéing gambas and plating *Carciofi alla Nonna*. Every knife, every bottle, bowl and ladle Salva used was returned to its exact place so it might be reached for again without the slightest glance.

What impressed me most, despite the speed, was Salva's attention to presentation. Each time he whacked the small brass bell on the wall at the kitchen door, the finished plate Bruno carried out into the street was a visual delight. I understood now why Bruno had bought every bit of mint, chive, basil and other fresh green herb he could – Salva used them all to subtle, colourful effect, as well as sprinklings of black poppy seeds, drizzlings of olive oil, dribbles of red pesto and scatterings of pink peppercorns. He could take a ricotta and tomato salad and make it look like a feast.

By nine o'clock the place was full and even Bruno was panting to keep up. 'Every winter I put on four or five kilos,' he told me as he prepared a tray of kir cocktails at lightning speed behind the bar. 'And every summer I work them off.' Then he was gone.

The pace increased until I thought Salva was going to come apart. He did not stop vibrating on the spot for three hours. Then, sometime around 10:30 – Vaison is still a provincial town, after all – there was a first perceptible lag. By a quarter to twelve it was all over, and Salva, looking like a distance-runner after a marathon, came out to the bar.

'What was it you wanted to ask me?' he said, taking a sip of cold white wine.

I couldn't remember. I had never seen a kitchen-artist show his mettle under pressure. If this was what Bruno and Salva regarded as a relaxed restaurant life, I could not imagine their more stressed former one.

'What keeps you going?' I asked the question that was really on my mind. I wouldn't have been surprised if he'd told me about some fashionable new designer-drug.

'My grandmother,' Salva replied. He was a man of surprises.

'When I was growing up in Puglia,' Salva said after another long slurp, 'my father ran a small-town trattoria. It was a simple, rough place, full of men who came to drink and gamble rather than eat. But my grandmother made the most wonderful food to keep their stomachs happy at the same time. I'll never forget the dishes – I was in the kitchen with her night after night. It's the memory of those things I keep trying to capture when I cook. Of course I never do. But it doesn't stop me trying.'

As with Odette, so with Salva – remembrance was the fuel which cooked the dinners at Leonardo.

∽

'Provençal cuisine is cooking which leads to the enchantment of all the senses. Its colours and odours play a role as important as taste itself. It is cooking which enlivens the spirit instead of leading it into stupor. Even before you touch it, it is cooking that makes you happy.'

So read the quotation at the top of the menu posted in front of Le Cigalou. Not 150 yards around the corner and up the street from Leonardo, it, too, was a cheerful, brightly-decorated restaurant. It was only 9 a.m., much too soon after breakfast to start thinking of food. But already my spirit felt enlivened.

Like Leonardo, Le Cigalou was small and had a reputation for good, authentic, made-from-scratch cooking. Like Leonardo, it too was run by a couple who lived by, for, and above their restaurant. But unlike the trattoria, Le Cigalou was strictly local – it specialised in traditional Provençal dishes.

Courgettes aux câpres; mille-feuille d'aubergine; salade verte avec ses toasts de pistounade; tarte à la sardine et aux tomates, poivrons rouges marinés – this was just one of the plates, a selection of cold Provençal summer dishes, that I saw listed at the head of the menu. I gazed on. I was trying to decide whether this sounded more appealing than the melon, cured ham, fig and goat-cheese platter that came next on the menu, when I heard a voice behind me.

'They're both good when it's hot like this – they go really fast at lunchtime.'

She might have been reading my mind. It was Nicole, the public half of Le Cigalou's two-woman team. Like Bruno she ran the floor, serving food, running trips to the bar and making up bills for customers. I had met her when I'd arranged to spend a little time in Le Cigalou's kitchen. As well as reading minds she was zippy, energetic and had vast stamina. If restaurants in Provence seemed to be all about pleasure, I was beginning to realise that these other traits were also necessary for anyone who wanted to stay in business.

'Why don't you go straight to the kitchen?' she suggested, looking at her watch. 'Martine is waiting for you – she's already started lunch preparation.'

Automatically I made for the back of the dining room behind the terrace.

'Up the stairs!' Nicole called out, pointing to a front door on the sidewalk beside the restaurant. 'It's not very convenient, but the kitchen is on the first floor, above the dining room and beneath our apartment. Everything goes up and down by dumb-waiter.'

And that was the last I saw of Nicole, of tables and customers and the outside world for the rest of the morning. From a command-and-control point of view Le Cigalou's kitchen might not have been very strategically placed. But I liked it. Regular restaurant commotion seemed far away. Cut off from the bustle and stresses that usually make their way into a kitchen along with hurried waiters, it was a haven of peace with an atmosphere all its own.

It was more than just quiet isolation, though. Both women at the Cigalou were casual and easy-mannered. In other, earlier lives Nicole had been an accountant, Martine a commercial marketing agent for a large firm in Paris. Both had come to Provençal restaurant-cooking looking for escape. But where Nicole bounced on springs, Martine worked with a calm concentration not many restaurant cooks command.

Somewhere at the centre of her disposition was a deep reservoir of attentive concentration for whatever job was at hand. It was not nervous or aggressive, but brought a kind of serene productivity to the whole clean, well-looked-after kitchen. It seemed to rub off, too, on Martine's young helper, Sounia, a pretty Moroccan woman with large, dark eyes and a scarf tied gypsy-style around her head. With less than three hours to go before the restaurant opened for lunch, the two women were working with a measured, unruffled efficiency that got lengthy tasks done quickly.

And that – the lengthy task – Martine said, is one of the great challenges of Provençal cuisine. As she and Sounia bustled about the kitchen from one job to another, she told me what Provençal cooking meant to her.

'Take this sardine-and-tomato pie,' she said as she opened an oven door to check on a baking-pan full of ripe, red tomato-halves. 'Like most true Mediterranean cuisine, it's unsophisticated cooking. It has simple peasant origins. But simple does not mean effortless, and peasant does not mean poor in quality or character. For the pie to succeed the ingredients have to be top-quality and absolutely fresh. Anything less than fillets of just-caught sardine, each one carefully scaled, de-boned, and de-finned, can spoil it. It's plenty of work.

'It's also plenty of time. Lots of Provençal meals are one-pot meals – *daubes* and *pot-au-feu* and *civets* and *estouffades*. What they lack in complex procedure they generally make up for with long, slow cooking. It is time that binds all those pronounced flavours so they hold together smoothly. Time was something Mediterraneans used to have.'

She pulled on oven gloves and pulled out the heavy baking pan to inspect its contents, then closed the oven door again. 'I suppose you could just throw raw tomatoes and sardines into a pie-shell and stick it in the oven. But it wouldn't taste the same. These tomatoes are first being cooked *confit*, conserved through slow heat – they're baking at just 100 degrees with olive oil, garlic, thyme and a bit of sugar. It takes about four hours for them to lose their acidity and become mild and soft and full of flavour. Then you can put them into pastry, lay the fresh sardine fillets on top, spoon on the confit pan-juices, and bake the whole thing.'

There seemed to be little that didn't require lengthy effort. As the clock ticked on I watched Martine and Sounia assemble a dozen different dishes for lunch. Not all Provençal preparations are unsophisticated. There was a *papeton* – a light mousse of aubergines, egg whites and cream. There were fennel-halves baked in chicken stock, white wine and saffron. There were raw pastes of green olives, basil, garlic and lemon; cooked sauces of black olives, cream and Noilly Prat. But they all took time and attention.

At twelve noon precisely the intercom on the kitchen wall started squawking orders and the dumb-waiter began its relentless rise and fall. It was like a hungry mouth opening wide, demanding to be fed more and more quickly. Without showing any signs of stress Martine and Sounia shifted smoothly into high gear.

They had the same speed as Salva, but a different kind of energy. Where Leonardo's chef worked like a nervy, high-strung artist under pressure, these women were deliberate, purposeful and collected. One after another, gigot of lamb, rabbit stews and skate salads disappeared into the maw of the dumb-waiter. There was no rush, no raised voices, no sense of urgency. Once, when the gas on top of the range cut out at a critical moment, Martine uttered one syllable, '*Merde!*' But it was gently uttered. The two worked almost wordlessly, moving in the restricted space of the kitchen with the kind of unscripted choreography that only comes with practice. It was a pleasure to watch, and I think Martine and Sounia got some pleasure from it, too.

And then, just as abruptly as at Leonardo, the lunch service was over. As diners lingered over coffee below, as Sounia wiped down surfaces and Martine replaced items in shelves and cupboards and refrigerators, I complimented them. I said I had never seen such calm and quiet efficiency in a kitchen.

Martine smiled. 'It is just another way of getting things done,' she said. 'I didn't invent it, you know.'

'You aren't going to tell me,' I said, irony creeping uncalled into my voice, 'that you learned it from your grandmother.'

'That's exactly what I'm going to tell you,' she replied.

She folded a dishcloth and hung it on a rack. 'I'm not saying my grandmother taught me everything I know. She didn't teach me very many dishes at all, in fact. But she gave me a taste for a way of cooking – for the time and organisation and attention to detail it requires. She was Marseillaise and meticulous. She would get up at five o'clock to buy the best and freshest fish for bouillabaisse. She would make cannelloni the day before she planned to serve it, because day-old cannelloni is better than just-made cannelloni. She taught me that cooking takes every bit of care you've got.'

Outside, I walked through the blinding glare of somnolent, mid-afternoon streets. Here, again, was another restaurant whose every plate was prepared *confit* – conserved, slow-cooked, and sweetened by decades of remembering.

⌒

I had questions. Were those swinging kitchen doors in Provence above all escape-routes to an alternate lifestyle? Did all chefs between Nîmes and Nice have sweet little grannies who'd spent their lives in the kitchen? Even Jacques Médecin had had a grandmother who'd appropriated recipes from Mietta, her cook, and passed them down as family lore. But it seemed improbable. There had to be more conventional, more straightforward approaches to cooking. To understand the Mediterranean through its food I needed another try. I needed a job.

What I had in mind was waiting on tables. There could be no dipping rose petals in egg whites, no kitchen-choreography for me. That took years of talented dedication. Besides, my own grandmother had only been a so-so cook. But there were other kinds of sleeves-up involvement that might give other satisfactions. It would have to be an informal place, ready to put up with a willing but untrained enthusiast. It would have to be friendly, simple, and free of gastronomic pretension. It would have to serve good food. Nothing else would do – it would have to be a family-run, mom-and-pop restaurant.

Did *maman-et-papa* establishments exist in the sophisticated south of France? They did. I found what I was looking for at the bottom of Mont Ventoux in the little town of Malaucène. Run by the Sénèque family, Le Siècle was the kind of bar-restaurant, traditional rather than trendy, that you still find in Provençal places not yet overrun by *chic*. The name itself, Le Siècle – The Century – is popular all over France. There are hundreds, maybe thousands of them scattered about the countryside. They vary in style, and are old, middling and new. But this one really did have a century's worth of solid, satisfied eating and drinking behind it.

It sat on the main street, a thoroughfare boasting more restaurants than you might think a small and out-of-the-way place like Malaucène would warrant. Among the oldest of them, Le Siècle had originally been a country hotel. Other, more modern hotels had lured the public away but the bar-restaurant still flourished, the most popular watering hole in the village. In winter, with Mistral winds gusting outside closed doors, village locals sat on stools at the mirrored bar or at the dining room's padded, booth-like *banquettes*. In summer, visitors from all over packed the outdoor terrace.

On my first morning at Le Siècle Jacqueline Sénèque showed me the restaurant's own yardstick for measuring the slow progress of the century. Out on the terrace a vertical pole, part of a metal structure supporting a blue canvas awning, protruded from the trunk of a large plane tree. The tree had been planted in the early 1900s. When she was a small child, Jacqueline told me, the plane already had a respectable girth, but she could still easily run between tree and pole. The years had continued to pass, the tree had continued to grow, and now in the new century it surrounded and swallowed up the metal pole's entire lower half. Who knew? said Jacqueline – in another hundred years, when Marie's children had their own children, it might disappear altogether.

Jacqueline was the woman who ran the bar, and along with Vincent, the cook who ran Le Siècle's kitchen, the establishment's co-owner. Having married Jacqueline's daughter Sarah, who supervised the dining room and terrace, Vincent was also Jacqueline's son-in-law. You couldn't get more mom-and-pop than this. Marie – Vincent and Sarah's daughter – was also a fixture at the restaurant. While at four years old she ran nothing at all, she had pig-tails, was very pretty and extraordinarily energetic – there was nothing she didn't have her nose into.

The Sénèques were close to each other, in the way most Mediterranean families are. And, in the way of small-town inhabitants, they were also close to the friends and neighbours who were constantly dropping by. Just as attractive, from my own perspective, the Sénèque family were on relaxed and easy terms with the help they employed in the busy summer months. They had been a little surprised by my out-of-the-blue offer to carry dishes and scrape dirty plates for free; usually it took months to find anyone to work at all. But they entered into the spirit of it, accepting that foreigners sometimes do odd and unaccountable things. Soon I was bustling around with the busiest of them.

And bustle we did, especially at lunchtime. Le Siècle was bigger than Leonardo or Le Cigalou; at a midday meal service in July and August the terrace alone could easily serve seventy. Dinners tended to be longer, more relaxed affairs, but the legendary two-hour French lunch seemed headed for extinction. Diners ate and ran.

It is not every town that has holidaymakers anxious to move off a cool and shady restaurant terrace in the middle of a hot summer's day. But then not every town has a Mont Ventoux towering above it. Malaucène is a take-off point for mountaineers, hikers, birdwatchers, nature-lovers and long-distance motorcycle tourers. It is particularly popular with cyclists – heroically, they like to measure themselves against the mountain that is one of the most demanding of stages on the Tour de France, itself an event now a century old. At lunchtime all these people found themselves on the terrace of Le Siècle, ravenously hungry, pressed for time, and raring to get going again.

I'd never seen such an odd mix of diners. One moment I'd be serving a party of elderly and fastidious amateur entomologists learning the habits of the Mediterranean high-altitude bark-borer beetle. The next I'd be waiting on a table of German motorcycle-heavies clad in black leather.

If you were judging by colour alone you couldn't beat a team of race-cyclists for exoticism – leaning their titanium-frame machines against the terrace railing, they would invest the tables with bright fluorescent spandex clothing, aerodynamic miracle-alloy helmets, and rainbow-reflecting wrap-around eyewear. But if, on the other hand, you were evaluating Le Siècle's inhabitants for sheer outlandish nature and foreignness of character, there was no one quite as exotic as the restaurant staff itself. Apart from me, all of them were Bulgarian.

Ziynep was small and shapely, with thick, straight black bangs squarely framing her pale face. Although she barely spoke French – she pronounced her words like a female spy in a James Bond film – she was popular at all the tables, especially with men. Pavlin was dark and handsome in a wild, Balkan sort of way. He wore a perpetual scowl on his face, and although he was just nineteen he was big and heavy-handed; already you could imagine him laying down the law in some rough mountain-village back home. Although he was more fluent and a better waiter than Ziynep, he wasn't as popular on the terrace. Illyana worked the salad-station at the back of the kitchen, assembling endless plates of lettuce, mixed raw vegetables and decorative garnishes at high speed. She spoke even less French than Ziynep, and although local village Casanovas were constantly buzzing around her on her days off, was too shy to say a word to any of them.

It was Alexsanar, the last of the Bulgarians, who I found the most convivial. Alex assisted Vincent in the general mêlée of kitchen production. He was modest, friendly, enthusiastic, very bright, and endlessly curious about everything he came across. And he learned fast – if Vincent showed him on a Monday how to make *lapin poêlé au muscat de Beaumes-de-Venise*, by Wednesday Alex was competently banging out rabbit lunches by the tableful.

We were the equivalent of a Guatemalan staff in a New York City restaurant – young, inexpensive, semi-skilled immigrant labourers ready to work hard on jobs no one else was willing to look at. If you asked Vincent he was categoric – you couldn't hire local French kids to work summers for love or money. It was too hot in the kitchen and state welfare didn't make restaurant-work worth it anyway. The Bulgarians were something else. They delighted in Vincent's 40-degree kitchen. Anything was better than life in Bulgaria.

But finding out how to prepare a *lapin poêlé* was just the beginning for them. Far from home, they were also discovering an attitude they had never known in their own difficult existence, a way of life with its own special approach to the enjoyment of physical things.

'What do you think?' I asked Alex as one evening we watched a party of French diners spend a full twenty minutes in debate over the relative merit of the offerings on the menu. Only then did they order.

'*C'est positif*' said Alex with a smile of pleasure. In Bulgarian restaurants you take what you can get. '*C'est même très positif.*'

⁓

August was now fast drawing to a close but the hot weather

persisted. One of my favourite times of day was driving to Malaucène in the early morning, when the smells of field and pine-forest were still fresh and cool, then setting tables with Pavlin.

At first he resented me, largely, I think, over the matter of tips. Already he was pulling in less than the slinky Ziynep, and suddenly, without warning, here was a third unknown waiter with whom he'd have to further share the terrace and its tippers. Pavlin warmed to me a good deal, though, when I reassured him I was just his helper – whatever tips were left on the tables we served were obviously his.

And so I followed the handsome, scowling mountain-brigand about the terrace, getting him to show me how it all worked. Together we set out trailing petunia plants on their upright wine barrels by the sidewalk; rolled the soft-ice-cream machine to its place beside the cash desk; pegged olive-branch-patterned tablecloths to a couple of dozen terrace tables; filled salt and pepper shakers; laid places with cutlery, water- and wine-glasses. Pavlin was unrelentingly precise about it all – he would scrupulously check everything I did, moving a glass half an inch to the right, repositioning a fork a smidgen to the left.

The days at Le Siècle started early, rarely slowed down, and ended late. But morning was also a time when I could hang around the kitchen watching the preparation of the day's menu. And it seemed to me that each time I was in there Alex had learned one more task, mastered one more dish.

I watched him making *mille-feuilles d'aubergine*. It wasn't a difficult job, but it was finicky – a construction of sliced aubergine, mozzarella cheese and Provençal tomato sauce laid in multiple layers in ring-moulds and baked. It sounds simple enough, but making three dozen of them before going on to prepare another six or eight dishes took nimble fingers. Alex's first attempts were failures, too loosely packed to stand up straight when the moulds were removed. But very quickly he got the hang of it, and soon Vincent was able to leave him to get on with it.

Whatever he was doing Alex asked questions. They were incessant. Could any other kind of fruit be used in the tarts he was baking? What part of the pig made up the *poitrine fumée* he was wrapping around little bundles of green beans? Could the lavender seeds he was scattering on the *crème brûlée* be used in other desserts as well? On and on the questions went, lunchtime getting ever closer, until the first orders started coming in and it was time to take up battle-stations.

Lunch at Le Siècle was nothing like lunch at Leonardo or Le Cigalou. It was more like trench warfare. This was a battle of attrition which pitted staff against invading waves of diners. The objective was to bombard them with the maximum number of lunches in the minimum amount of time. The strategy was to maintain a fluid front – not to bog down in time-wasting and delayed orders, but to keep meals moving. We worked under a constant barrage of barking waiters and incoming orders. In the white heat of conflict the kitchen was an impressive place – clamoursome, crowded, unbearably hot and in constant motion. No sooner had I returned loaded with dirty dishes and slung them in the sink than I was over the top again, armed with a *filet de rouget à la tapenade* or a couple of *poulardes aux morilles*.

Sometimes things went wrong. Sometimes Ziynep mistook an order and time was wasted replating dishes. Sometimes Pavlin stomped violently around the kitchen shouting '*Bordel! Putain!*' because poor Illyana was late with salads. Generally, though, the war was fought with courage and manners. After a couple of hours the oncoming waves would slow, and then retreat. The real victory, of course, lay in keeping patrons satisfied. Invariably they walked away happy and replete, never suspecting they'd been in a war zone in the first place.

Evenings were less hectic, but my last evening at Le Siècle was the quietest of all. There is no accounting for the work rhythms that restaurants have to live with. The place would go full tilt night after night and then suddenly, for no rhyme or reason, a slack night would come along. A few customers would show up, Pavlin would take some *poulardes* and *mille-feuilles* out to the terrace, and the rest of the staff would hang around drooping. In theory they should have been happy for the breathing space. It didn't matter – a dead restaurant is never a happy restaurant.

Early on we'd had a big table of post-office employees on holiday. Behind their counters they're the most niggling and inflexible of all French bureaucrats. But on the terrace they'd been expansive, charming, gallant – such is the power of food. Then there was nothing. I was grateful for Alex's sake. Escaping the heat of the range on the back doorstep of the kitchen, we got chatting. He'd been working so hard for such long hours that he'd lost weight and was looking pale. Nonetheless, he was his usual cheerful self. We talked about wine for a while – he was always happy when the talk was French food talk. And then, because I asked him to, he was happy to contemplate his future.

Once, Alex's family had been well-to-do – until the communist collapse his parents had been party members and active in the Bulgarian intelligentsia. Now that world was gone and in a poor, corrupt country Alex had no such cosy future ahead of him.

But he had big plans nonetheless, and they were based on French cooking. No matter how bad things got at home before they got better, Alex was going to open a French restaurant on the Black Sea there. And it was going to be a good one.

Did that sound far-fetched, a fine French restaurant on the tatty resort-coast of an impoverished Balkan nation? It should have. But somehow, coming from this pale young man, a dishcloth over his shoulder as he sat in the dark, it didn't. Alex, I had the feeling, might just pull it off. He was that kind of person.

I left Malaucène early that evening, feeling worn out

myself, and with the car windows all the way down drove slowly home. Once again a blessed coolness had descended on the rolling Vaucluse countryside. With the town behind me I sniffed at the odours, all but suppressed in the heat of the day, now emerging on the cool night air. They smelled of the good things growing all around.

I hadn't known that grapevines, bean fields and olive orchards had any smell at all. But spending time in restaurants sharpens the faculties, opens them to tastes and colours and odours only vaguely suspected before. Spending time in restaurants teaches practical lessons too. I had found out how to carry four full plates of food at the same time. I had learned how to uncork a wine bottle in front of diners without doing what I do at home – jam it between my legs. After one very messy incident I had even discovered how to avoid collisions with waiters coming through double kitchen-doors – you just stick to the right.

But there was something more. I had also learned that those double kitchen-doors are the fastest route to contentment. Of all the physical senses taste is the most immediately satisfying, and in its pursuit kitchens come alive with creative powers. It didn't matter if your grandmother was a good cook or not. It didn't matter if you'd inherited an old rural tradition like Odette's, an edgy artistry like Salva's, a serene calm like Martine's. Alex came from a line of apparatchiks in a country whose best-known culinary achievement was yoghurt. Yet after just a few weeks of making *mille-feuille d'aubergine* he was determined to build his life around such things. You could throw all the hot weather and state welfare you liked at Alex. He would still make a fine, hard-working chef.

About halfway home I slowed down even further and then pulled the car over. It was dark out there, and I couldn't see what was growing in the roadside field. But I could smell it, and it was irresistible – row after row, lavender plants stretched away into the night.

I got out of the car, crouched and pulled some stalks through my fingers, detaching a few small, sticky seeds. I didn't need many, just enough to give a subtle Provençal flavour to a dessert I had carefully watched Alex making. I couldn't wait to get back to Aix and impress Jany with my own *crème brûlée à la lavande*.

Nine

September came and the summer, six months before just a whisper of things greening and a promise of pleasures to come, was over. Jany and ten million French schoolchildren went back to school. Holidaying Parisians, Bruxellois and Amsterdammers went back to Paris, Brussels and Amsterdam. Shopkeepers raised their blinds, removed the *Congé Annuel* signs so gleefully taped to windows a month before, and returned to work. Sunburned, tired, replete, Provence exhaled the long-held hot breath of air that is summer and started breathing normally again.

The wonderful thing was that summer was not really over at all. In up-to-the-minute Aix, of course, life resumed the rhythms of the post-holiday season. For the first time in months you could stroll the Cours Mirabeau without being jostled by a thousand elbows. You could see your dentist, have the plumber fix a tap, hire a lawyer if you had to. Once more, with a bit of luck, you could even find a parking place in downtown Aix. But these different phases of the year and the abrupt changes between them were artificial, alterations in a human schedule dictated by governments and economies. Nature, quite naturally, ignored them. It transitions were smoother. The picking of grapes, the turning of leaves, the slow slide toward autumn rains – these were things that would not even begin for another month.

In the meantime the season pursued its course, winding itself down only gradually. Most of its concessions were welcome. The sun's fierce bite and the white glare of noon were gone. The days were gentler now and the skies, emptied of heat-haze and dust, were clearer than ever. Freed of the frantic energy of holiday crowds but still warm and sun-filled, September was in many ways the finest, most relaxing month of the Provençal summer.

Like the season, I too was hesitant to bring things to an abrupt halt. For I still hadn't made up my mind about the future. If society in general had to return to a productive life, so did I. But I was not ready quite yet. I had tasted all sorts of Mediterranean flavours in the last little while, and not only in restaurants. Back-country hill-farmers, port-city immigrants, chestnut-forest non-conformists, art-loving Cézannians, Gregorian-chanting monks, even large Camargue marshbirds – all had given me provender to sample and savour. Now I needed to sit down and digest it. In the kind of contemplative siesta that should follow all good meals, I needed a quiet, shady place to linger over Mediterranean life and think about what it might possibly mean to me.

But where? In our little apartment out on the Route du

Tholonet the atmosphere had changed as much as it had on the Cours itself.

Waking to an alarm clock, armed with leather briefcase and red correction pens, Jany was now a different creature, a *professeur de collège*. We had spent the summer wandering around Provence with nothing more to worry about than what we might be having for lunch; now, with large classes of less-than-joyful adolescents barely in hand again, Jany was facing such tasks as the charting of irregular verb conjugations. Not even her blackboard mastery of that rounded and regular scholastic hand, taught to every French schoolchild in the 19th century and still satisfyingly old-fashioned today, made her feel entirely equal to the job. In a couple of weeks both Jany and her students would calm down, but for the moment life at the Collège Mignet was a rude shock. She returned home most afternoons with her cool blown, wild-eyed and reeling.

It was not the most peaceful setting for contemplating the rhythms of the Mediterranean world. Soon I found myself planning escape. What I needed was a place of calm and reflection. A touch of brightness would be nice as well, for by September much of the countryside was tired, bleached out and browned-over by months of scorching sun. And last and most important, I wanted to be somewhere that captured the essence of the land.

Did such a place exist? It did indeed, but I had to think about it for a while, for it did not in fact exist on land at all.

In this gentle season there was no calmer, brighter, more Mediterranean place than the blue waters of the sea itself.

⌢

I drove down to the coast on a fresh and sunny Monday morning as everyone else was getting on with workaday life. The closest stretch of Mediterranean lay just half an hour due south of Aix, but this time it was not the busy urban pulse of Marseilles that I was seeking. About halfway to the city the *autoroute* split and I veered westwards, driving inland but parallel to the coast along the rocky chain of the Estaque hills.

My route took me past warehouse complexes and residential housing tracts, through a spaghetti of motorway flyovers and cloverleaves, past airports and high-tech industrial parks. Where they weren't covered by development the hills were weathered and white and denuded, typical of the kind of eroded landscapes found all over the Mediterranean from Turkey to Spain. Once the slopes around Marseilles had been covered with thick forests of oak and cypress. The last of them had fallen to the axe-blade centuries ago, raw material for the boatyard-builder's galleys. Modernisation had not stopped biting into the land since.

Things only seemed to get more concentrated as I headed towards the petrol refineries and steel-mills at Fos-sur-Mer, heart of the industrialised Midi. But just past Aérospatiale, the French partner in the building of that modern aluminium galley, the European Airbus, I ducked off the *autoroute*. Following a series of roads that grew progressively narrower, steeper and more curved, I made my way down through the hills to the coast. There were unexpected surprises, vestiges of an earlier, less technological age, to be found there still.

My destination was a tiny seaside place called Méjean and in it, a house I had hunted down through Jany's old-girls' network. In France the teaching profession has as often as not been an upwardly mobile one, a way out of rural isolation or working-class constraint. It was surprising how many of Jany's teaching colleagues had inherited, through parents or grandparents, properties or old houses scattered through the remotest parts of Provence. Too far away to be convenient, too cherished to be sold, they were used now as holiday homes. Jany had friends with chalets high up in snowy pastures in the southern Alps, with slate-roofed farmhouses lost on the windswept hills of Haute Provence, with ancient stone dwellings hidden deep in the forests of the Var. Brigitte was different – her family had passed down to her that far rarer possession, a *cabanon* in one of the Marseilles *calanques*. Now back to work at school herself, she had made a loan of it to me.

I came up over the last rise, slipped down around the last few bends, and the little world that was going to be mine for the next few days hove into view. I was enchanted, not because Méjean lived up to my expectations, but because it didn't. For those with access to them, *calanques* and *cabanons*

356

are highly prized, partly because they so little resemble the rest of the Mediterranean coast. Neither Méjean's topography nor its buildings had much to do with that parasol-shaded, suntan-oil-slicked littoral that makes up the rest of seaside southern France. Not far away on the Côte d'Azur there were a thousand waterside things to distract the eye – crowded promenades, seaview restaurants, palatial yachts, noisy beach-bars, casino roulette-wheels and all the rest of the tourist whirl. This place was different. The wide blue gulf that stretched away to the south may have been empty and silent, but it was nonetheless the sea itself that won all claims to attention here.

The *calanque*, the deep, fjord-like indentation around which the little community was built, only emphasized Méjean's ties to the sea. Born 10,000 years ago, the Marseilles *calanques* were formed when melting glaciers raised the level of the Mediterranean and flooded the river valleys etched into the area's steep and rocky coasts. Such are the geological origins of the *calanques*, but what's harder to explain is the feeling a *calanque* can give you when climb down its sides, take your clothes off and dive in. Rock and sea and sky – these were the simple components of the classical Mediterranean world, the natural elements that surrounded its ancient inhabitants. In the *calanques*, bathed in the clearest of southern lights, they sometimes seem to emerge again as living elements. Even if you have never been to the Mediterranean before, these are places that can stir old memories.

But nature was only one element making up Méjean – the other was entirely human. Parking the car, I loaded up with spare clothing and bags of groceries, and made my way towards the tiny port. The homes on each side of Méjean's single street had a crude, thrown-together look about them. It was as if none of their parts were compatible and no one house were built with any of the others in mind. It was hardly surprising in structures first built as primitive overnight shacks by Marseilles fishermen. Mismatched shutters and corrugated roofs, salvaged doors and second-hand window-frames, brick, rock, breeze-block, rough stucco and rusty old ironwork – all and any materials were considered good enough by these inspired amateur constructors. And if their working-class descendents had turned their *cabanons* into holiday homes to escape the stink and clutter of industrial-ized Marseilles, the haphazardness continues. But in the end, as anyone who stays in a *cabanon* discovers, there is yet another component holding everything together – sociability.

I let myself in through a metal-grilled door, passed a tiny ground-floor terrace where a neighbour greeted me from over a late breakfast, and climbed a steep flight of steps. Upstairs, snuggled into the tree-shaded, sloping rock sides of the *calanque* wall, was my own *cabanon* terrace. But I was not alone. Built flush against this terrace was another, where a woman stood hanging laundry on a line. Above me, perched on wooden stilts, was a third little loggia, where a man lounged on a deckchair reading a newspaper. We said our *Bonjours*, introduced ourselves, exchanged pleasantries on the fineness of the weather.

In the restricted space of a *calanque* elbow-to-elbow existence is inevitable – from rooftops, through open windows, on terraces and in stairways you share in the intimate lives of your neighbours. You hear what they are saying, see what they are doing, smell what they are cooking. Of course they know just what you're having for dinner, too. They are also fully up-to-date on your Tante Mimi's phlebitis or cousin Jean-Baptiste's fling with that little hussy from the Monoprix cosmetics counter. It is the kind of promiscuous living most of us would shy away from. But in the holiday atmosphere of the *calanque* it is just a happier, more concentrated form of that closeness that Latin families are comfortable with anywhere.

I rummaged about and soon got things up and running – the electricity turned on, the water mains opened, the fridge humming. The atmosphere was simple and rustic – all about the bunk-beds, the cupboards piled high with pots and pans, the long dining table lined with chairs, was this same atmosphere of homey gregariousness. On a shelf I found a family photo album. And in its pages I discovered a house unfamiliar with lone residents like me – it was used to side-by-side living, to life lived communally by uncles and cousins and grandmothers and constantly changing parties of family friends.

Here they all were, smiles fixed forever, one generation

after another – slim Mediterraneans, plump Mediterraneans, tanned and bathing-suit-clad Mediterraneans. In couples and groups and entire expeditionary forces they fished, played *boules*, drank pastis, hiked the cliffs, dived from boats, ate vast outdoor summer lunches. The pleasure lay entirely in doing it together. You could almost *hear* the voluble, unending sociability of it all – the only silent photos were those showing contented Mediterraneans sleeping their way through long afternoon siestas.

I may have been alone in that little *cabanon* in the rocks, but it didn't feel like it. I was part of a large and happy company.

⌣

Where the *cabanons* ended the sea began. From Brigitte's door I walked twenty-five paces to the water and stood looking outwards. Sheltered behind a rocky breakwater sat the port, a little square of sea bordered on three sides by quays and filled with a motley collection of small pleasure boats. Beyond was the *calanque* itself, steep-sided and irregularly shaped, broadening 500 yards out to a wide mouth; there in the middle sat a submarine reef, its saw-toothed rocks emerging from a wash of waves. On the far side of the reef lay open water, the Mediterranean, its emptiness stretching to the horizon. Four hundred and fifty miles due south lay the shore of North Africa. These days it is little more than an hour's flight away. But in the age when this sea was the middle of the world it lay a good deal further off – a week's sail, at least.

There was barely a soul about. I strolled, thinking of Brigitte's stories of a livelier summertime Méjean.

In full season the little port, the *calanque* and the open sea were all crowded. The port was the busiest of all – its quay-sides were covered with sunbathers, its boats draped with men delving in the innards of marine engines, its breakwater dotted with fisherman casting into deep water. There were other, non-maritime pleasures here, too. Squeezed between the quay and the *calanque* wall was a narrow *boulodrome*, a great sacrifice of space in this small, steep place. But wherever they find themselves, young men need somewhere to challenge and defeat each other, and in the cool of the late afternoon they gathered here as all *boules*-players gather, in a clamour of clanking steel and good-humoured abuse. Still more popular and noisy was Le Mangetout, a little outdoor restaurant that was cheap and cheerful and each evening crowded with *calanquais* and outsiders alike. For the moment both were entirely deserted.

In high summer the outer *calanque*, too, had its own enthusiasts, both above and below the surface. The *calanque* waters, among the clearest around, were a favourite haunt of divers. Snorkelers could pop up out of nowhere at any time, fat sea-bream skewered and flipping on the sharp-tipped points of spear-guns. Diving deeper, whole schools of frogmen would show their slow progress out to the reef with an upwelling trail of silver bubbles.

But no one needed special equipment to swim at Méjean.

Here and there around its rough edges little groups of adventurers would colonise the waterline in hot weather. It was not an easy place to swim. Having let themselves down steep slopes with the help of tree branches and rocky handholds, having stepped cautiously on slippery rocks and avoided the perils of spiny black sea urchins, determined bathers would launch themselves into the freedom of deep water. It was all worth it – there is little to compare to floating in the water of a *calanque*, with nothing but high rocks above and the deep blue of the abyss below.

But now nothing was crowded at Méjean, neither port, nor *calanque*, nor open coast. At summer's end there wasn't a single towel on the little beach on the far side of the harbour, not a bench occupied on the quay.

Even the boats behind the breakwater had been left to float quiet and unbothered. *Le Petit Bleu*, a dinghy no bigger than a bathtub, bobbed about leaky and unbailed. The cabin cruiser *Coucounet* lay forlorn, its hatches shut and locked tight. The *Tire-Cul* was so abandoned that it had no rigging left to rattle against its tall metal masts. Only a fishing boat, the *Petou*, looked as if it were still in business. Old and worn, it had recently been painted a bright blue and white. Its stern-well was crowded with empty boxes ready for the catch, its little half-deck piled with fine-meshed nets and strands of fresh seaweed. But now it, too, lay at rest.

I stood for a minute or two surveying the boats, the empty quays and the flat sea, and then walked back to the *cabanon*.

That was fine by me. If all Méjean could lie silent and still as a pin after a long, busy season, then so could I.

∽

Black olives from Nyons, white wine from Puymeras, bread, tomatoes, goats' cheese, a dried sausage – back in the *cabanon* kitchen I packed a picnic lunch any Mediterranean would have recognised. I had decided I might as well do it right. Into my rucksack, too, went a blanket to stretch out on and an old cushion for my head. Dutifully, I also threw in a book, a volume which, like one I'd taken up the Trabassac Valley, I'd kept for a quiet moment.

I started along the path that led upwards behind the *boulodrome*. In seconds a sharp hillside spur had obscured the little port and its *cabanons*. There were no flat spaces ahead, no man-made lines, but instead a tumbling landscape of strong colours and sensations. The worn rock, tinted here by some subterranean chemistry, took on a reddish hue. Against it the twisted pines growing from the slope's cracks and crevices glowed a vivid green. I looked upwards. The sky might have been an inverted bowl of porcelain – it had the brilliant, depthless cast of a high-temperature glaze.

Brighter still was the water running away from the edge of the *calanque*. Seen from sixty feet up it was no longer opaque and glittery, but startlingly clear. Sunlight bounced from a sea-bed made of rock and weed and sand – here the water was turquoise, there electric blue. Further out it darkened to cobalt, finally growing dull where the sea-bottom sank and then disappeared altogether.

I was not ten minutes from the port, but it didn't matter. There was nothing and no one about, and I might have been on my own desert island. I scrambled down and found a place where a shady pine grew from a little shelf twenty feet above the water. There was just enough space to throw a blanket.

I spread out my picnic. I shucked off everything but a pair of old shorts, and relegated my watch to the deepest pocket of my pack. Leaning my back against warm, smooth rock, I took a handful of olives and sat looking out to sea.

I was happy. Through the open spaces in the branches overhead I could feel the sun on my skin, a slow, warming radiation. The sandpapery grain of stone against my back, the rub of dry pine needles beneath my heels felt just as good. I could sense the atmosphere itself, a smooth, warm envelope of air. Every now and then a cooler breath, refreshed by its passage over the water, would waft deliciously in. There was the odour of pine gum and sun-heated rock in the air. Suspended there, too, was the droning of cicadas – it waxed and waned, fading to nothing at times, swelling mysteriously to a loud crescendo at others. But it was the sea that did the real soothing here. It slapped softly back and forth in the rocks below, its surface spreading smoothly away to infinity.

For the moment I couldn't see another human being. Far out on the water, though, I spotted a tiny white sail, and it was enough to remind me of what in fact was all around. In the northern landscape I came from the human presence was negligible, the surrounds untouched. Here in the Mediterranean every rock, every hilltop, every forest that once existed and now existed no longer had been claimed, fought over and transformed by the hand of man. This sea and everything around it was imbued with an age-old presence.

Even olives were. I looked at the black and wrinkled little fruits I was eating, and was reminded of an impressive list compiled by Lawrence Durrell. For Durrell the taste of olives seemed to have evoked half the cultural inheritance of western man: 'The whole Mediterranean – the sculptures, the palms, the gold beads, the bearded heroes, the wines, the ideas, the ships, the moonlight, the winged gorgons, the bronze men, the philosophers – all of it seems to rise in the sour, pungent taste of these black olives between the teeth. A taste older than meat, older then wine. A taste as old as cold water.' [16]

I was not sure I was getting quite the same heady mixture from my own handful of Nyons olives. Had Durrell been eating some superior Cypriot or Alexandrian variety I had yet to sample?

Of course not. He had immersed himself, like the very olives he had eaten, in a deep, briny bath; all his life, through its landscape and history, culture and geography, he had soaked up the Mediterranean. He had listened to the cries of its street-vendors and the songs of its poets. He had lived, worked, written, gotten drunk, built houses, grown gardens, had families in half a dozen countries around its shores. In spirit he had become a Mediterranean himself. In the taste of black olives he was simply getting back from the Mediterranean what he had put in.

Now I was hungry, too. I moved on from olives to bread, from bread to cheese to wine and the rest of it. And with each new taste I added to my own small list of references and associations. I cannot say that with each bite of tomato I entered a realm of golden beads and bearded heroes. My dreams were simpler. For me they conjured up visions of a stone house and a search for it among the ruined churches and wild summer thunderstorms of Haute Provence.

But it didn't matter. For there was something more significant about this business of Mediterranean appropriation. In the end it seemed to me that neither landscape nor history, culture nor geography were guarantees of Mediterraneanity. Anyone at all could be a Mediterranean. It was not a question of birth. I had met Italians and Greeks and Provençaux who were becoming less and less like true Mediterraneans all the time. And I had met northerners who, like Durrell, moths drawn to light, were. For me it always came back to the same question – the ever-rarer ability to live by and through the senses.

But it wasn't just the physical senses alone. Anyone could buy their way into over-the-top Mediterranean sensuality. Instead it was the strong ties, the fierce attachments that those senses could generate. They all had it, the people I had lived around this summer. It was Gerard Chauvin's senses that attached him to his land and his work. It was a strong physical sense of family and place that kept Odette tied to her clan at Le Marronnier. Marseilles lived through a fusion with the sea, Sully Rauzier through his allegiance to the things of the Cévenol past. The art-students of Aix pushed their senses further still, emulating a long-dead Provençal painter in his search for hidden harmonies in colour and form. The monks of Ganagobie had been even more rigorous; reduced, pared, filtered of all that was extraneous, their own sensations had transported them to a reality that lay far beyond colour and form.

And what of the cooks I had met? Looking to the rocks and the gently surging water below, I thought of yet another list I'd come across.

'Take two or three stones from a spot where the low tide does not reach,' began a recipe remembered by one Predrag Matvejevic, a Croat born not far from the Mediterranean. 'They should be neither too large nor too small, and dark from having lain at the bottom of the sea. Cook them in rainwater until everything in the pores has had a chance to seep out. Add a few bay leaves and some thyme, a teaspoon of olive oil and a teaspoon of wine vinegar. You will not need to salt if you have chosen the proper stones. Stone soup is known on virtually all the islands of the Ionian Sea, from the Adriatic to the Tyrrhenian. It was made by the Illyrians, the Greeks, the Liburnians, and probably the Phoenicians, the

Etruscans, and the Pelasgi. It is as ancient as Mediterranean poverty.'[17]

Lawrence Durrell could wax poetic over olives and I could dream on about tomatoes. But here were Mediterraneans, their sensual life reduced to one thing only – hunger – inspired to find sustenance in sea stones. The real roots of sensual existence are as far removed from today's indulgent self-satisfactions as we can imagine. For painters and priests and hard-scrabble farmers, for Provençal cooks and drinkers of stone soup, the life of the senses is engagement with the world. It is connection that gives meaning.

My own hunger now satisfied, I drifted into a reverie, a still and silent contemplation of the sea. I had been meaning to read, but ended up content to simply watch the slow passage of the day and the progress of boats on the horizon. In these surroundings there was no need to distract my mind at all. It was quite happy as it was. Anyone watching might have said I was being lazy. In fact I was engaged in a fine and delicate balancing act, fitting precisely into the centre of this faultless blue afternoon without ever noticing myself at all.

⤶

> ... *There's nothing better*
> *than when deep joy holds sway throughout the realm*
> *and banqueters up and down the palace sit in ranks,*
> *enthralled to hear the bard, and before them all, the tables*
> *heaped with bread and meats,*

and drawing wine from a mixing-bowl
the steward makes his rounds and keeps the winecups flowing.
This, to my mind, is the best that life can offer.[18]

In the same way my quiet *cabanon* was loud with the spirits
of laughing holidaymakers, so too, for the next few days,
was my rocky little shelf beside the sea crowded with happy
banqueteers. I would rise each morning, pack myself a picnic
lunch, stroll past the port and climb the steep path above
the water. I had no idea if deep joy held sway elsewhere in
the land, but in the little realm of the *calanque* things were
as festive as could be. My palace walls were made only of
fissured red rock, my roof of a branch of pine. My table was
merely a blanket. I had to double as my own retainer – I, the
steward, made sure that I, the guest, had a cup kept properly
flowing. But the spread of food was genuine and my supply
of wine held good.

What made it all work, though, was the presence of the
bard. At last I had settled down to reading, and spent my
days with Homer.

What better poet to read on the shores of the Mediterranean? What better voyage to read about than the first and
best of all Mediterranean voyages? It is in *The Odyssey* that
Homer has his hero say that poetry and feasting are the best
life has to offer. Life, admittedly, has changed somewhat in
the twenty-seven centuries since the blind poet, declaiming
before shadowy crowds in torch-lit feast halls, told the story

of Odysseus. But from where I sat he didn't look to be too far wrong about life's greatest pleasures.

In Homer's poem Odysseus makes his claim at just such a celebration of wine and words. The happy feast is given in his honour by King Alcinous, ruler of the Phaeacians on the island of Scheria. But it comes only after Odysseus, at the end of the Trojan Wars and a further ten long years of wandering, is rescued from shipwreck.

The storm that causes it is one of the most violent in all the stories of the sea. It takes place as Odysseus, having escaped the embraces of the goddess-nymph Calypso, is sailing home at last. But he runs afoul of his foe Poseidon, brother of Zeus and lord of the oceans. With his trident Poseidon rams the clouds together, churns the waters and stirs up vast waves. Throwing lightning bolts around like matchsticks, he calls in gales and thunderheads the way US combat colonels call in air cover. Destruction rains down on Odysseus's ship.

Homer outdoes himself describing the terrifying scene. It is the most mighty of storms – it lasts for three days and 200 stirring lines of poetry. Odysseus's mast is snapped and his sail hurled across the sea. He is thrown from the decks, dragged down by giant breakers, sees his ship smashed to pieces. He sits astride a plank for two days and nights, 'riding it like a plunging racehorse' as the howling storm carries him forward.

Things only gets worse off the island of Scheria – Odysseus confronts treacherous headlands, perilous cliffs, roaring breakers, sheets of spray, jagged reefs, boiling surf, razor-sharp rocks. 'Like pebbles stuck in the suckers of some octopus dragged from its lair,' Homer hisses, 'so strips of skin torn from his hands stuck to the rock face.'

The shipwrecked sailor, however, finds his way through all these dangers. At last discovering an open passage to the mouth of a river, he swims ashore. He crawls up on the river-bank, brine gushing from his nostrils, more dead than alive. 'Man of misery, what is next?' he whispers to himself. 'Is this the end?'

For most men it probably would be. But Odysseus is no ordinary man. He is a Greek epic hero, and like all his kind has an uncanny way of triumphing against the odds. He is brave, resourceful, intelligent and skilled at war. He is so physically attractive that nymphs of all sorts stoop to every low trick to seduce him – if Odysseus hadn't lashed himself to his ship's mast the singing Sirens, as homicidal as they were erotic, would have lured him to his death. But irresistible females aside, Odysseus does not generally fall into traps. For he is, above all, the most wily and calculating of men.

'I am Odysseus', he introduces himself to King Alcinous at the feast, 'son of Laertes, known to the world for every kind of craft – my fame has reached the skies.' Such a boast of conniving character might appear odd coming from a clean-cut hero. But it has to be said that no voyager on these old Mediterranean waters would have lasted very long at all without at least some cunning and guile. Such ancient seas were places of lawlessness and constant uncertainty – no one could tell what challenge the next ship or unknown island might bring.

But Odysseus also faced threats far more dangerous than those brought by simple mortals. The ancient world was still an extraordinary place where men and gods were often tangled in each other's affairs.

It was a relationship that required all sorts of skill to manage. For in those days not only could certain men claim god-like qualities; lounging about on the summit of Mount Olympus, the gods could behave in just as petty and small-minded ways as men themselves. They bickered, fought, caroused and slept around. Not that sleeping at home was any guarantee of good behaviour, either – from time to time they weren't above impregnating their own daughters and sisters. There were times when the heavens themselves were hardly large enough for their carrying-on.

Then the gods descended to earth, and woe to the man who through no fault of his own got in their way. If a deity chose to use a mortal to further his own ends in some Olympian feud then good character alone was of no use. All man's strivings – his virtues, his moral conduct, his struggle for earthly justice – counted for little. His only hope lay in a heavenly fixer – an Artemis, an Ares, or an Aphrodite. Without some sort of benefactor up there, the fate of ordinary men was a matter of indifference to the gods.

Sacrifice helped, and *The Odyssey* is full of men, sometimes fearful, sometimes thankful, burning ox's shinbones in honour of the gods. But being a towering, larger-than-life hero – someone a little like the gods themselves – also attracted divine attention. Through his resourceful character Odysseus had gained himself just such a benefactor: Athena, daughter of Zeus and patron of nothing less than human resourcefulness itself.

Who else but powerful Athena could have opposed Poseidon's raging anger, calmed the waters, and helped Odysseus safely to shore? In fact the goddess has been watching over Odysseus ever since he set out on his journey home at the end of the Trojan Wars.

On I read. I was no more a reader of classical Greek poetry than I was of German philosophy. But now, sitting through one near-disaster after another, I was riveted. *The Odyssey* was a page-turner. The man made Indiana Jones look like a wimp. I had forgotten the passage of time. I had forgotten my uneaten picnic. I had even lost touch with the little port that lay close by. Halfway out of my own Mediterranean world, I was halfway into Odysseus's. Now he was in a serious fix and I wondered how, even with Athena's help, he was going to get out of it.

Is the castaway rescued by some peasant local, a fisherman or swineherd? There isn't much heroic style in that. And so, relieving Odysseus of his pain and suffering as he lies washed up on the shore, Athena puts her protégé to sleep. Then off to the palace of King Alcinous she flies. There in the bedroom of Nausicaa, the king's young and beautiful daughter, she insinuates herself into the princess's dreams. Athena needs a pretext for a meeting – she persuades Nausicaa that the very next morning would be the perfect time to pack her dirty laundry into a cart and haul it down to the river for washing.

To some later generations this seemed so unlady-like a proposal that one of Homer's ancient translators, a certain Aristophanes of Byzantium, actually altered his version of *The Odyssey* to ensure that it was Nausicaa's maids who handled the offending laundry. But neither Homer nor Athena has time for social snobbery. So great are their creative powers they can make royal laundry-washing look plausible, even fun.

There is greater impropriety to come, for they also have a taste for scenarios that hint at the low-budget sex comedy. Once the laundry is clean and lies drying on the grass by the river, Nausicaa and her maids undress, bathe, rub each other down with olive oil, and have a picnic. Then, still stark naked, they begin a lively round of beach-ball.

I wondered how a modern Mediterranean princess would react if, unsuspecting and undressed, she were suddenly confronted by a wild-looking man, bruised and torn, just as naked as she was? I doubted that Stephanie of Monaco – the only Mediterranean princess who came readily to mind – would be caught dead washing her laundry in public, naked or not. Her bodyguards, though, would certainly have flattened an undressed intruder in seconds. And in fact even Nausicaa's maids run screaming in panic when Odysseus, woken by sounds of play and female laughter, stumbles blearily out of a waterside thicket.

But in an age of wonders the gods can work any transformation they like. With her divine powers Athena makes her protégé even taller and more handsome than he already is. She gives him curly hair – apparently a fool-proof item of male seduction in those days – 'like thick hyacinth clusters full of blooms.' At this point it doesn't matter who is wearing what – Nausicaa ends up gazing in wonder at this god-like creature and falls deeply in love. It is only natural after that for her to offer the stranger the help of her father, the king.

In the end there is no limit to the good fortune heaped on Odysseus in the land of the Phaeacians. In a world that is violent and insecure, Alcinous respects the old codes of hospitality. He orders a feast to celebrate this chance arrival from the sea. A dozen sheep, eight boars, and a pair of oxen are soon grilling on the coals. Guests, the greatest of Phaeacian lords and sea captains, are called on to welcome Odysseus – down at their assembly place by the port men like Swing-Aboard, Racing-the-Wind and Greatfleet compete with him in games. Races are run, dances are danced, lavish gifts are bestowed on Odysseus. At the great feast songs are sung by a blind bard, a poet not unlike Homer himself. It is all in Odysseus's honour. But the honour that pleases him most is the solemn promise the king and his banqueteers make – their undertaking to return him safely home.

When I came to the end of the feast-scene in King Alcinous's palace I closed *The Odyssey* and for a while sat dreaming.

Out at the wide mouth of the *calanque* I could see the submerged reef with its protruding, saw-toothed rocks. The sea right now was calm and flat, and not the slightest surge broke over them. But in my mind's eye, at least, it was rocks just like these which I had seen lashed by boiling surf only minutes before. In fact the whole rocky coast here, the cliffs, the headland, even the drowned river itself, might have been part of that stormy scene from *The Odyssey*.

Of course I knew that this was Méjean. But as if in a mirror seen through some luminous reflection dancing off the water, this was also an old Mediterranean seascape where wonderful things had long ago happened. The *Odyssey* had made that world come to life. At that moment, in fact, I wouldn't have been surprised to see Odysseus himself suddenly climb up from the water below my feet.

It set me thinking. How is it, after nearly 3,000 years, that Odysseus remains such a lively and engaging character? It can only be because he resembles something in all of us today.

He is a man who is incessantly knocked around by fate. Along his journeys he has seen more than his share of the nasty surprises life can dish out. Being larger than life, his own surprises are of a suitable size – he faces man-eating monsters and ship-eating whirlpools, a Cyclops who destroys crewmen in a single bite, magic bags that open to release all the winds of the world. Odysseus has even made a gloomy trip down to the land of the dead. Yet through all these trials and sufferings he not only survives – he consistently comes out a winner. He is a hero. And we all need heroes, for they give us hope.

But there is another Odysseus that is still part of us, too. This is not a man who purposely sails in search of adventure; this is a man who is sailing in search of home. Far away on the island of Ithaca, lamenting his long absence and praying for his return, are his wife Penelope, his son Telemachus, his aging father Laertes. Even his dog, Argus, sits waiting and pining. In the end *The Odyssey* is not a book of travel-adventure, it is a book about return. Odysseus has had more than his share of the world, and ultimately all of his efforts are directed to getting back to his own place and people.

And it was this Odysseus, Odysseus the non-hero, that I enjoyed most of all. He's a man who is tired and just wants to go home. I could identify with that. I hadn't faced a Cyclops or cannibals. I had never been shipwrecked. My own adventures were hardly heroic. But I'd been on the road a long time and I wanted to get to a place of my own. Once again I picked up *The Odyssey*. Against all the odds, I had the feeling, Odysseus was going to make it.

$$\backsim$$

The weekend arrived at Méjean, and with it came not just Jany but a two-day spell of full-blown summer.

It was just as Brigitte had said. The *cabanons* filled up with Marseilles families happy to escape the city. The Mangetout filled up with chatty lunchtime diners, the *boulodrome* with boastful youths, the port with greasy-handed men tinkering with motors. Bare-breasted young women lay sumptuously sunning on the quays, casting fishermen dotted the breakwater, and out in the *calanque* snorkelers finned and splashed about like porpoises at play.

After such a quiet time it was all too much for me. Following a hectic week at school Jany, too, was perfectly happy to escape the human race. So we put on our walking shoes and tramped out of the *calanque* along the *chemin des douaniers*, a path once used by customs patrols, that wound its way through wild country high above the open sea.

There is a point above Méjean where walkers arrive at the summit of a high headland overlooking the *calanque*. Suddenly the sea opens up, and there, across the Bay of Marseilles, lies the city itself. At this distance it is too far to make out clearly, but in bright sunshine its buildings climb away from the water a radiant and shimmering white.

Now I am not sure quite what it was – a simple effect of the noontime light, maybe, or eyestrain resulting from too many hours of reading. But as I topped the headland and Marseilles came into view it no longer looked to me like any modern place. It looked more like a city of glistening marble. Immediately I put the idea out of mind to concentrate on the path ahead, now narrowing to a steep and slippery trail. The hours went by, the path rose and fell along cliffs fragrant with wild thyme. We gulped huge breaths of fresh sea air. We scrambled, swam, picked bunches of herbs to make fresh *tisanes* at home. Each time I raised my head, though, I saw the same thing – an ancient seaside city, vibrant and noble, its halls, ramparts, temples and marble palisades shimmering in the sun.

On the way back in the late afternoon it got even worse. From the top of the headland above Méjean we looked down to the mouth of the *calanque*. Out on the water far below I could see a boat. It was the *Petou*, the blue and white fishing-boat that usually sat moored at the quay. Now as the sun sank behind it the little craft was setting nets – or at least that is the only rational explanation I had. For as the high-prowed boat advanced, the solitary fisherman in the stern was paying out yard after yard of net by hand. And as he did so the sun's rays were catching his momentarily-raised mesh of fine nylon filament. From up on the headland it looked like a hanging curtain of fire. Slowly circling, the *Petou* seemed to be laying a ring of living flame in the water. Obviously, I thought to myself for just one fraction of an unthinking second, the man is performing some sacred rite of propitiation.

Had I taken too much sun in the last few days? Quaffed too much Puymeras wine? It was all nonsense, of course, and I didn't even mention it to Jany as we walked down into the *calanque*. Perhaps I'd just been over-exciting my brain, reading too much *Odyssey* in a setting that too closely resembled it.

This had to be the explanation, I began to think, when later that evening we sat down to dinner at the Mangetout.

Most of the casual day-trippers had gone and our fellow diners on the terrace by the water were *calanque* regulars. There was nothing exceptional about them – they were small-boat owners, *boules* players, casual fishermen, *cabanon* residents. They were simply relaxed men and women enjoying outdoor meals in the cool of the evening by the lapping water.

But as our dinner arrived and we began devouring the tiny *mangetout* fish that one eats whole from head to tail, my attention began to wander. Jany was telling me a story of some common-room teaching intrigue, but it wasn't making sense. Soon it faded altogether. In its place I had the vivid impression I was sitting in an old Mediterranean assembly place, the kind where the Phaeacians fêted Odysseus down by their own port.

The tables were still plastic restaurant tables, not quarried slabs of Scheria granite. The boats nearby had no drilled stone mooring posts, no stepped masts or leather oarlock-straps. The Méjean décor had not changed at all. I examined our wine. It didn't come in a Greek double-handled jar – the bottle was entirely normal, the year of the vintage clearly marked. There was no doubt – we were firmly anchored in the early 21st century. Yet a much older Mediterranean also seemed present. I finally traced its source – it lay in the people themselves.

I looked at diners eating, drinking and talking, watching the bobbing boats or gazing upwards as the first evening stars appeared. Without making any effort they seemed focused and relaxed at the same time, devoted solely to the enjoyment of the here and now. There were at least a couple of noble, straight-backed Nausicaas sitting at nearby tables, and a scattered handful of laughing girls who could have been her companions. There were any number of Swing-Aboards, Greatfleets and Racing-the-Winds present, too, busy telling the day's tales of great deeds accomplished in little boats and at valiant games of *boules*.

Their expressions were mobile, their faces shining, their eyes alive. They might all have been animated by Athena herself. Their pleasure was the pleasure of being alive, of being together and being a part of the simple things of life. It was as ancient as Homer's tale – hidden in this rocky *calanque*, as it was hidden in unaccustomed corners all over Provence, the old Mediterranean life was alive and well.

'Tell me what I just said.'

'What?' I replied, slowly coming to.

'Tell me what I just said,' Jany repeated. 'I don't think you've heard a word I've said in the last five minutes. Are you feeling all right? I think you've been away too long.'

'Do you know,' I said, thinking as much of the last decade as of the last week. 'I am sure I probably have.'

I made a sign to the waitress to bring the menu. 'Just a couple of more days,' I said to Jany, 'and then I should be back. In the meantime, try a little dessert – the *fondant au chocolat* is supposed to be fabulous.'

～

The weekend was over and the crowds, Jany with them, had left. I didn't go with her because there was one last thing I needed to do.

From the moment I had seen that little blue and white fishing-boat, the *Petou*, circling on the swell I had wanted to be out there on it. Small-boat fishing is one of the oldest ways of making a living in Provence. It is also one of the hardest – it's what Mediterranean emigrants from Alicante to Palermo ran away from a century ago. Yet this man persisted, and I wanted to know why.

In the Provençal language *Petou* is an affectionate nickname, a term of endearment for one who is small. And at just over twenty-three feet the boat that lay moored outside the paint-flaked *Club Nautique de Méjean* at the end of the quay was no giant. But then I knocked on the door of a storeroom and discovered that her owner, too, was small. Entering from bright sunlight into a dim interior I could not see him at all at first. Then, half-hidden amidst piles of floats and bins of rope, tubs of engine grease and nets piled high to the ceiling, I made out Méjean's last professional fisherman.

Like his boat, he was short and stocky, broad of beam and solidly built. And he, too, was named Petou. Whether the nickname had originally been his and was then transferred to his boat, or *vice versa*, I never found out. It didn't matter much – they were exactly the same.

No, of course he would not mind taking me out to set nets, Petou said when I explained I was only a poor northerner, a friend of Brigitte's and in love with the Mediterranean. We could go when I liked – he went out twice a day. And so I joined Petou and *Petou* that very afternoon.

'What's that ... that *thing*?' With diesel engine banging rhythmically and mooring ropes aboard, we had pulled away from the quay. I had meant to hold off all queries for a while, but my curiosity had the better of me. The thing in question stood erect at the prow of the boat, a bow-end extension of its wooden keel. Up it swept a foot or more above the deck, a strong, graceful curve ending in a realistically-carved phallic knob.

'Ah yes, that,' smiled Petou. Now dressed in overalls, yellow slicker and rubber boots, he was looking every inch a fisherman. 'I often get asked about that. It is called a *capian*. All the little fishing boats around Marseilles have one. It brings good luck.'

'But why that, exactly?' I persisted. A convenient, pocket-sized rabbit's foot would have been more discreet than this lucky charm.

The fisherman shrugged. 'They've been part of fishing boats here forever. They say the Greeks brought them when they arrived. Even the modern, non-wooden fishing-boats being built these days – they're horrible things – have plastic penises. Who knows? Maybe the Greeks thought a virile fisherman was a lucky fisherman.'

I nodded sagely. It was very likely so. But still it struck me as extraordinary – here we were, more than 2,500 years since the first sailors had settled on these coasts. And yet today fishermen were continuing about their business as if nothing had changed.

It wasn't just the phallic prow. If their marine engines have given the little coastal fishing boats of Marseilles a modern sound, their basic design is ancient. The *Petou* was a *pointu*, so called because both bow and stern, rising slightly from a wide beam amidships, were pointed. A cousin of all the little fishing boats from the *gozzo* of the Mezzogiorno to the *caique* of the Levant, the *pointu* is a classic Mediterranean craft. They may not be the most elegant-looking of boats, for they tend to tubbiness. But if they have survived changes of history perhaps it is because they are good at surviving changes of weather, too – in the Mediterranean rough seas can blow up out of nowhere in no time.

But now the wind had fallen, as it often does at sunset, and the water was smooth. Solid and stable, the *Petou* rode her way across a softly rolling plane of glittery blue and silver. Not ten minutes from the quay, on the far side of Méjean's reef and directly below high cliffs, the skipper threw his engine into neutral and prepared to set his nets.

I had thought we might go further out to sea or along the coast. But no, said Petou, he rarely sailed more than a kilometre or two from port, and always fished close to land. That's where one caught what little boats like this fished for, all the finny creatures you would find in a first-class bouillabaisse.

Standing in his stern-well, Petou tied a rope to a heavy metal weight and lowered it. When it touched bottom he engaged the engine. Moving his craft slowly forward, he lifted the net lying piled in neat folds at the bottom of the boat, and hand over hand fed it out into the water. Paying the net out while simultaneously keeping the boat on the right course – a broad, sweeping U – took some doing. It was trickier still, Petou assured me, in a cold and howling mid-January Mistrals. Unless a violent onshore wind piled waves straight into the *calanque* and made it impossible to get out of port, Petou fished day-in and day-out through every kind of weather.

It wasn't everyone's idea of a living, he admitted. For the last seven years his had been the only commercial boat to fish out of Méjean. There were other small fishing boats along the coast, of course, and an entire fleet of them in Marseilles. But nobody was living the high life. Costs had risen and fish-stocks fallen. In far-away Brussels the European Commission was dictating the numbers – everything from the mesh-size of nets to the issue of new licences. It was OK for the big trawling fleets, said Petou – they could absorb the shocks, negotiate with governments, bargain for subsidies. But for the little man like him, fishing was a life on its way out.

So why bother, I asked?

Once again Petou shrugged his shoulders.

'We'll see tomorrow morning when we pull the net up,' he replied.

Petou attached a ragged black marker-flag and buoy to the rope leading down to his net. One hundred feet below, a gossamer wall of filament forty-five feet high, weighted at the bottom with lead and buoyed at the top with floats of cork, now stretched 3,000 feet along the sea-bed. We turned the boat and headed for home.

It was chilly when I rose with the sun the next morning, and for the first time I felt the slightest hint of warning. Watching the light grow as I sat on the breakwater waiting for Petou, I breathed in a message carried on cold, fresh air. Soon, it was saying, a new season would come drifting in; autumn might not arrive today, nor even in the next few weeks. But changes were ready at hand. It was time, I thought, that I had changes of my own ready.

As we headed out past the reef the sea looked the same to me as it had looked the day before. But it, too, was subject to time's changes. Petou was looking closely at the water and doubtfully shaking his head. We were approaching full moon, that irresistible pusher and puller of seas, and he was afraid the currents had been even stronger than he'd expected. Currents are no respecters of nets – they twist and tangle them, bend them flat like reed-beds in the wind. They are the Mistrals of the deep.

At his marker-flag Petou pulled up one end of his net and wound it onto the revolving metal drum that sat at the bow beside the *capian*. A touch of a hydraulic lever and the wheel began turning, hauling in the net. Petou piled it back into the bottom of the boat as neatly as it had come out, stopping the drum whenever it was necessary to disentangle a fish.

It wasn't necessary very often. First up was an ugly, grey-green sea cucumber, a being of no great interest to anyone but itself. Back it went into the water, and back to work went the hydraulic drum. Gradually, yard by yard, the net came in. There was a *beaux-yeux* – a 'beautiful-eyes' – all of four inches long. Five minutes later there was a pink bream. It was followed shortly by an octopus, a writhing, sucker-sticking creature Petou punched and pummelled on the deck until it no longer threatened to drag its way over the gunwale and back to the sea. There was nothing after that for fifteen minutes. Then, in quick succession, up came two small scorpion fish, their spiny pink dorsal fins tangled in the net. They were followed by a *sar*, a *daurade royale*, and a grey mullet. And that was it. For one day's work, Petou growled, there was just about enough to feed the neighbours' cats.

The funny thing was that he did not seem upset at all. He wasn't saying anything, but I could see that, like me, he was enjoying the morning sun, the cool air, the gentle rise and fall of the boat beside the cliffs. Nothing seemed to bother him much, not the newly-torn hole in his net, not the weeds the current had tangled in it, not the cheeky seagull that tried to steal his fish and then for extra measure shat on his deck.

'Why should I complain?' he asked as he finally hauled up the last of the net. 'It's not me who decides what comes out of the water – it's the sea. One day I'll have nothing, the next I'll have enough to sell to my customers and to take home to my wife. In the meantime I enjoy life on the water, all of it. That's why I bother carrying on fishing. It's what I like.'

Who could argue with that? But there was something I learned about Petou that morning that pleased me even more. He had grown up by the water and had always enjoyed fishing. But he was no old salt who'd never known anything else. Until Petou had been made redundant a decade before he had worked a few miles up the road in the quality-control offices of Aérospatiale. He had begun his working life checking lists, not nets. Anyone can be a Mediterranean. Anyone can become a Mediterranean.

Petou was right about the neighbour's cat. There was a grey tabby waiting for us as we glided around the breakwater and back into the quay. There were two human customers, too, regular buyers of Petou's. I watched him hand over the fish they were interested in. There were just a couple apiece.

'It'll take us a while to get rich at this rate,' I joked as we stepped ashore and shook hands goodbye.

Petou stopped and looked at me, serious for the first time.

'What do you mean *get* rich?' With a sweep of his arm he gestured at his boat, the port, the rocky *calanque*, and beyond it, the sea.

'Look around,' he said.

⟿

I spent the rest of the day in *far niente*. I swam from the breakwater, dozed on the rocks, chatted to a neighbour. I had no thoughts in my head at all. I was happy just to be part of the quiet life of the little port. Only in the late afternoon did I wander back to begin tidying up at Brigitte's *cabanon*. The stacking and storing of outdoor furniture, the spreading of dust-sheets on sofas, the lowering of split-cane blinds cracked and discoloured by fierce summer suns – these were all rituals that had been performed a thousand times before.

When everything was in order, when the *cabanon* door was locked and my car loaded and ready to go, I trudged one last time up the path on the hillside above the port. I had a ritual of my own to observe.

On the high headland at the mouth of the *calanque* the cliffs were steep and fell sharply to the sea below. I scrambled up a rocky pitch to one of these sudden edges and there found myself a perilous little niche to settle into. I could see everything from here – the *calanque* far beneath me, the coastline stretching away on either side, and out at the world's edge the broad blue sweep of horizon that enclosed it all.

Far in the distance I could see the city of Marseilles, bright once again in the clear light of the sinking sun. I knew it had no magic. There were no glittering temples, no marble palisades. This was just a very old, slightly down-at-heel city, a place of human variety which, despite its problems, somehow got along. And there again, on the other side of the headland, was the *Petou*, the sharp *tuk-tuk-tuk* of its engine faintly audible even from up here. The boat emerged from the port and described a wide circle as its master began lifting his nets out into the water. And I knew that there, too, lay no enchantment, no ring of propitiatory fire. This was just a man who pulled fish from the sea in an effort to make life satisfying.

But it did not matter that these simple things no longer seemed miraculously transformed. To me they remained wonderful just as they were. Nor was there much point in trying to figure out how one thing – a fishing boat, an old city, a wounded stag, a much-painted mountain, a plate of *ratatouille*, a churchful of smoky incense – might have a second, more-than-physical existence. The moment one tries to analyse the life of the senses, to pull it apart and rationalise it, is the moment it loses its power.

But power it undoubtedly has. Months before, I had sat on another boat on grey northern waters in London trying to figure out a new life for myself. I couldn't. Instead, I had let myself be carried along to old Provençal places where the life of the senses still prevails.

And gradually, having abandoned the effort of trying to distinguish what makes people different and keeps places apart, I had begun to see what it is that connects and holds them together. The point about writers like Nietzsche and Homer, I suppose, is that it doesn't take much for us to start uncovering these hidden Mediterranean things. They are naturally inside us. They always have been. If we continue to use our senses to understand the world, they continue to give it meaning.

I made my goodbyes to the sea, then looked northwards at the white stone hills that climbed up behind Marseilles. On the far side, invisible but not far away, lay Aix-en-Provence and a teacher tired by a long day's work. I stood, clambered carefully down the rocks, and walked back along the trail. Jany was probably already worrying why I was late. I was going home.

Notes

1. Colette, *La Treille de Muscat*, cited by Michael Jacobs in *A Guide to Provence* (Viking, London: 1988).
2. Lawrence Durrell, *Provence* (Arcade Publishing, New York: 1994).
3. Friedrich Nietzsche, *The Birth of Tragedy* (Oxford University Press, Oxford: 2000).
4. Emile Zola, *L'Oeuvre,* cited by Evmarie Schmitt in *Cézanne in Provence* (Prestel-Verlag, Munich: 1995)
5. Paul Alexis, cited by Jean Arrouye in *La Provence de Cézanne* (Edisud, Aix-en-Provence, 1982) (my translation).
6. Cited by Jean Arrouye in *La Provence de Cézanne*.
7. Flannery O'Connor, 'The Nature and Aim of Fiction', in *Mystery and Manners – Occasional Prose* (Faber and Faber, London: 1984).
8. Roger Fry, *Cézanne – a Study of His Development* (University of Chicago Press, Chicago, 1989).
9. Fry, *Cézanne – a Study of His Development*.
10. Fry, *Cézanne – a Study of His Development*.

11. Rainer Maria Rilke, *Letters on Cézanne* (Fromm International Publishing, New York: 1986).

12. Fry, *Cézanne – a Study of His Development*.

13. Schmitt, *Cézanne in Provence*.

14. Claudia Roden, *Mediterranean Cookery* (Penguin BBC Books, London: 1998).

15. Jacques Medecin, *La Bonne Cuisine du Comté de Nice* (Solar, Paris: 2003).

16. Lawrence Durrell, *Prospero's Cell* (Faber and Faber, London: 2000).

17. Predrag Matvejevic, *Mediterranean – A Cultural Landscape* (University of California Press, London: 1999).

18. Homer, *The Odyssey* (translated by Robert Fagles), (Penguin, London: 2001). All further *Odyssey* quotes from the same translation.